Trials & Tribulations

Trials & Tribulations

The Red River Settlement and the Emergence of Manitoba 1811-1870

by J. M. BUMSTED

GREAT PLAINS PUBLICATIONS

Copyright © 2003 J. M. Bumsted

Great Plains Publications
420 – 70 Arthur Street
Winnipeg, MB R3B 1G7
www.greatplains.mb.ca

All rights reserved. No part of this publication may be reproduced or transmitted in any form or in any means, or stored in a database and retrieval system, without the prior written permission of Great Plains Publications, or, in the case of photocopying or other reprographic copying, a license from CANCOPY (Canadian Copyright Licensing Agency), 6 Adelaide Street East, Suite 900, Toronto, Ontario, Canada, M5C 1H6.

Great Plains Publications gratefully acknowledges the financial support provided for its publishing program by the Government of Canada through the Book Publishing Industry Development Program (BPIDP).

Design & Typography by Gallant Design Ltd.

Printed in Canada by Friesens

CANADIAN CATALOGUING IN PUBLICATION DATA

Main entry under title:

Bumsted, J.M., 1938-
Trials and tribulations: the emergence of Manitoba, 1821-1870/J.M. Bumsted.

Includes bibliographical references and index.
ISBN 1-894283-39-2

1. Red River Settlement. I. Title.
FC3372.B86   2003   971.27'401   C2003-910140-1
F1063.B86   2003

To my daughters

Table of Contents

Preface	9
1 - The Settlement Begins	11
2 - The Departure of Selkirk to the Flood of 1826	36
3 - From Flood to Full Government	58
4 - Resisting the HBC Monopoly	76
5 - Between the Storms	112
6 - The External World Intrudes	137
7 - The Morbid Symptoms of Pre-Confederation	165
8 - The Road to Rebellion	189
Select Bibliography	215
Index	234

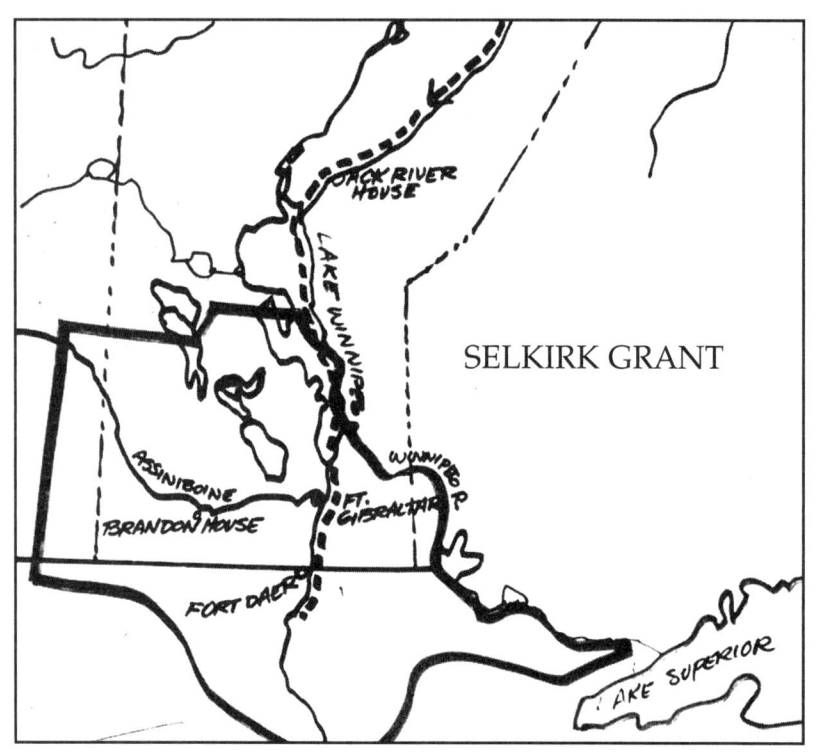

Lord Selkirk's land grant, 1811

Preface

In many ways this history of the Red River Settlement has been the hardest book I have ever written. I gained some understanding of the problems of such a history several years ago, when I wrote an historiographical essay on the settlement. In that essay I had observed how few efforts at synthesis there were. Although I did not speculate overmuch on why this was so at the time, I knew perfectly well that a large part of the problem was connected with the absence of a proper political dimension, which meant that a history of Red River could not be hung on a either a political or constitutional narrative. In an earlier incarnation I had specialized in Early American history, and I was certainly familiar with the ways in which the early histories of colonies like Rhode Island or Virginia had been put together, relying heavily as they did on the development of political machinery and infighting between governors, assemblies, and councils. In my work on the early history of the Island of Saint John, I was able to use as a scaffolding the Colonial Office Papers at the Public Record Office.

Red River, meanwhile, had neither a properly articulated government nor a series of files at the Colonial Office. In some senses this lack was an advantage, for it meant that whatever the resulting history looked like, it could scarcely be dominated by old-fashioned political and constitutional developments, but would have to look elsewhere for its themes. I found those themes in a variety of places, such as the changing patterns of the mixed-bloods and the encroachment on the outside world on the settlement. On the other hand, one of the disadvantages of weak plot lines is the difficulty of being able to distinguish the important from the trivial. This is a problem which particularly besets the inexperienced local historian, for whom every piece of information seems equally relevant and who is never able to throw any bit away. I can assure the reader that this book does not attempt to encompass everything that we

Trials and Tribulations

know about the Red River Settlement. Some discrimination has been maintained, albeit with difficulty.

As is usually the case with historical research, innumerable librarians and archivists have assisted me in the pursuit of an understanding of Red River. I am particularly indebted to the staffs of the Legislative Library of Manitoba, the Provincial Archives of Manitoba, the Hudson's Bay Company, the National Library of Canada, the University of Manitoba Archives, and the St. John's College Library for assistance above and beyond the call of duty. Thanks to the decentralized library system at the University of Manitoba, it is not only possible but necessary to trudge long distances between branch libraries in order to borrow books. I thus got quite a lot of additional physical exercise on a regular basis, for which I am eternally grateful. I am also greatly indebted to my publisher, Gregg Shilliday, for constant support and encouragement in the completion of this project.

J.M. Bumsted
Winnipeg, Manitoba
January 2003

-1-

The Settlement Begins

The Red River Settlement was born in London in May of 1811, when the General Court of the Hudson's Bay Company (HBC) voted a grant to Thomas Douglas, Fifth Earl of Selkirk, of 116,000 square miles of land within its chartered territories. In return, Selkirk was to pay a nominal rent, and provide some services to the Company, chiefly in recruiting servants for North America. Although the grant did not say so specifically, the General Court also understood that Selkirk was planning to establish a settlement somewhere within its bounds. His Lordship's motives in promoting and accepting this land grant were, like most things in his career, quite complex. Selkirk's family had gained control of the Hudson's Bay Company in 1810, and intended to rejuvenate it. But Selkirk was also impelled by the opportunity to

Métis hunter on the plains.

transplant dispossessed Highland Scots to the wilderness of North America, a process with which he had been involved since the beginning of the century.

For the site of his settlement, Selkirk had already chosen the region at the fork of the Red and Assiniboine Rivers. His opponents in the rival North West Company (NWC) were persuaded that this decision was taken because he knew that the territory was the chief source of provisions for the east-west canoe routes of their fur trade. Equally likely was the fact that the area contained enough natural provisions to sustain a pioneer settlement.

In any event, the region was extremely difficult to access, hundreds of miles from the nearest market or source of supplies, and the Nor'westers had indicated that they would oppose the settlement by any means available. Moreover, British colonists were unlikely to be able to cope with the unfamiliar conditions of the prairie west – isolation, insect infestations, an extreme winter climate, and the potential hostility of some of its local inhabitants.

The typical account of the beginnings of Red River suggests that Selkirk's principal settlers were Highland Scots, mainly recruited from the Kildonan area of Sutherlandshire. Certainly, in Alexander Ross's and Donald Gunn's pioneer histories of Red River, the "Selkirk Settlers" and Highland Scots became virtually synonymous. But if "Selkirk Settlers" includes any colonists recruited by Selkirk, his agents, or his trustees, the Kildonaners were only one of several ethnic groups involved. Other early settlers in Red River included a good many Irish, some 'Canadians' from Quebec (of whom Jean-Baptiste Lagimodière and his family were the most prominent), and a few Scandinavians. In addition, there were some mercenary soldiers (mainly Swiss from the de Meuron and de Watteville regiments), and, in 1821, a large continent of Swiss settlers recruited after Selkirk's death, but under terms authorized by him. In 1818, a listing of "Names of the Settlers in Red River" included 45 Scots, 46 de Meurons, 6 Canadians, and 5 uncategorized names which appear to be of Scandinavian origin.

From First Arrival to First Dispersion

The first party of Highlanders (and a few Irishmen), hastily recruited in 1811, was forced to winter at the Bay, and arrived at the Forks at the end of August 1812. These arrivals (six Scots, four Orkneymen, and eight Irishmen) were not actually settlers, but servants recruited on limited-term contracts. Another party recruited in Scotland and Ireland in 1812, again composed mainly of "servants" intended to prepare crops and buildings, rather than of actual settlers, arrived at Pembina on 27 October 1812. Both parties had to be fed without any benefit of a harvest, relying mainly on buffalo hunted on the plains.

Selkirk had appointed Miles Macdonell as governor of the settlement, and before he had a chance to assess the agricultural potential of the region, Selkirk informed him that a much larger party of settlers, to be recruited in Kildonan, would be dispatched in 1813. These Kildonan settlers were the by-product of an attempt by Selkirk to raise a Highland regiment for service in North America. Their transatlantic voyage was a disaster, and after wintering in the north, the youngest and fittest of the party arrived in Red River on 22 June, 1814. By this time, the servants had built a fortified house, which they called Fort Douglas, on the west side of the Red River, almost immediately opposite to the North West Company's Fort Gibraltar.

Word of the arrival at the Bay of the new group of Kildonaners spurred Macdonell, in January of 1814, to seize the settlement's entire supply of pemmican. Further, he banned its export from the region. Macdonell was convinced that the settlement needed all the foodstuffs it could produce, but the North West Company also needed the pemmican, and charged that Macdonell was exceeding his authority. The result was a series of confrontations. Eventually, Macdonell agreed that the fur traders would be entitled to half the pemmican. The Nor'westers capitulated.

Those North West Company partners who had permitted the pemmican to be seized were censured at the annual meeting of the company's partners at Fort William in 1814. This confrontation prompted Alexander Greenfield Macdonell to write, "Something serious will *undoubtedly* take place – nothing but the complete downfall of the Colony will satisfy some, by fair or foul means." Every Nor'wester in the district returned from Fort William with military appointments, swords, and uniforms.

One fur trader, Duncan Cameron, showed himself publicly in full military dress, declaring himself a captain in His Majesty's service. Cameron circulated among the Selkirk people over the winter of 1814-1815, stirring up their discontent. He had much fertile ground on which to work. Nothing had gone right for the settlers. Difficult journeys to Red River had been followed by provision shortfalls, and an absence of proper housing. Promises made had not been kept.

Trials and Tribulations

Miles Macdonell was anything but a charismatic leader. To make matters worse, he was not even a Highlander, but a British North American of Highland descent. The difference was crucial. He never understood the settlers and had little but contempt for them. He handed out muskets, and expected people who had never held a gun in their lives to be able to fight if necessary. Moreover, he was less of a presence than an absence, as he was often away from Red River. As his successor once observed, his attitude was that he "was surrounded by envious men whose chief wish was to throw obstacles in his way, and whose greatest pleasure would be to see him fail in all his plans."

Support for the governor rapidly deteriorated in the spring of 1815, leaving him virtually alone to face the combined opposition of his own people and the Nor'westers. In the midst of this dissent, Duncan Cameron offered to liberate the discontented settlers from their bondage and transport them to better lands in eastern Canada.

Once the contracts of the settlement's servants expired at the beginning of June, Macdonell was largely abandoned by his own settlers. Only a handful of people remained loyal. In one confrontation, one of the cannons which he ordered fired exploded, seriously injuring several men. This accident took all the heart out of those still supporting the governor. They met, and advised him to surrender to the NWC, even writing him a public letter to that effect. Under this pressure, the governor allowed himself to be taken prisoner. Meanwhile, on 18 June, the Nor'westers sent off their canoes, bound for Upper Canada, with 134 settlers aboard. Macdonell would follow soon afterwards. The remaining settlers – some 28 males – were harassed by armed parties of mixed-bloods.

The Saulteaux, led by Chief Peguis, eventually escorted this small party of loyalists, including a handful of women and children, out of the settlement. One of their number entered in his journal on the evening of their departure, "We have been driven from a country whose fertile soil, wholesome climate, natural production & beautiful scenery promised to us and our children ages of happiness." These colonists, led by Peter Fidler, Postmaster at Brandon House, proceeded to Jack River above Lake Winnipeg.

From the First Dispersal to the Second Dispersal

While the settlers were being wooed away from Lord Selkirk at Red River, former Nor'wester Colin Robertson had collected a large party of fur traders on behalf of the Hudson's Bay Company. They left Lower Canada in May of 1815, for the Athabasca country, where they were to compete directly with the North West Company in the centre of the richest fur country in North America. As Robertson's brigades headed west, they began to pick up news of the settlement's dispersal from eastbound NWC canoes.

Robertson did not hesitate for a moment. He left his brigade and went ahead to Red River, where he learned from the mixed-bloods of the recent events. Going to the rendezvous point at Jack River, Robertson agreed to lead the party of loyal settlers he found there back to Red River, and on 19 August 1815, Robertson, 40 settlers, and 17 employees arrived back at the Forks. They discovered that while various parties of marauders had done considerable damage to the crops, there was still something to salvage – about 400 bushels of wheat, 200 bushels of barley, and 500 bushels of potatoes. Small huts were hastily thrown up for the winter. When Nor'westers Duncan Cameron and Alexander G. Macdonell arrived back at Fort Gilbraltar from Fort William, they discovered that the settlers had re-established themselves. In addition, the settlers' new leader – Colin Robertson – was popular and decisive, rather than detested and ineffectual like Macdonell. His declared motto was "When among wolves, Howl."

Robertson learned in October that the mixed-bloods were threatening Brandon House, and he responded swiftly to what he took to be a resumption of hostilities. He and a small squad seized Fort Gilbraltar and took Duncan Cameron prisoner. In the process, he obtained possession of some of the arms seized in the spring from the colony. A few days later he sent Jean-Baptiste Lagimodière east with dispatches for Lord Selkirk.

In the meantime, Robert Semple and a party of 84 new settlers arrived at York Factory on 17 August. Semple was an American Loyalist who had been appointed Governor-in-Chief of the HBC territories. Semple had initially intended to visit the Forks in the spring, but he was delayed until 3 November. His early letters to Selkirk were quite encouraging. Leaving Robertson in charge of the settlement, the governor set off to tour the neighbouring HBC posts.

As for Lord Selkirk, he had spent several frustrating years serving as Lord-Lieutenant of Kirkcudbright, and as a member of the British House of Lords. By late 1815, he and his family were on their way to Montreal via New York. In the American city, he learned of the dispersal of his settlement. He arrived in Lower Canada by early November, prepared to negotiate with the North West Company on behalf of the HBC, and to pressure the colonial government into action in the west. The talks with the NWC led nowhere, and Selkirk was completely frustrated in his

Trials and Tribulations

dealings with the government of Canada. Red River was beyond the control of colonial government, of course, and local officials tended to be sympathetic to the North West Company.

Before long, Lord Selkirk began thinking about the use of a private military force in the West, most particularly the enlistment of soon-to-be disbanded Swiss soldiers serving in North America who could be recruited as settler-soldiers. Interviews with his former settlers now in Upper Canada confirmed that they could not fight. His efforts to relieve his settlement were redoubled in early March, when Jean-Baptiste Lagimodière brought him news of the re-establishment of Red River by Colin Robertson.

Selkirk immediately requested of the Lieutenant-Governor of Upper Canada, Sir Gordon Drummond, permission to recruit an officer and a few soldiers to accompany him into the interior, where he planned to evict the Nor'westers. Drummond granted Selkirk's request. Unfortunately, most of his plans were sent west with Lagimodière, who was an experienced bushman, but not a very discreet messenger. As he travelled west, he told whoever would listen in the taverns of Upper Canada of his mission. Not surprisingly, he was captured by Nor'westers near Fond du Lac (now Superior, Wisconsin) on 16 June, and his dispatches were eagerly read at Fort William.

Drummond then had second thoughts about the armed guard, and rescinded his permission. Selkirk ignored this setback, and entered into negotiations with officers of the disbanded Swiss regiments to recruit soldier-settlers for his settlement. He did not expect long service, he wrote one of the officers, but merely a year's employment. As many as 80 men from each of the de Meuron and de Watteville units were enlisted. Whatever the moral and legal implications of the hiring of the mercenaries, as a practical measure it was a brilliant stroke.

By early May of 1816, Selkirk had two separate expeditions heading westward to relieve Red River. One, consisting of men and livestock, was led from Upper Canada by Miles Macdonell. The other party came from Lower Canada, commanded by Captain Frederick Matthey of the de Meuron regiment. It consisted of over 60 former de Meuron soldiers, most of them still armed and wearing their regimental uniforms. Selkirk himself remained in Lower Canada, still trying to convince the government to assist him. Unfortunately, events in Red River would not wait.

According to Peter Fidler, rumours that the mixed-bloods of the region – encouraged by the North West Company – were once again planning to drive away the settlers were rampant after Christmas of 1815.

J. M. Bumsted

At the end of February 1816, Colin Robertson wrote to Governor Semple that some action was to be feared. He advised Semple that in the spring the settlers should not be allowed to occupy, or farm their land. Instead, they should remain within Fort Douglas until the period of expected danger had passed. In early March, HBC men observed that a new flag had joined the NWC on one the flagpoles of Fort Qu'Appelle, on the Saskatchewan River. This "flag of the Half-breeds" was "about 4 ½ feet square, red & in the middle a large figure of Eight horizontally of a different colour." At about the same time, mixed-bloods from all over the West began to assemble at Fort Gibraltar.

In the advance planning for the settlement of Red River, no attention had been paid to the mixed-bloods, or their "freeman" associates, as important players in the region. These people were not yet known as "Métis" or even "mixed-bloods," but usually were called "half-breeds" or "bois-brulé." Selkirk had acknowledged that the friendship of the First Nations people would have to be cultivated, and that Aboriginal land title would have to be respected. But his early writing on Red River, the fur trade, and the First Nations, offered no suggestion of the existence of the mixed-bloods. Nor did any of his instructions to Miles Macdonell recommend a policy for dealing with them.

In contrast, early entries in Macdonell's journal noted the presence of these local residents, whom he employed as hunters to provide food for the settlement. However, Macdonell did not treat them as a distinct people with their own aspirations and interests, and he bullied them and attempted to regulate their activities. Macdonell would increasingly come to appreciate that the mixed-bloods and freemen were the main warriors of the NWC. Accepting that they were a potent force was hardly the same as understanding them, however.

The leaders of the settlement, and their employer, were eventually forced by the events of 1815 and 1816 to recognize the importance of the mixed-bloods. Selkirk's description of these people in 1818 is worth noting, for it epitomizes the Selkirk/HBC/Red River interpretation of their role in the region. Selkirk introduced them in his *Memorial to the Duke of Richmond* in the context of the increasing success of his settlement in 1814: They were "a set of men...judged fit instruments for acts of violence, viz: the sons of their Canadian, and other servants by Indian women, a great number of whom are reared about their trading posts." These men were brought up to be dependent on the NWC, and it was only after 1814 that they were "taught to consider themselves a separate tribe of men, and distinguished by a separate name, with a view of ascribing their violence to the native Indians." Selkirk emphasized,

Trials and Tribulations

"These half-breeds have been described as a Nation of independent Indians, but they are in fact with very few exceptions in the regular employment and pay of the North West Company." Such an understanding hardly equipped Selkirk and his agents to formulate an adequate policy for dealing with this "New Nation," however it had been brought into existence.

In early 1815 Colin Robertson decided to seize Fort Gibraltar again, claiming that if he delayed he would not have sufficient strength to do so. He wrote Semple of his intentions, but acted before he received any reply. Duncan Cameron was again placed in custody, and Robertson later testified he found in Cameron's room an open letter, in the Nor'wester's handwriting, inviting Indians to the Forks to pillage in the spring. This letter led Robertson to seize the remaining papers at Fort Gibraltar and ship them to Fort Douglas for careful scrutiny.

Among these papers were a number of HBC letters, which had been intercepted, opened, and obviously read. Robertson also found a circular letter from Cameron and Alexander G. Macdonell, written from Qu'Appelle, in February 1816, which said, "the spirit of our people particularly the Halfbreeds will require to be roused, and we think that the appearance of a few of their color from the nearest posts would again have the desired effect." A number of other letters related to the events of 1815. Here, Robertson insisted, was clear evidence of NWC duplicity and instigation.

On 18 March, John Siveright, a clerk of the NWC at Fort Gibraltar, asked Robertson whether he intended to stop the winter express as it passed the Forks. Robertson replied that he had three men ready to seize the express, but he would be satisfied with examining the letters from Qu'Appelle, Swan River, and Fort des Prairies, and if they contained no evidence of plans against the settlement, the express could proceed. Otherwise, he would detain it until Semple's arrival.

The express arrived the following day, and when Robertson opened a letter from Alexander G. Macdonell at Qu'Appelle, he read: "A storm is gathering to the Northward ready to burst on the heads of the rascals who deserve it; little do they know their situation; last year was but a joke. The new nation under their leaders are coming forward to clear their native soil of intruders and assassins." This letter did not suggest that the "new nation" was being instigated or encouraged by the Nor'westers, but in another letter Macdonell wrote, "Sir William Shaw is collecting all the Halfbreeds in the surrounding departments, and has ordered his friends in this quarter to prepare to take the field; he has actually taken every Halfbreed in the country to the Forks Fort des

Prairie, it is supposed they will when collected together form more than one hundred, God knows the result." Other correspondence from the three posts was in the same vein. Robertson carefully bundled the entire express up and put it away without opening any more of the letters. Or so he would later claim.

On 19 March, at Pembina, Sheriff Alexander Macdonell (no relation to the Nor'wester) received a letter from Robertson informing him of the capture of Fort Gibraltar. Macdonell, accompanied by Messrs. White, MacLeod, Pritchard, and several constables, immediately proceeded to the NWC post, where he formally arrested its occupants and seized their arms and ammunition. The Nor'westers were sent to Fort Douglas in the custody of P.C. Pambrun and John McLeod. In the meantime, Robertson had heard that two of the cannon taken from the settlement the previous spring were hidden at Bas de la Rivière, which had been the site of La Verendrye's Fort Maurepas. He sent John MacLeod and a party of five men to search for the artillery, but they were unable to find it.

Governor Semple arrived back at the Forks from his western tour at the end of March. Semple sent a formal letter to Robertson on 12 April, approving of his actions in seizing Fort Gibraltar, arresting Cameron, and opening the letters in the express. The measure was demanded by the conduct of the Nor'westers, the governor wrote, and the seizure of the express "was a step arising out of the former and which has happily furnished its own justification to the fullest extent."

Robertson advocated sending Cameron and the intercepted letters to Hudson's Bay, and thence to England, but Semple insisted "that he did not see any harm the said Cameron could do as a Prisoner." This disagreement appears to have marked the opening of the quarrel over policy between Robertson and Semple that would end with the former departing the settlement in early June. From Robertson's perspective, Semple (whom the fur trader persistently referred to in his writing as "Mr. Simple"), placed too much trust in the honourable behaviour of both friends and enemies in a place that was "a hotbed of Hypocrisy, desertion, and party spirit." Robertson did not approve of the release of all of the traders arrested except Cameron, for example, despite their solemn promises not to disturb the tranquillity of the settlement.

Robertson continued to advocate the dispatch of Duncan Cameron and the captured express to England. He also recommended that Forts Douglas and Gibraltar be consolidated in order to make defence easier. Perhaps most important of all, Robertson continued to insist that all the settlers should reside at or near one of the forts, and should not be placed upon their farms until after the menace was over.

Trials and Tribulations

In early May, James Sutherland, an HBC trader, set out with his furs from Qu'Appelle for the Bay, having been assured by G. Alexander Macdonell that he could proceed unmolested down river. Sutherland and his party were subsequently stopped by a large party of Francophone Canadians and mixed-bloods led by Cuthbert Grant. According to Peter Fidler, the attackers had "their faces all painted in the most horrid & terrific forms & dressed like Indians and all armed with Guns, Pistols, Swords & Spears, & several had Bows & Arrows; and made the War-whoop or yell like the Natives in immediately attacking their Enemies."

The cargo of furs and provisions was seized. Sutherland and his party were forced to sign an agreement not to bear arms against the NWC before they were freed, having been kept prisoners for a week. Upon learning of this incident, Governor Semple decided to send Duncan Cameron and the captured evidence to the Bay, which was done on 18 May.

The settlers who had wintered at Pembina returned at the end of April, and Semple immediately located them on their land. They were assigned separate lots, given seed, and encouraged to plant extensively, even though rumours of potential destruction swirled all around them. At the end of May, a number of settlers came to Colin Robertson, still in charge of Fort Gibraltar, and asked him to shelter them until the danger had passed. Robertson answered that they must apply to Governor Semple, who then told them to remain on their lands. The differences of opinion between Robertson and Semple had now reached an open break, and Robertson debated about leaving.

While Robertson and Semple were disagreeing over what should be done, Brandon House was attacked on 1 June by a party of mixed-bloods, Canadians, and Aboriginals. The HBC fort was defended by only a few HBC servants, and Peter Fidler later described the scene: "A little after noon about 48 Canadians, half-Breeds, & Indians, but mostly half-Breeds appeared in the plain all in horse back with the half-Breeds flag flying, this little army marched in regular order in an oblong square; one was near the middle beating an Indian drum & accompanying it with an Indian Song, the greater part of the rest bearing Chorus."

They ransacked the post and celebrated for days, while the residents of the post – most of whom were fur-trade families living in buildings surrounding the fort itself – moved out on to the plains to take shelter with the Cree and Stone peoples. The attackers eventually moved down the river toward the Forks. No-one had been seriously injured in the incident, although Brandon House had been stripped of its rum, tobacco, and ammunition. Up to this point, the "new nation" had intimidated fur traders and settlers alike, had destroyed property, but had not actually hurt anyone.

Word was brought to Fort Douglas of the destruction of Brandon House on 9 June. The Aboriginal who reported this news also claimed that Alexander G. Macdonell and his crew were heading down the Assiniboine publicly proclaiming their intention of destroying the settlement at Red River. Governor Semple finally decided that Colin Robertson's long-expressed fears were justified. Two forts could not be defended. He marched to Fort Gibraltar, still occupied by Robertson, to order its destruction and the movement of its palisades to help protect Fort Douglas.

Although Robertson had now seen most of his recommendations accepted by Semple, the major one of keeping the settlers within the fort remained unresolved. Robertson later argued that he did not want to have to stay in Fort Douglas with Semple while the two men were still at loggerheads. He requested permission to depart Red River to go to the aid of the HBC traders he had sent to the Athabasca. The request was granted. Robertson left with the parting words, "the Colony is nearly ruined, – time will show who has been the cause of it."

At Lake Winnipeg, Robertson had second thoughts, and he returned to within fifteen miles of the Forks. He wrote Semple again offering his services. The governor declined them, writing that Sheriff Alexander Macdonell had been put in charge of Fort Douglas in his absence. Robertson then resumed his journey. On 16 June, an Aboriginal named Moustache arrived at Fort Douglas, claiming to have escaped from the mixed-bloods who were encamped at Portage la Prairie. He said that a heavily armed party would arrive at the Forks in a day or two. The chief of the local Saulteaux offered to assist the settlement, but Semple said it was not necessary.

On 19 June, at about 7 p.m., a party of armed men on horseback was seen on the prairie to the north-west of Fort Douglas by a man using a spyglass in the watch house of the fort. The party consisted of about 60 mixed-bloods, some free Canadians, and Aboriginals, with the mixed-bloods in the majority. The horsemen would subsequently maintain that they were attempting to go around Fort Douglas and the settlement, but there was nothing but open prairie all around them. They could have made a much wider sweep to the north-west had they wished to avoid a confrontation. The armed party had just about reached the lots of the settlers, who were weeding potatoes in the fields, when Governor Semple recruited a small number of volunteers from the fort to

Trials and Tribulations

accompany him to meet the intruders to "determine their intentions." Six officers from the fort were included in the group.

Semple was particularly concerned for the safety of the settlers in the fields, which was understandable given his refusal to keep them within the fort. William Coltman, the commissioner who later investigated the Seven Oaks incident for the British government, was convinced that the governor's disagreement with Colin Robertson – in which Semple was now being proved demonstrably wrong – aggravated Semple's lack of sense and caution on this day. Semple had called for an artillery piece, but refused to wait for it. Several witnesses said that the governor had a paper which he intended to read to the intruders.

On his way to meet the mixed-blood party, Semple was met by settlers running to the fort, and was informed that some of them had been taken prisoner. Indeed, Alexander Murray, Alexander Sutherland, and William and Alexander Bannerman were detained before a shot was fired. Alexander G. Macdonell later testified that "I have reason to think that it would enrage the Governor against the North West servants to see these settlers taken prisoner so inoffensively attending their own lawful labours." One of the retreating settlers warned Semple to be careful, to which he replied, "I am only going to speak to them."

Semple and his party marched single file along the west bank of the Red River past a number of settlers' houses, until they reached a bend in the river at a place called Seven Oaks. John Pritchard, one of the few survivors of the subsequent melee, insisted that Semple's group was unaware how numerous the other party was. Pritchard and others from the settlement also claimed that the mixed-blood party were dressed as Indian warriors in full war paint. At Seven Oaks, the horsemen surrounded the governor's party in a half-moon.

Most testimony agrees that at this point, a Canadian named Bouché or Boucher rode up to Semple and asked him what he wanted. John Pritchard insisted that the question was asked in an "insolent tone," which may have further aggravated the governor, who after a brief verbal exchange, attempted to grab either Boucher's gun or the reins of his horse. A single shot rang out, and a full scale fire-fight erupted. In this clash, the settlers were at a distinct disadvantage. They were not soldiers, and were unfamiliar with guns, while their opponents used them almost daily.

Semple was wounded in the thigh, and one or more settlers killed. Semple told Cuthbert Grant, "I am not mortally wounded, and if you could get me conveyed to the fort, I think I should live." Grant promised to do so, but he did not remain with the governor. At this point Grant completely lost control over his forces, which not only continued firing, but ignored various attempts on the part of the settlers to surrender. What followed was nothing short of a massacre. Semple himself was fatally shot by an Aboriginal named Machicabaou, and before the killing finally ended, twenty-one settlers were dead, including a number of the settlement's officers and leaders, while only one of the mixed-blood party was killed.

To compound matters, the bodies were stripped and mutilated. It was this part of the incident at Seven Oaks that Lord Selkirk and his friends always regarded as particularly repugnant, and he spent many years seeking redress for this conduct. One of the few settlers to escape was John Pritchard, who was physically protected by a Canadian named Lavigne he had known when employed by the NWC. Pritchard eventually made his way back to Fort Douglas.

It has never been definitively established who actually fired the first shot. Later testimony claimed that it came from the ranks of the settlers, but it must be pointed out that most of the surviving witnesses were of the mixed-blood party. Seven Oaks was clearly a spontaneous eruption of violence between two armed forces emotionally prepared for trouble, rather than a deliberately planned incident of mass murder. In the aftermath, the mixed-bloods were probably as shocked at what had happened as were the settlers.

Up to this point, the confrontations in Red River had not claimed any lives. From a legal standpoint, the absence of premeditation might lessen the nature of the offence, but cannot exculpate those involved. Neither can the likelihood that Semple's people fired the first shot. Cuthbert Grant's party was armed, and in the process of engaging in criminal activity – kidnapping and the display of armed threats, at the very least – when the incident occurred.

Only a handful of the mounted party was involved in the post-battle slaughter and mutilation. Nonetheless this brutal behaviour horrified the world beyond Red River, confirming in the minds of many the notion that the mixed-bloods were little short of savages. Lord Selkirk would become obsessed with the legal pursuit of those involved at Seven Oaks, although he never achieved a single conviction in the courts for their acts. The mixed-bloods might have had an even worse press if most people had not been convinced that they had been put up to their actions by the NWC.

At daybreak on the morning after Seven Oaks, Sheriff Alexander Macdonell, who had assumed command, attempted to rally his forces after the disaster of the preceding day. Initially, the remaining settlers

Trials and Tribulations

agreed to defend Fort Douglas, and their position was strong. With the assistance of the Saulteaux, Macdonell buried the dead.

Then, John Pritchard arrived with a message from Cuthbert Grant and Alexander Fraser, demanding that the fort be surrendered, the settlers removed, and all property abandoned. Alternatively they would murder all the settlers. Pritchard drafted, and circulated a petition, supported by others, calling for capitulation. Most of the settlement signed. Sheriff Macdonell understandably felt abandoned, and suspicious of Pritchard, who had mysteriously escaped death at Seven Oaks. On 20 June, he negotiated an agreement with the "chiefs of the Halfbreeds," allowing the settlers safe passage out of the Red River Valley. This hasty surrender was perhaps premature, given that the settlement was a fortified position and the fact that the mixed-bloods had no artillery. However the Seven Oaks incident had clearly demoralized the settlers, and they had no taste for further bloodshed.

Two days later, after making out a full inventory of all the public property at Fort Douglas, Macdonell turned everything over to Cuthbert Grant, who signed a nine-page document acknowledging receipt of the goods. He wrote, "Received on Account of the North West Company, by me Cuthbert Grant Clerk to the North West Company, Acting for the North West Company." By signing the receipt as a clerk of the NWC, rather than as a chief of the mixed-bloods, Grant suggested that he did not himself believe that he was acting solely as an autonomous leader of his people. Grant now refused to allow the settlers to depart, since he had received orders from Alexander G. Macdonell to detain them until his arrival from Qu'Appelle. Sheriff Macdonell observed that this would deprive Grant of the honours of the victory. Grant finally agreed to keep his word, and ordered the settlers to leave immediately. Sheriff Macdonell loaded his people, and as much baggage as could be carried into eight boats, and the little flotilla started down the river towards its ultimate destination at the Bay.

One of the Sheriff Macdonell's concerns was for the remaining documents which Colin Robertson had intercepted at Fort Gibraltar, which were now in his custody. Fearing that his party would be searched for this incriminating evidence, before his party disembarked, Macdonell instructed one of the females of the settlement to tie the letters around her middle under her skirt.

On 23 June, the fleet of settlers met a large brigade of Nor'westers heading south under the command of Archibald Norman McLeod. The brigade of eight canoes had left Bas de la Riviére on 19 June, having been previously armed and instructed in "the manual and Platoon exercises" by mercenaries Charles Reinhard and Frederick Heurter. Accompanying the canoes was a bateaux carrying two brass three-pounder cannon mounted on field carriages. Heurter later testified that when he remarked on the relative weakness of this force, he was informed that this was only one of a number of parties that were converging on the Forks to attack the settlement.

McLeod ordered the boats from Red River to stop, and ordered a general search of their effects. His orders were to search everywhere, stated Heurter, especially in trunks and boxes, looking for "all account Books letters & papers of whatever nature." There were no keys for Governor Semple's trunks, which were broken open with an axe. Meanwhile, the girl with the letters hidden around her waist stood unobtrusively on the shore.

The acting governor and the settlers were eventually allowed to proceed, although several, including John Pritchard, were detained as prisoners. Sheriff Macdonell was persuaded that the detention of Pritchard was really a ruse by the Nor'westers to disguise the fact that he was a turncoat, who had been spared at Seven Oaks to sow dissension. Pritchard did not know of the presence of the documents. The settlers apparently escaped without actually taking an oath never to return to Red River, although Sheriff Macdonell had to post bail for an appearance at Montreal before he was released. Peter Fidler and his family were also heading from Brandon House to the Bay, and they were also halted and threatened with death should they return to Red River.

After releasing the settlers, the NWC brigade continued to the Forks. There, Messrs. McLeod and McKenzie assembled all the mixed-bloods, and congratulated them on their efforts. They also distributed presents. Each of 40 mixed-bloods got a capot, a pair of green trousers, a cotton shirt, a silk handkerchief, a leather jockey cap, and a feather. The remainder were told they would receive their rewards in the autumn. The two Nor'wester leaders also harangued the Saulteaux for not being supportive. They then ordered a schooner, laboriously constructed by boatbuilder Donald Livingstone, to be destroyed. According to Frederick Heurter, the entire assemblage then moved to Seven Oaks to view the site of the battle, with more praise given to individuals who had distinguished themselves in the action, including those who had committed the acts of brutality. Most of the NWC partners then departed for the West, leaving Alexander G. Macdonell and Archibald McLellan in charge of what remained of Red River. In late June of 1816, therefore, the NWC appeared completely victorious, and in control of the region. Their triumph, however, would be short-lived.

Trials and Tribulations

Lord Selkirk on the Offensive

The Earl of Selkirk had finally departed Montreal for Red River on 18 June, 1816, in company with a personal physician, and a number of other companions. At Drummond's Island, near Sault Ste. Marie, he learned of the incident at Seven Oaks. He determined to head west via Fort William to interview the witnesses he understood had been brought to the NWC post. On 11 August, the Selkirk party met up with Captain Frederick Matthey and his party of de Meurons at Thunder Bay, 15 miles east of Fort William. The 12 canoes of the Matthey brigade contained four former officers, and 100 former enlisted men of the de Meuron regiment, still in uniform and under military discipline.

The de Meurons easily occupied Fort William on 13 August. Selkirk, as a duly appointed magistrate, began interviewing witnesses from Seven Oaks. Despite the denials of the Nor'westers, Selkirk thought he had a case for conspiracy, although much of the evidence was circumstantial. He understood that he was treading on thin legal ground, but he expected to be supported by government. Whether his basic assumption – that the behaviour of the North West Company had so passed beyond the bounds of acceptability that both government and public would react against it once the "facts" were put before them – was accurate, did not occur to him for a moment. The supposed culprits in the Seven Oaks business were sent east.

The Earl's associates, headed by Dr. John Allan and Miles Macdonell, had been leaning heavily on Daniel McKenzie, the one NWC partner remaining at Fort William, over his culpability in the events in Red River. McKenzie was clearly not well. He had to be allowed to make notes to himself over a period of several days in order to produce a coherent statement of his activities. He was afraid he would be left holding the bag for the Seven Oaks business, and Selkirk's people did not disabuse him of his concern. Selkirk and McKenzie came to an agreement on 19 September, to send Selkirk's grievances against the NWC to two or more arbitrators chosen by the Lord Chief Justices in the King's Bench and Common Pleas, Westminster. The parties were to indemnify each other for damages, with a decision to be reached by 1 December 1819.

This was a reasonable way to settle the dispute between Selkirk and the NWC, and it would later be recommended by the commissioners of investigation. Whether McKenzie was the appropriate person to make this agreement was another matter, however. Even more dubious was the consignment by McKenzie to Selkirk of all the furs, and the sale of all property at Fort William.

Daniel McKenzie was probably not sufficiently in command of his faculties to understand what he had done, even without his subsequent claims of inebriation, bad treatment, and intensive interrogation. He had been forced to "dry out" before coming to terms with Selkirk, a move that Dr. Allan advised against. When Allan pointed out that this transaction could be misrepresented by the NWC, Selkirk replied, "it would be absurd to abstain from doing anything merely to avoid being misrepresented by the NWCo. who had already misrepresented his best actions, and would invariably misrepresent his conduct however unimpeachable it might be." Selkirk went further, when he wrote to one legal acquaintance in London, "I flatter myself that the step which I have taken, tho' perhaps unusual, is not so far out of the common path, as to be in any degree improper."

Indeed, had McKenzie been more a more responsible individual, it would have been a complete stroke of genius. As it was, Selkirk's bold action, which also included a complete take-over of the NWC posts on the canoe routes between Fort William and Red River, exposed the weakness of the corporate structure of the NWC, and completely disrupted its trade. The chaos he created would take years to undo. Indeed, it could be argued that the Nor'westers never did recover from this act of corporate guerrilla warfare.

On 10 and 11 September, two groups of de Meurons were dispatched up the Kaministiquia to rendezvous at Lac la Pluie under the command of Captain Proteus D'Orsennens. Four weeks later, on 9 October, D'Orsennens reported that he had occupied Fort Lac la Pluie in the name of the HBC, using warrants issued by Selkirk. The de Meurons had been forced to break down the gate of the fort, but had met little resistance within. A number of Nor'westers were placed under arrest. Selkirk's aims, which were to re-establish the Old Grand Portage along the proposed international border, and to control the canoe routes to the interior, had now been achieved. Whether D'Orsennens could carry out Selkirk's next step, which was to send a winter expeditionary force to retake Fort Douglas at Red River, was another matter.

On 2 December 1816, Selkirk wrote a lengthy letter to Captain D'Orsennens at Lac la Pluie. The Earl wrote of the "old contests between the Engl Colonies & the French of Canada," in which winter marches had been common. In addition, it was impossible to reinforce D'Orsennens, and for him to pull back would be a "retrograde" step. Since government intervention could not yet be trusted, Selkirk felt that the best step was a surprise winter march to Red River, capturing the artillery and dispersing the rebels.

Trials and Tribulations

At Lac la Pluie, Captain D'Orsennens had considerable difficulty in responding to what was more than a suggestion, but not an order. Most of those under his command were opposed to the adventure. Their arguments were many. They pointed out that the distance was too great for men to carry a sufficient quantity of supplies, and the hunt was too precarious. The presence of Miles Macdonell advocating the scheme was no help, since many argued that he was desperate to redeem himself from his earlier embarrassments. Word from Aboriginals that Fort Douglas had been taken by men from York Factory – later proved erroneous – seemed to make the attempt unnecessary. In the end, the shortage of provisions at Lac la Pluie decided the matter. They had to get to Red River, or starve. D'Orsennens held out to his underfed de Meurons and Canadian voyageurs the promise of feasting on the smoking limbs of fresh buffalo meat if they could reach their destination.

The difficulties of supply were to some extent resolved by forming a depot about halfway between Lac la Pluie and Red River at an NWC trading post at the south-west extremity of Lake of the Woods. A small party with four sledges drawn by most of the horses at Lac la Pluie set out for this depot with supplies of flour, wild rice, and a keg of spirits. Concerns about getting there were obviated by the unexpected appearance of a qualified guide who knew the territory between Lake of the Woods and the Red River. This was a man named John Tanner, who had lived among the Aboriginals for many years and was known as "the American." Tanner had been captured as a child in Kentucky by a war party of Ottawas, and raised as a native at Michilimackinac. He had later followed his people to Lake of the Woods. Tanner could no longer speak English, although he had some memories of his childhood, and wanted to visit his natural family again.

The party of 25 de Meurons, and a slightly larger number of Canadians set off on foot on 10 December. Each man had snowshoes, but there was not enough snow to facilitate their use. Nonetheless, the weather proved extremely co-operative, with bright sunshine, moderate temperatures, and little wind. Each two-man team was allotted a hand sledge, on which they could carry their baggage and provisions. The rations were quite spartan, consisting of 30 pounds of bread per man baked into three pound loaves, plus some wild rice and Indian corn. The expedition carried only 15 pounds of meat, and a small quantity of rum. Three draft oxen were yoked to a sledge to carry the two pieces of artillery brought from Fort William. A bull, two cows, and a heifer were driven ahead by William Laidlaw, who had accompanied Selkirk from Montreal, and would later become manager of the Selkirk farm at Red River.

Miles Macdonell accompanied the men on a small cariole drawn by a horse, one of the few remaining at Lac la Pluie. Traversing the ice of Lake of the Woods, the group reached the supply depot without mishap except the loss of one draft ox, which slipped on the ice and had to be killed. The dead ox provided a welcome supply of fresh meat, which was distributed to the men in rations of 12 pounds per man. The Canadians ate their meat within two or three days, while the de Meurons managed to make their portion last for more than two weeks.

The party of 60 Canadians and de Meurons was joined outside Lake of the Woods on 24 December, by a small group of Aboriginals led by Chief Pin-panche, who acted as scouts to make sure that the expedition was not discovered by the Nor'westers as it made its way to Pembina. On 31 December, Fort Daer was captured by parties led by Captain D'Orsennens and Lieutenant McDonald. They found no Nor'westers, and only a handful of Canadian freemen and their families occupying the buildings. However, all the buildings at Fort Daer were full of piles of frozen buffalo meat. The little army feasted, and consumed the two kegs of rum which Miles Macdonell had carried on his cariole. Macdonell was happy to find that Fort Daer was fairly intact. There were, however, no fresh horses to be found anywhere in the neighbourhood. This march had demonstrated that winter, while formidable, need not prevent all military activity.

On 2 January, D'Orsennens set off for the Forks, still accompanied by Tanner. He would have to act quickly, since the presence of such a large party of men could not be concealed indefinitely. Weather conditions quickly deteriorated to near blizzard conditions, and intense cold. While the weather proved an obstacle, slowing the party to the point that it took over a week to make the 70 miles to Fort Douglas, it was also blessing. The Nor'westers were not likely to be out and about in such conditions, nor would they expect anyone else to be.

At the La Salle River, south of the Forks, the party was startled by Chief Peguis, and nine members of his band of Saulteaux. Only with difficulty did D'Orsonnens prevent his men from firing. He had just as much trouble preventing Peguis from discharging his firearms in a salute to the newcomers. Either action might have given the alarm to the opposition. That evening, the men ate the last of their provisions, plus a few buffalo tongues furnished by Peguis, and warmed themselves at the fire. Macdonell once again produced some spirits which "afforded an encouraging dram to all hands." Many of the de Meurons, inexperienced with winter conditions, attempted to thaw their shoes and socks in front

Trials and Tribulations

of the fire. This was only partly successful, and the footgear was still wet when put on the next morning. As a result, 17 de Meurons experienced frostbite. These were the only casualties of the march, however.

D'Orsennens led his men up to Fort Douglas at six a.m. on 10 January. They could hear the barking of dogs, and could see sparks from the chimneys within, indicating that fires were being supplied with fresh logs. The attackers had fashioned crude scaling ladders from trees, most of which turned out to be too short. While the invaders were attempting to sort this out, Seraphim La Mar, whose house was close to the walls, came to his door and called out a challenge. Louis Nolin tried to buy time by replying in French. Unconvinced, La Mar repeated the challenge, and Nolin again answered ambiguously in French. By this time, Tanner had managed to scale the wall, and flung open the gate. Nolin quickly brandished his pistol, and forced La Mar into his house.

D'Orsonnens and Miles Macdonell headed to the quarters of McLellan, who came out of his bedroom trouserless. McLellan complained that the intruders had entered the fort like robbers. D'Orsennens replied that Macdonell certainly had a right to enter his own house, and asked McLellan how he justified his possession of the property of others. The Nor'wester replied that he was only a lodger, and the fort was actually in the possession of the mixed-bloods. However, a number of incriminating documents were found in his quarters. McLellan, Seraphim La Mar, Soussants Voudrie, and François Mainville were kept under confinement. Joseph Cadotte was released after a "very humble and submissive apology for his conduct," and immediately set off to collect a band of mixed-bloods to retake the fort.

Fort Douglas contained very few provisions, and was devoid of tools and agricultural implements. It did house several pieces of colonial artillery and a quantity of small arms. Some of the invading party was sent back to Fort Daer to collect the buffalo meat. Those left at the Forks scavenged desperately for food from the surrounding trading posts of both the NWC and HBC. Sleds sent from Bas de la Riviére with food intended for the Nor'westers were captured, and it was learned that only six men were at the post. Laidlaw and a small party subsequently captured the fort at Bas de la Riviére without any resistance, finding more guns than food.

A group of mixed-bloods led by Cuthbert Grant arrived in the area shortly after the seizure of Fort Douglas. They killed some of the cattle in the settlement and imprisoned some Canadians returning to the fort with provisions. But despite a numerical advantage they did not attack the fort. Miles Macdonell had sent a copy of a proclamation he had issued to

Grant calling for the laying down of arms by all participants in the fur trade war. Grant is supposed to have thrown a copy of the proclamation in the fire, saying "voila encore une de ces sacres proclamations." But he likely was influenced by it nonetheless, as well as by an awareness of the risks of violence. When Joseph Cadotte advocated a raiding party against Fort Daer, Grant rejected the idea, saying "We are not barbarians."

Not all of Selkirk's military initiatives were as successful as the reconquest of Red River. Lieutenant Antoine de Graffenreid with 22 de Meuron soldiers and a handful of Canadians got lost in the woods while attempting to reinforce La Pluie. When their provisions were finished, Graffenried reported, they were forced to boil and eat their snowshoes and one of the dogs with them. Finally finding the fort and getting food from it, Graffenreid's men did "nothing but cook and eat all day." His men could not follow D'Orsennens to Red River, wrote Graffenreid, and he himself felt "the want of liquor more than I could believe." Graffenreid subsequently got lost again while trying to get from Lac la Pluie to Fort Douglas. Such experiences only demonstrated how fortunate the Red River expedition really had been, particularly in the employment of "the American" to guide the way.

The Coltman Commission

In October of 1816 a commission of investigation into the western conflict, headed by William Bachelor Coltman, was appointed by Sir John Sherbrooke, governor of Lower Canada. Sherbrooke had despaired of finding anyone credible enough to serve, because of the pervasive influence of the North West Company. Coltman emerged at the last moment. Born in England, he had resided in Quebec since 1799 and was not closely associated with the NWC.

While at Fort William, Lord Selkirk had refused to acknowledge several warrants served in dubious circumstances by Upper Canadian constables for his arrest. An angry colonial secretary, Lord Bathurst, responded to NWC accounts of this refusal with instructions to Sir John Sherbrooke to prefer an indictment against Selkirk and to arrest him post-haste. These categorical instructions of Bathurst would influence the actions of colonial officials in Canada for several years, since they could be interpreted as an official repudiation of Selkirk's conduct. In principle it was true that the British government could not condone the actions of a peer of the realm leading a private army and resisting Crown warrants. But at the same time, the British government had for years refused to

Trials and Tribulations

bring law and order into the territories where Selkirk was operating. The colonial secretary was probably most angered by a realization that Selkirk had forced the government's hand.

On 1 May 1817, Selkirk and a small party left Fort William for Red River, arriving at the Forks on 21 June. There he had an interview with Nor'wester John Shaw, who demanded a return of all company property. Shaw insisted that the mixed-bloods were not under the control of the North West Company. They were regarded as was any other band of Aboriginals, he said. He later told Selkirk that he considered his own son William as "merely an Indian." Commissioner Coltman arrived at the Forks on 5 July. He persuaded Selkirk that he was indeed impartial, but the Earl had serious questions about whether the commissioner properly understood the situation. Selkirk tried to explain matters in a letter of 7 July. Most of the disorder resulted from the habit of the Nor'westers to take the law in their own hands. If Selkirk's people had responded in kind, it was because there was no alternative. The Nor'westers needed a practical lesson about the impropriety of their conduct, Selkirk maintained.

At the Forks, Lord Selkirk was quickly disabused of any hope he may have had that Coltman would move to investigate the outrages committed against his settlement in 1815 and 1816 by immediately calling witnesses and hearing testimony. Instead, the Earl found himself haggling over the restoration of property and other matters he regarded as peripheral, while individuals who had played a leading role at Seven Oaks were allowed to come and go as they pleased. Worse still to his mind, he learned that Coltman in effect was granting immunity to most of the mixed-bloods in return for their evidence. Conscious of his heavy losses in the Athabasca district, Selkirk understandably wanted a simultaneous restoration of all property throughout the Indian country. Simon McGillivray insisted that restitution start immediately with Red River. Selkirk maintained that only property illegally seized should be returned, while the Nor'westers wanted everything included since to make inventories of what belonged to each company was a "manifest absurdity." The NWC also insisted that all servants hired by either party while still under contract to the other be restored. This was actually a quite one-sided demand, since all the servants thus hired, including Frederick Heurter, were defectors from the NWC. Coltman added insult to injury by refusing to take Heurter's evidence on the grounds that he had left the NWC service and was not a neutral witness.

After many days of bargaining and the exchange of numerous letters frequently written in leaky tents by the various parties involved,

Coltman had managed to arrange with Selkirk the return of all contested property to the NWC. Coltman and Selkirk exchanged over 50 letters and memoranda between July and September 1817, most of them in the first half of July. Selkirk fought fiercely to have the question of the property purchased from Daniel McKenzie adjudicated in the courts, but eventually surrendered the point. The order on restitution was signed by the parties on 15 July. On that same day, Coltman reported in a letter to Sir John Sherbrooke that the proof was decisive that Selkirk obeyed "legitimate authority." The Earl had also demonstrated his peaceable intentions by his refusal to interfere with NWC canoes bound for the Athabasca, despite many rumours of violence committed against HBC traders in that western region. Coltman added that he was not clear whether Selkirk's reasons for refusing to obey the earlier warrants were "well founded," but "with his Lordship's views of the character and proceedings of his opponents, they were not unnatural, and must I think be allowed considerable weight in extenuation on a future bona fide surrender." This judgement went a long way to exonerate Selkirk from charges of the flaunting of legal warrants.

Selkirk did not make much progress with the commissioner on the matter of legal action for earlier depredations against the settlement. Coltman did meet on 10 July with a delegation of mixed-bloods to retrace *in situ* the movements of 19 June 1816. He had Peter Fidler a few days later draw up a map reflecting the testimony of the participants. In an affidavit sworn before Coltman, Fidler managed to make an editorial comment on his map and the mixed-blood testimony, noting that there were no natural impediments to the mixed-blood party making a wider sweep around Fort Douglas than they had done. Coltman also took many depositions from the mixed-bloods and Canadians. Selkirk's lawyer would later complain that the commissioner allowed the witnesses long preambles of "mitigation and extenuation of the atrocities committed in Red River." The Selkirk people were continually upset by Coltman's refusal to detain legally any of those involved in the violence. Both Selkirk and Captain D'Orsennens offered to execute the warrants already outstanding against the culprits, but were refused by Coltman. The commissioner's rationale for this tolerance of lawbreakers was twofold. In the first place, he would not have had the co-operation of the mixed-bloods in his fact-finding investigations had he gone around arresting them, either before or after they had testified. Secondly, he truly believed – and would repeat many times – that most of what had happened, while horrible, was not really actionable in the courts.

Trials and Tribulations

Lord Selkirk did succeed in getting Coltman to attend a two-day conference with a number of Aboriginal leaders from the Red River region who were at the Forks. He also managed to convince the commissioner to discuss with the chiefs the question of a land concession to the settlement. On 17 July, Coltman wrote to Selkirk, "It appears to me as far as I can see that the Indians wish the Settlement for their own advantage & would scarcely require any consideration for allowing to the Settlers an exclusive possession of a reasonable portion of land." He added, "something will however perhaps be expected as the subject has been so much talked of & certainly an annual present seems best, as it is evident that the interests of the Colony would require the Indians' friendship to be ensured in this manner, even if they gave up their lands voluntarily."

Coltman promised to get the Aboriginal sentiments "faithfully recorded," but understandably wanted nothing to do with the negotiations concerning any deed of land. These negotiations were carried out independently on 18 July by Selkirk and a number of officers from the settlement with five of the Saulteaux and Cree chiefs who were attending the conference, including Peguis. In return for an annual quit rent of two hundred pounds of "good merchantable tobacco," the chiefs granted to the King an area extending six miles in all directions from Fort Douglas and Fort Daer, as well as land extending two miles from the banks on either side of the Red and Assiniboine Rivers. This land was to "have and to hold forever" and was for the use of Selkirk and the settlers he established on these lands. Whatever other effect the transaction had or would have, it made clear that the resident Aboriginals were in 1817 well disposed to Selkirk's settlement.

Despite the frequently annoying presence of the commission, Selkirk did succeed in putting his settlement back on its feet, particularly after the settlers had returned to the Forks on 19 July and after the arrival of his attorney Samuel Gale a few days later. Gale took over much of the detailed negotiation with Coltman, casting a suspicious eye on most of the commissioner's activities. Sheriff Alexander Macdonell recorded the meeting between the founder and his people laconically: "about 11 o'clock forenoon he came to the Frog Plains and conversed with the settlers." As well as arranging the treaty with the Aboriginals, Selkirk allocated land for a church and a school. He also announced that those loyal settlers who had suffered in the recent depredations – 24 families – would have their land forever free from any debt to him. Land surveys of Peter Fidler, which allowed farm lots of 220 yards along the river and 1,980 yards back from it, were confirmed by the Earl, and lots were given to the de Meurons. Ten thousand acres of land was set aside for the Roman Catholic Church, a substantial amount given the nature of the Aboriginal cession. Selkirk also negotiated with the HBC for the establishment of a company store at Fort Douglas. The Earl was under no illusions about what he had done. While he had some hopes for the future, he wrote Lady Selkirk that "we are thrown back into all the difficulties of the first stage of a settlement." All the work and expense of the past six years were lost. There were few tools and not even a dependable supply of provisions.

The founder's presence and actions in the summer of 1817 acquired the status of mythology in the settlement, as Alexander Ross would record in his history published nearly 40 years later. Despite the exhilaration of dealing in person with his colony, Selkirk could spend little time with his settlers. It was necessary to return east to deal with a myriad of problems there. Selkirk fought unsuccessfully to prevent the Nor'westers from continuing to hold Fort Gibraltar within gunshot of the Forks, arguing to Coltman that without the elimination of the NWC, it would be most prudent to remove the settlers across the American boundary to Pembina, "where at least they will not have to apprehend hostility from subjects of the same Government and where if they be liable to be attacked it will not be considered an offence to be prepared for resistance." On 9 September Selkirk departed Red River, riding south on horseback to the St. Peter's River and carrying on by boat to the Mississippi, arriving in St. Louis on 27 October. Within three years he would be dead.

-2-
From the Departure of Selkirk to the Flood of 1826

For the Red River Settlement, the period between 1817 and 1826 falls into two parts. Between 1817 and 1821, Lord Selkirk, and after his death the executors of his estate, made some serious efforts to develop the settlement and to increase its population. The development process reached its height in 1821, with the expenditure of thousands of pounds on a project to transplant Swiss settlers to the plains of the West. With the failure of the Swiss operation, however, the Selkirk executors began running the settlement without spending money on it, in the hope that it would eventually prosper. Benign neglect seemed to be working, at least until the flood of 1826. From the beginning, the settlement was characterized by considerable ethnic complexity, and had to endure recurring hardships. The result was a constant current of social unrest.

The Settlement Re-established Yet Again

With Lord Selkirk's departure from Red River on 9 September 1817, the settlers were once again left on their own to face a western winter. The re-establishment of the settlement in 1817 had been the third in three years. Thanks to Selkirk's intervention, and William Coltman's investigations, there was a fair chance that the mixed-bloods would not cause excessive difficulty over the ensuing winter. But the remaining settlers – more than 50 Scots, and about the same number of de Meuron soldiers – were not likely to have an easy time. The crops, particularly the potatoes, had failed miserably. The de Meuron officer left in charge, Graffenried, blamed the crop disaster on bad seed. Alexander Macdonell would subsequently write Selkirk that the crop had been spoiled by frost, and then blown down by a high wind, an explanation with which the newly arrived farm manager William Laidlaw concurred.

Macdonell had saved all the harvest for seed, he wrote, keeping back nearly 100 bushels of wheat, 12 of barley, and 308 bushels of potatoes.

In any event, Graffenried reported, on New Year's Day 1818, that most of the Scots were living at Pembina, dependent for food on the buffalo. The German soldiers remained at the Forks and came to Pembina for rations. A shortage of rum and tobacco was a double disaster. Without these commodities to trade it was almost impossible to get meat from the Indians, and their absence made the soldiers restive.

Lieutenant Graffenried was extremely disappointed. The settlement had not advanced, he wrote Selkirk. "The crops having failed so completely has dampened the settlers hopes, the want of goods. Particularly tools of every kind, the disappointment of [not] getting horses of which they have given up all hopes, everyone sees the colony is not supported by the Company, all this must be very discouraging to every settler, the Meurons speak of going down next summer, they have been promised a great deal that could not be performed." A day later, HBC trader Donald McPherson, wrote that he could not understand why the officers of the Hudson Bay Company "are in generall so much prejudiced against the Collony & his Lordships proceedings in this Country." His reference was at least in part to the extortionate prices the HBC was charging for provisions at the settlement. Colin Robertson subsequently put the matter succinctly when he wrote, "Red River and Athabasca has hitherto served them [the HBC] as a Kind of Sewer where they could conveniently throw in a few hundred pounds, which enabled them to make an economical balance, at the expense of the two drains."

While the settlers carried on with short rations, and Lord Selkirk made his way back to Canada, his people in Lower Canada set under way a major operation which they hoped would help with the pacification of the region. Samuel Gale conceived the project, during a trip to Montreal from Red River. Why not request the Church in Quebec to provide missionaries for the French mixed-bloods and Aboriginals in the Red River area? Gale enlisted Commissioner Coltman to advance the scheme, and Coltman convinced Governor Sherbrook to back it. Quebec Bishop J.O. Plessis was easily brought on side, and allowed a collection to be taken in every parish in his diocese on behalf of the project. After several months of preparation, Plessis nominated Fathers J. N. Provencher and Sévère Joseph Dumoulin to the mission. Their instructions, issued on 20 April 1818, were "to recall from barbarity and the disorders which are the consequences of it the Savage Nations dispersed over the vast Country," and particularly to prepare all women for legitimate marriage.

Trials and Tribulations

Back at the settlement, at about the same time as the orders were issued to the missionaries, the ice in the rivers broke on the 10th of April. The Pembina people returned to the Forks at mid-month. A few days later, a plains fire swept from James Sutherland's house northward, driven by a strong southerly wind. A number of houses were burned, and many settlers lost property. Despite this disaster, planting began on 28 April, with barley started on 9 May, and potatoes a few days later. William Laidlaw began building a house at "Hayfield" farm. The settlers were hampered by a lack of animals and tools, and many of the de Meurons continued to talk about leaving the country. Only William Laidlaw had decent tools and animals. He had obtained an English plough at York Factory and had six good horses to pull it. He sowed 27 bushels of wheat, six bushels of barley, four of oats, and 74 bushels of potatoes.

Fathers Provencher and Dumoulin left Montreal in mid-May, accompanied by the schoolmaster William Edge, and a guide named Captain J.B. Lorimer. The party paused at Sault Ste. Marie in early June to collect ten families of mixed-bloods (including the family of Louis Nolin), and then travelled on to Red River in a brigade of seven canoes headed by Frederick Matthey. The missionaries reached Fort Douglas on 16 July 1818, and soon set to work building a large house in St. Boniface to serve as chapel and residence. Some problems emerged from the fact that the church had been promised much of the same land as the de Meurons, who had already built their houses on "German Street," now Taché Avenue, in present day St. Boniface.

The missionaries had arrived in Red River only two days after Colin Robertson, who was again heading west to the Athabasca country. Robertson reported to Selkirk that the settlement seemed prosperous. "The old Scotch Sentiment of Peace & Plenty is at last realised on the fertile plains of Ossiniboia," he proclaimed. The weather was fine, and crops were abundant. Things were not perfect, of course. A few days later, Father Provencher wrote to his bishop that a tame buffalo bull, and a cow, along with an 18-month calf, were the only domestic animals remaining at the settlement. The bull and cow, reported Alexander Macdonell, had been broken to the plough. Cuthbert Grant, commented other correspondents, had killed the last surviving imported bull, upon his return to Red River a few months earlier.

Other correspondence from the settlement, in August of 1818, certainly suggested that matters were improving at the Forks. Frederick Matthey, who had been appointed by Selkirk as his superintendent at Red River arrived on 1 August at the head of the canoe brigade from the

Sault. He reported to Lord Selkirk that he had "directed the Brigade to pass the usual way, in line of Battle like a Squadron of Cavalry the flag in the center – the canoes within 1 or 2 yards of one another – paddling in perfect good time, on one good Voyageur Song only the female in their best atirers most of them Paddling." At Point Meuron he had met the 11 NWC canoes: "on perceiving our flag of the White, they stopt within a gun shot of us – we continued our charge and song, each Canoe pointing to an interval in the other Brigade, so that we passed like Magic through their fleet, with a few hands shaking, and in a very friendly manner their Voyageurs and Bois Brules were evidently touched at the sight of so many Canadian children."

Matthey thought that the mixed-bloods now understood that the roots of the settlement went deeper than had been supposed. William Laidlaw reported in late July that the year's crops were the most bountiful and heavy ever seen in the settlement. However, the de Meurons had virtually no crop, he added, but then most hadn't even turned the soil over. A list of settlers, dated August 1818, showed 45 Scottish heads of families (representing 155 people), six Canadians (representing 26 people), and 51 de Meurons (most of whom were still single, although a handful had taken Aboriginal wives), for a total of 232 souls. On 30 August 1818, Frederick Matthey would report to Selkirk that there were 153 Scots, 45 de Meurons, and 26 Canadians – 224 people in 57 houses – exclusive of the Orkney people in the employment of the HBC.

No one familiar with Red River could possibly have believed that such good fortune would continue, and, indeed it did not. The day after Captain Matthey and the NWC had conducted their canoe pass-by at the Forks, the grasshoppers arrived in full force in the tiny colony. There have been a number of Manitoba varieties, and it is not known which was responsible for the 1818 devastations. The grasshoppers devoured the potatoes and barley, cutting off the heads of the ripe grain as if with an ax. Frederick Matthey reported, "everything has disappeared, [the grasshoppers] having dug the earth to eat the stems of the Potatoes under ground – in some places they were two and three inches thick on the ground."

All observers emphasized that the infestation, while serious, was less than total. Alexander Macdonell reported that potatoes on the plains were left untouched. Matthey observed that wheat, far enough advanced, had been spared on both sides of the river. He expected a crop of 500 to 600 bushels. Father Provencher reported in September that "the wheat has been cut at Red River, the potatoes are in fine condition, the soil here is excellent, and I believe that in ten years there will be a great

Trials and Tribulations

abundance of wheat. By next year, unless some accident prevents, all the settlers will have more wheat than they need, both to eat and to sow."

On the other hand, the Scots had lost cabbage, carrots, and turnips. Matthey explained that the de Meurons were disheartened less by the grasshoppers (they had virtually no crops to lose) than by the partiality of Macdonell in favour of the Scots, the want of tools and goods, as well as by exorbitant prices and the lack of animals, both horses and cattle. All observers agreed that the Nor'westers returning from their trials in Montreal were well behaved. Not until 1819 did anyone in the settlement learn of the boundary agreement worked out between the British and the Americans in 1818, which set the international boundary at the 49th parallel, thus putting much of Selkirk's grant in the United States.

The Catholic mission in the settlement had flourished from the outset, although the missionaries bombarded their superiors in Lower Canada with questions about how to deal with the "novelty" of local conditions. What was it absolutely necessary to know in order to be baptized and married? Could priests say the mass in moccasins, which were otherwise worn every day? What should be done with *engagés* who traded a gallon of rum for two horses? Ought one to baptize those whose fathers were bigamists or inveterate drunkards? What penalty should be exacted from those involved at Seven Oaks "who admit having killed some one in that engagement?" The good fathers worked their way through these concerns, and by January of 1819, had managed to construct a house with a chapel large enough to hold all their parishioners. Construction of buildings also proceeded at Pembina, although Provencher eventually learned that his chapel there fell on the American side of the line. Shortage of carpentry tools and nails was a constant problem, but the missionaries were buoyed by the reception of the people, both mixed-bloods and Aboriginal.

In the early summer of 1819, at Michilimackinac, Colonel Robert Dickson signed an agreement with one Michael Dousman, for the delivery to the settlement of 76 milk cows, 20 oxen, and four bulls, at a price of $80 (U.S.) each for cows, and $100 each for bulls and oxen. While Lord Selkirk himself had suggested that Dickson make such arrangements, he had placed a limit of $5,000 on any contract. Dickson, who was notorious for his profligate spending, blithely ignored Selkirk's conditions. He paid $500 in advance, with no guarantee in case of failure to deliver. Dousman assigned the contract to Adam Stewart, who hoped to inflate it still further. The cattle were supposed to reach Big Stone Lake in 1820, and William Laidlaw actually went there to meet them. But the cattle never got beyond Prairie du Chien, where most of them died. Stewart went to

St. Louis after a second herd of 175 head, which were driven north in 1821, but these also fell victim to Aboriginals at Prairie du Chien later in the year.

The crops of 1819 were considerably more of a failure than those of 1818, which resulted in shortages of both bread and seed. Both Captain Matthey and Father Provencher reported that epidemics of measles and whooping cough had cut a heavy swath of death through the children of the settlement. The shortage of grain perpetuated the annual migration from Red River to Pembina. Meanwhile in London, the Hudson's Bay Company, in October 1819, decided to send John West, a Protestant missionary of Anglican background, to Red River. Lord Selkirk, who was by this time dying of consumption, may have been too ill to remind the HBC of his commitments to the Scottish settlers regarding a Presbyterian minister. He expressed his concern that "sentiments of jealousy and hatred on the subject of religious differences" would gain ground in a colony "composed of people of different languages."

That winter, in order to alleviate the shortage of seed, an expedition was sent to Prairie du Chien to obtain seed, returning to the settlement in June of 1820 in flat-bottomed boats. This expedition cost Lord Selkirk over one thousand pounds, but it was an early demonstration that river navigation to the United States, which would later become the life-blood of the settlement, was possible.

Lord Selkirk died in France in April of 1820. His brother-in-law, Andrew Colvile, wrote to Alexander Macdonell that Selkirk's demise would make no difference to the settlement. The executors would carry on as Selkirk would have wished, and would send new settlers as soon as possible. In the meantime, Macdonell was to measure off and deliver to John Pritchard 100 acres for the Buffalo Wool Company, a scheme that Pritchard had promoted to exploit the buffalo as an export commodity. Governor George Simpson thought Pritchard a "wild visionary speculative creature without a particle of solidity and but a moderate share of justice," but allowed that the scheme was a good one.

A buffalo skin was expected to yield six to seven pounds of hair, of which two pounds would be suitable for export. The rest could be used for coarse cloth, blankets, and mattresses. Thus, local labour could be employed to produce local products as an export commodity. This was the first of many such projects in Red River. It would eventually fail miserably, partly because Pritchard was a bad manager, but mostly because of a major problem with some the wool. As it turned out, buffalo wool was impervious to bleaching, and therefore could not be dyed, so the only possible colour was dark brown.

Trials and Tribulations

A fair amount of wool was shipped to England for test purposes, and Lady Selkirk herself directed the manufacturing effort. However, the wool's short strands were best suited for simple items such as shawls, and there was a very limited market for dark shawls. Lady Selkirk tried, unsuccessfully, to set a new fashion in Scotland for mourning shawls. Nonetheless, the buffalo were still useful as domestic animals at the settlement, and they were used for this purpose for several years, until the arrival of cattle. The first successful mating of buffalo in captivity occurred at Red River in 1821.

The Anglican clergyman John West landed at York Factory on 14 August 1820. He arrived in Red River in early October, describing the settlement as "a number of huts along the margin of the river" and the colonists as "a compound of individuals of various countries." He began a school in November in a log house on the Red near the modern St. John's Park. His schoolmaster, George Harbidge, had come with him from England. By 1822, the school had an apartment for the schoolmaster, lodging for the Aboriginal students, and facilities for the day students. On Sundays it was the parish church. A farmer was subsequently hired to live next to the school and "take care of the Milk and provide Hay for the Cows, draw with his horse all the firewood... and go with the Cart for the Fish..." West hoped that children of "country" marriages who had been orphaned or abandoned, could be educated at the school, but George Simpson opposed such a plan "until Agriculture and not the Chase becomes the main pursuit of the Savage Tribes."

West was not likely to be successful as a parish minister. His real interest was in missionary work among the First Nations, and he was a terrible preacher. According to Deputy-Governor Nicholas Garry, "he unfortunately attempts to preach extempore from Notes, for which he has not the Capacity, his discourses being unconnected and ill-delivered. He likewise mistakes his point, fancying that by touching severely and pointedly on the Weaknesses of People he will produce Repentance..." Moreover, the Anglican was clearly unpopular with George Simpson, who felt that West's educational and missionary plans for the Aboriginals were too ambitious.

Meanwhile, in 1821, there was a significant announcement: the HBC and the NWC agreed finally to merge. Nicholas Garry was sent to facilitate the merger at the local level. Garry arrived at Red River on 4 August 1821, just after the first small herd of oxen and cows driven by Alexis Bailly from Prairie du Chien. He was not greatly impressed with what he found at the Forks. He visited former HBC employee Robert Logan, who lived in a "small miserable Hut" with his Indian wife and seven children. He found 70 acres under cultivation at William Laidlaw's, but reported that the grasshoppers had totally devastated the crop, which left "a most desolate melancholy Appearance."

German Street, the home of the de Meurons, was more promising. Houses there were "comfortable and clean, the Crops excellent where the Grasshopper had not been, nothing in the World could be finer." While he did not think much of the human efforts at habitation, Garry was impressed with the black soil and the meadowlands. "Excellent soil," he reported after one ride, "most luxuriant Meadows, the Verdure not finer even in England, not a Stone or Piece of Gravel." He did not record what he thought of the catfish he was given for dinner at the HBC fort. Nor was he ever in Red River during the winter.

Everywhere he went, Garry heard complaints from the settlers, but none seemed terribly serious. Since he spoke German fluently, he was able to converse with the de Meurons in their own language. Garry's journal offered little evidence of anything but the gradual recovery of the settlement from its earlier devastations. He calculated that there were 221 Scots, 65 de Meurons, and 133 Canadians scattered along the banks of the Red and Assiniboine, with 500 largely French-speaking mixed-bloods concentrated around Pembina. As one settler wrote to Andrew Colvile that summer, "A Code of Laws, and a Governor Semple to administer the same, is the only thing necessary to secure the peace of this country, and the prosperity of its inhabitants." Unfortunately, the situation was about to become considerably more complicated, thanks to the arrival of a large party of Swiss settlers in the autumn of 1821.

The Swiss Settlers

The story of the Swiss settlers really begins in 1819, when a former de Meuron halfpay captain named Rudolf de May wrote Lord Selkirk from London on the suggestion of Captain Proteus D'Orsennens. A native of Bern, Switzerland, de May offered his services procuring settlers from Switzerland for Red River. With Selkirk ill, the negotiations with de May were taken over by Andrew Colvile, and the two men came to an understanding in October 1819. Although he was an astute businessman, this operation would not show Colvile at his best. The problem of transplanting settlers, as it had been for Lord Selkirk, was the inability to control events at either end of the process. Colvile relied upon distant agents to fulfill fairly tight deadlines and impossible

Trials and Tribulations

requirements. Neither de May in Europe, nor Alexander Macdonell were able to meet Colvile's expectations.

To some extent, Colvile may have misled himself into thinking that the earlier problems in Red River had been caused by the origins of the settlers (from the Highlands of Scotland), the exigencies of the fur trade war in North America, and perhaps even Selkirk's lack of attention to business detail. In truth, these were but collateral matters. The essential problem was that successfully transplanting European settlers en masse across vast distances was a very difficult undertaking, as a series of governments would learn to their chagrin over the next century and a half.

Colvile was promising transportation to the settlement, and providing £20 per adult, no inconsiderable sum in the years after the Napoleonic Wars. de May fleshed out these promises with some account of the destination in a prospectus he had printed in French and German in the spring of 1820. As a promotional publication, de May's effort was in keeping with the standard strategy among emigration promoters of the day. He described the positive features of Red River in glowing term, and either downplayed or conveniently forgot about the negative ones. He extolled the virtues of the rich soil of the prairies, not covered with thick forest, which would have to be cleared, saying it was extremely fertile and well suited for grain and other crops. There were "boeufs sauvages" literally begging to be hunted; the lakes and rivers abounded in fish; the settlement was well supplied with houses and a fortress; conditions for raising Merino sheep were ideal. The climate was moderate and very healthy, with winters neither very cold nor very long. Aside from the entirely misleading description of winter, there was no mention of the isolation or primitiveness of the place, the shortage of wood, or the difficulties of getting to it (or away from it).

The commitments which the Earl of Selkirk was prepared to make to the settlers, according to the pamphlet, were extensive. They would be transported to the settlement at his expense, where they would be provided housing until they could build their own homes. They would be furnished with provisions, and advanced seed grain. They could buy equipment on site at reasonable prices. They could get 100 arpents of land "en toute propriété et pour tourjours pour lui et ses decendans" in return for an annual payment of produce. These promises demanded resources well beyond the capability of Red River to provide, although Andrew Colvile had assured Captain de May that such promises could be met. Colvile, unfortunately, believed the assurances of his agents at Red River that everything was constantly improving. Having never been to North America, he had no conception of how rough an approximation of these commitments would actually be possible. But they were actually condensed by de May into a single-paged contract, to be signed by both parties.

Despite the enthusiasm of his brochure, and the offer of a contract, Captain de May was forced to deal with a Swiss population that was quite skeptical of his project. He was forced to extend credit, and to accept applicants who had been in workhouses. Difficulty in assembling a full party, and in obtaining an observer who would accompany the emigrants (to report to the Swiss government on their treatment and progress) continued through the year 1820 and into 1821. Eventually, Walter von Huser was obtained as the observer. The continued negotiations between de May and Colvile nearly broke down on several occasions over lack of trust. Not until 24 February 1821, did Colvile write to Alexander Macdonell announcing that 250 to 260 settlers would arrive at Hudson Bay in the autumn, They would have to be provisioned over the winter. He trusted that a good many 100-acre lots had been laid out with proper boundary posts.

This extraordinary letter was the first definite word the settlement had heard of the arrival of a substantial party of new settlers. Even had the letter been sent to Montreal, rather than to the Bay, it could not have arrived at Red River much before August of 1821. More likely, Macdonell would first read it when he received his mail off the same ship that was bringing the emigrants. Under such circumstances, it was impossible that proper preparations for the arrival of the Swiss could have been made.

de May had managed to collect approximately 170 potential settlers and transported them to Rotterdam, where the *Lord Wellington*, a vessel chartered by Colvile, was waiting. William Todd, the surgeon appointed to accompany the passengers to Hudson Bay, observed that the settlers' chests were much too large and heavy to be transported from the Bay to Red River. The fourteen-week voyage across the Atlantic went without serious mishap. The biggest problem was "bad water" which was regarded as a serious hardship for the Swiss, who were accustomed to "pure spring water." There was a brief encounter with ice, and a ramming of the emigrant's ship by another vessel after passing through Hudson Strait. The *Lord Wellington* limped into York Factory with its pumps running continuously.

On 5 September 1821, George Simpson, the newly appointed governor of the HBC's "Northern Department" wrote to Colvile that the settlers had arrived at York Factory. He was impressed with "Mr. Dehouser," but not with the settlers. "The present batch has been most injudiciously selected, men of bad character taken out of Jails and others

Trials and Tribulations

out of Work & Mad houses; instead of useful hardy agriculturists they are of all ages and unaccustomed to labourers work being chiefly Watch makers Jewellers pedlers &c &c. Your agent Captn' de May has certainly not done his duty conscientiously; I do not know how he is paid but conceive from the rabble he has sent out that it must be by head, many without looking to their abilities habits or morals." This assessment – and its criticism of Captain de May – is undoubtedly the most frequently quoted comment on the Swiss who arrived in Red River.

In the Bulger Papers at the National Archives of Canada is a document dated 31 July 1822, and entitled, "The State of the Swiss Colonists at Red River." It was probably prepared by Walter von Huser, who had spent a year with these people observing their progress. According to his name-by-name assessment, all but fourteen of the settlers were of the Reformed Church. The others consisted of six Catholics, two Lutherans, and six unspecified. Nearly half of the male heads of families were over the age of 40, and one-third was over the age of 50. Men of this age, particularly if previously engaged in sedentary occupations, would not fare well in the rough life of Red River. The party contained only nine farmers and two vine growers. Apart from these agriculturists, who represented just over one-quarter of those for whom occupations were listed, there were 21 other trades represented. Six settlers were clock-makers, but the remainder included a variety of individuals, most of whose skills would be useful in the settlement, including a joiner, a master carpenter, a locksmith, a nail-maker, a physician, a midwife, three weavers, and a schoolmaster.

The problem with the party does not appear to have been in the occupational mix. Walter von Huser was not much impressed with the character and morals of many of his fellow passengers, although we do not know on what basis his assessments were made. In any event, he described 33 (40 percent) of the adults as bad or worthless, 27 (33 percent) as fair and 20 (24 percent) as good, or very honest. One passenger was described as crazy, and another as simpleminded. All but one of the clock-makers were of bad character. In short, von Huser was favourably disposed to less than 60 percent of the passengers on the grounds of character.

George Simpson was doubtless led to his early assessment of the overall nature of the emigrants by a handful of troublemakers, whose vices were almost immediately apparent. One had tried to stab von Huser and was sent packing, while another died from drink the day after he landed. Simpson reported that Nicholas Garry was present at York Factory, was fluent in German and was able to read the printed prospectus. That document, insisted Simpson, was "rather highly coloured and leads them to expect more than can be realized in the present state of the Colony. I take the liberty of mentioning this as it may be the ground of future complaint." That there would exist a discrepancy between what the Swiss had been led to expect in Red River, and what they found, was, of course, a bit of an understatement. Even Walter von Huser was disappointed. In his letter from York Factory of 1821, Alexander Macdonell pointedly commented about the "strange Gentlemen... thrown upon us ... who are in the habit of living well and obliged to put up with our Country & not pleased, I am told this foreign Gentleman from Switzerland even did not consider York Factory very good in the eating & drinking way." In the event, virtually none of the promises made to these settlers were ever fulfilled.

Things did not begin auspiciously, as most of the emigrant's baggage had to be left at York Factory. By local standards, the Swiss journey from York Factory to Red River was a relatively normal and uneventful one, although for Europeans unfamiliar with the hardships of the region, it seemed harsh and frightening. One adult male and two children died before the party arrived at the lake. In his 1825 book, published in Switzerland, Rudolf Wyss reported that the settlers had to endure 300 hours of upstream travel in small boats, the men frequently dragging the boats with ropes from the shore. When the dragging was done, the rowing – as in galleys, Wyss observed – resumed. There were the inevitable portages, and halfway through the journey, the snow began. The HBC postmaster at the head of the lake was not very helpful with provisions, claiming that he was short himself. He gave the settlers enough barley and fish for four days, although it took them 18 days to cross the lake, just ahead of freeze-up.

Arrival at Fort Douglas brought little improvement for the newcomers. They were greeted with cannon volleys and each was given a glass of rum, but they were then informed that the grasshoppers had destroyed the crops and food was in short supply. From the beginning, the Swiss arrivals told the Red River authorities that they could not remain under such conditions. According to Wyss, the de Meurons took in many of their fellow countrymen, and shared what little they had. Wyss thought much of their interest was in marriage with the girls in the party, and within a week nine girls had become engaged. Over the winter of 1821-22, 15 marriages of Swiss girls and women to men of the settlement were celebrated.

Governor Alexander Macdonell reported the arrival of the settlers to Andrew Colvile by remarking that the newcomers were very

Trials and Tribulations

inadequately clothed for the winter. He added that they "are the greatest eaters I have ever seen." Some of the young Swiss were put to work pulling buffalo wool. Most of the party wintered at Pembina. George Simpson subsequently wrote that the winter of 1821-22 was an unpleasant one for the settlement. The buffalo virtually disappeared, and food was in very short supply. On 26 February 1822, a paper was signed by 14 Swiss and transmitted to Governor Macdonell. It complained about ill treatment, insisting that the houses were in ruins, and that the people were treated like slaves, being largely confined to the fort.

Reorganizing the Settlement and Dealing with Discontent

George Simpson, writing in May of 1822, stated, "Take the Colony all in all, and it is certainly an extraordinary place, the Great folks would cut each other's throats if they could with safety; there is nothing like a social feeling among them and the best friends today are the bitterest enemies tomorrow. Among the lower orders it is much the same, they have a certain feeling of pride, independence and equality among them which is subvertive of good order in Society: they are opposed to each other in small factions and every man in the Colony looks to his arms alone for safety and protection." This tendency toward a Hobbesian state of "war of all against all" became a constant theme of Simpson's correspondence from the settlement.

Governor Alexander Macdonell was relieved of his duties in the spring of 1822. His demise was caused partly by his inability to deal with the Swiss settlers, and partly by reports of excessive revelry. The two may well have been connected. According to Alexander Ross, "nothing was to be heard or seen around Fort Douglas but balling, dancing, rioting, and drunkenness, in the barbarous spirit of those disorderly times.... The challenges of empty glasses went round so long as a man could keep his seat; and often the revel ended in a general melee, which led to the suspension of half-a-dozen officials and the postponement of business, till another bouse had made them all friends again." By the summer, ex-soldier Andrew Bulger had arrived as Governor, locum tenens, of the District of Assiniboia, and secretary and registrar of Selkirk's colony. He was accompanied by John Halkett, Selkirk's brother-in-law, and a former pamphleteer on Selkirk's behalf, as representative of the Selkirk executors. Bulger was born in Newfoundland, and had served on the Niagara Frontier in the War of 1812. Within a few weeks Bulger was describing his new "life of slavery and exposure to the insults and threats of some of the most worthless of God's creatures, in one of the most miserable countries on earth..."

By early 1822, there were 126 houses and 160 garden plots in the settlement. But on his arrival, Halkett found all the inhabitants at Red River demoralized... us. He promised that Selkirk's committee would... ere would be farm animals and fixed prices for goods... fered reductions in interest, and concessions on rent. ... post at Pembina and asked Father Provencher to sh... ion there. Halkett heard the Swiss complaints and aba... ed indebtedness. He was unable to fulfill their dema... nediately, but hoped soon to be able to bring their ba... Bay. He would not implement the Swiss request tha... to leave the settlement, given their debts to the Selkirk...

Some satisfacti... ttlers in late August of 1822, when Adam Stewart arriv... 170 cattle, 50 more than had been ordered. Andrew B... ous problem in deciding how to allocate the cows, si... t enough to supply each worthy applicant with an a... to London: "I began with the married men of the c... om Lord Selkirk made promises of cattle in writing; ne... Scotch families which had been the longest in and su... the country; then the married Canadians from Mont... g served I was induced, in the hope of reconciling {th... untry to give a cow to each of them that had a family... German families and then the unmarried men of all... peared to have the strongest claims on Lord Selkirk... one to choose his animal, but distributed the cows by a... angement.

Andrew Bulger was... Andrew Colvile that "from the printed prospectus. ... gh the Swiss cantons by Mr. de May, it is but too a... wretched people have not been fairly dealt with. This... which Mr. de May has, in that prospectus, represente... e May might have replied that he had merely describe... lvile had told him, but the problem still remained. E... ed George Simpson in complaining about local law... By far the greater part of our population, I am assured... d depravity, and daring enough to despise our laws... our magistrates." Like Simpson, Bulger wanted son... orce at the settlement. "Nothing but the presence of... id the civil power can

Trials and Tribulations

prevent the country from becoming very soon a nest of thieves," he wrote, "for no honest man will remain in it..."

At the same time, Bulger also recognized that the monopoly of trade enforced by the HBC was a considerable stumbling block to the settlement's prosperity. On 12 September of 1822, he wrote Simpson, "If... the people are to be debarred from the exercise of privileges necessary to their existence and be permitted merely to till the ground, hopeless in my opinion, will be the attempt of Lord Selkirk's executors to establish a Colony on Red River." Two days later, John Clarke arrived as the new Chief Factor of the HBC, and almost immediately drew up a proclamation prohibiting "all trade with natives or otherwise." He subsequently broke into the house of one mixed-blood and confiscated a cache of furs. Clarke and Bulger fought all winter over a variety of matters, including the granting of land. Bulger advocated the establishment of a proper judicial system in Red River, the posting of troops, the legal admission of settlers into the fur trade, the introduction of a legal medium of exchange, and the necessity of a market for surplus grain. Without such reforms, recognizing the autonomy of the settlement from the Company, he warned Andrew Colvile in late 1822 to "spend no more of Lord Selkirk's money upon Red River..."

Colvile did not need Andrew Bulger's advice to decide to stop spending money on the settlement. The Swiss debacle, which had cost thousands of pounds, had convinced him that Red River would never provide a return on Selkirk's investment. He and George Simpson quickly agreed that there would be no more European migration to the settlement. Instead, new settlers would be found among the fur traders and their families, who had been made redundant by the merger of the HBC and NWC. This policy would not only save money, but would help ease some of the most serious problems resulting from the joining of the two great fur trading companies. As had always been the case, the settlement proved utterly unable to free itself from the incubus of the Hudson's Bay Company. Colvile paid far more attention to George Simpson than to Bulger. Simpson was, after all, Andrew Colvile's man in North America, and his counsel was more congenial.

Early in 1823, Bulger found it necessary to investigate efforts by the Swiss to depart Red River. To finance their departure, they had begun selling the cows they had received. Clearly, they were intending to walk away from their indebtedness to the Selkirk estate. On 10 February 1823, David Louis DesCombe testified before Bulger as to why he sought to leave the settlement: "The promises made to us in Switzerland have not been fulfilled. We were not nourished the first year, as was promised.

Our Baggage was left at the Sea, and even this Year the greatest part of it was left there also. We gave almost all we had last Winter for Provisions, and we suffered much misery. This Country is not what the Prospectus stated that it was. The winters are too long. We can never become farmers here. We cannot live here. We are not hunters, to obtain a little meat we run the risk of being killed by the Indians, or of being Frozen."

DesCombe had been a tenant farmer in Switzerland. He was 43, with three children. He did not know exactly where his family would go. "We have everything to dread – we may die on the road, or be drowned or killed by the Savages," he confessed, "but we cannot remain here. . . " That same day, John Dubach was also examined. He concurred that he could not continue. He was "not accustomed to that way of life," he said. He had paid Rudolph de May nearly 50 pounds for nothing but broken promises. Andrew Bulger decided to do nothing, and those Swiss who so desired were permitted to quietly leave.

The conflict between John Clarke and Andrew Bulger, representing the interests of the HBC and the Red River Settlement respectively, came to a head at the meeting of the Council of Assiniboia on 3 May 1823. Complaints against an HBC employee were met by Clarke with a declaration "that the Governor and Council of Ossiniboia are not authorized to interfere in the internal affairs of the Honourable Hudson's Bay Company, whether in civil or criminal matters." Where both parties belonged to the Company, argued Clarke, the Governor and Council of the HBC (which met at York Factory) was the proper body. The Council suspended its proceedings and appealed to the Company. By the summer of 1823, the authorities of Red River, regarded both the de Meuron and Swiss residents as discontented time bombs just waiting to explode.

Conditions did not improve. According to Rudolph Wyss, the houses of the settlers were of wood daubed with mud and clay. Only a few had wooden floors, and most lacked glass for the windows. In the summer of 1823, heavy rains soaked almost all of the houses, and many had to be abandoned. No sawmill was yet in operation. Wyss insisted that those in charge of the settlement put Selkirk's money in their own pockets while sending glowing reports on progress to the executors. The Swiss had no clergyman – yet another promise broken – and could not understand enough English to attend services at the fort. Swiss settlers constantly trickled away from the settlement to the United States.

In October of 1823, the Anglican missionary, David Jones, arrived at the Forks to replace John West. Welsh-born and decidedly Low Church, he was forced to stay at Fort Douglas with Governor Robert Parker Pelly,

51

Trials and Tribulations

who had replaced Andrew Bulger over the summer, while the church's buildings were "mudded" with Red River gumbo. A few weeks later, Jones met with Chief Peguis, and asked the Saulteaux to send some of his boys to the mission school. Peguis replied:

> "I have listened very much to what you say, and they are fine promises; we want our people to become like white people, to get plenty of Indian corn, wheat, and potatoes, for since you white people have got our lands, we are very poor. Before that we had plenty – our rivers were full of fish, and we always conquered our enemies, but now the white people promise much and give nothing. And now you come and want our children, but I do not know what to say, for I hear so many reports, one saying one thing, and another thing, that I am quite distracted and know not whom to believe. Last year a new chief came, now he is gone and another is come, I do not know what to do of all this changing, but I shall see how things go on. I will call my people together when I go home and tell them what you say."

The Saulteaux did nothing about the schooling question, perhaps because of difficulties with the schoolmaster and his wife. George Simpson described Mr. Harbidge as "ignorant, self conceited and moreover under the entire control of his wife," and Mrs. Harbidge as "above her station, assuming more of the lady than is necessary." Harbidge, who could neither keep order, nor teach arithmetic, was removed from his post in 1825 by David Jones, ostensibly for drunkenness.

The authorities in the settlement continued to worry about the lawlessness in the settlement. In October 1823, Pelly established a "police" force, with the HBC Factor as High Constable, two bailiffs, 20 part-time paid constables, and 50 special constables who would serve without remuneration. The cost of this force, which was eventually assumed by the HBC, was £100 per year. The constabulary was not called out very often, and justice was meted out quite gingerly. In 1824, a Saulteaux warrior who had murdered a woman of his own tribe was turned loose by Governor Pelly, who told the accused "that he has manifested a disposition subversive of all order, and that if he should not be punished in this world, he is sure to be punished in the next." Such an action was only partly because Aboriginals were regarded as outside the legal system. According to parliamentary legislation, capital crimes were to be tried in eastern Canada, and there were no facilities for the long-term incarceration of criminals in the settlement.

In May of 1824, Simpson wrote to Alexander Colvile that the councillors "have no public spirit nor general view towards the welfare and good government of the place, but are entirely influenced and actuated by self in every thought and action." What this really meant, of course, was that they did not agree with George Simpson's view of good government. They wanted a distillery to provide a market for surplus grain, for example, but Simpson insisted that "if distillation is once commenced, it will not be safe to live in this Settlement." More to the point, it would be difficult to prevent settlers with access to liquor from trading with the Aboriginals. Simpson was highly critical of the de Meurons, who were "ripe for outrage and violence whenever an opportunity offers." He was better disposed to the Scots, (their grumbling was "the characteristic of Highlanders") and the HBC's old Canadian servants ("the least troublesome and most attached to us").

His real concern, of course, was with the mixed-blood population of the region. Unless these people – who combined "all the savage ferocity of the Indians with all the cunning and knowledge of the whites," were brought to "industrious habits," and removed from the open plains, argued Simpson, they would eventually "be the destruction of the colony," an "alarming banditti who will have recourse to acts of violence and barbarity in order to gratify their love of plunder and revenge." In an attempt to control the mixed-bloods, Simpson reported, he had encouraged Cuthbert Grant to lead a number of families to settle at White Horse Plain, 19 kilometers west of the Forks, and the site of modern day St. François Xavier. Here Grant would settle migrants from Pembina, giving each a river lot 241 metres wide, and running 3.2 kilometres back from the river.

In 1825, Alexander Ross arrived on horseback at Red River. Ross had been born in Scotland, and worked in Canada as a schoolmaster before joining the Pacific Fur Company in 1810. He joined the NWC when it took over the Pacific Fur Company, and after the merger, the HBC, working mainly in the interior. His Indian wife, an Okanagan "princess," and his mixed-blood family joined him in Red River where he would reside until his death in 1856. "Instead of a place walled and fortified as I had expected," he wrote, "I saw nothing but a few wooden houses huddled together without palisades, or any regard to taste or even comfort. To this cluster of huts were, however, appended two long bastions in the same style as the other buildings. . . . Nor was the Governor's residence anything more in its outward appearance than the cottage of a humble farmer, who might be able to spend 50 pounds."

All things are relative. While the newcomer Alexander Ross was obviously not impressed by the settlement, resident John Pritchard boasted of "a line of well built houses" from the White Horse Plain to Netley Creek, of "an abundance of domestic cattle," and of "a prospect

Trials and Tribulations

of wheat exceeding anything heretofore produced in this Country." With the departure of Robert Pelly in 1825, HBC Chief Factor Donald McKenzie was appointed Governor of Assiniboia by the Selkirk trustees, thus ending the fiction that Red River and the Company were separate entities.

The winter of 1825-6 was an exceptionally hard one. Trouble began in the autumn when the buffalo hunt failed. The mixed-bloods had survived the homeward journey from the plains by eating their dogs and horses, their buffalo robes, their leather tents, and their shoes. Missionary David Jones, who recorded these hardships in his journal, commented, "May this severe lesson teach the thoughtless Canadian H. Breeds to turn their attention to diligence & industry on their farms." A heavy winter, described by several observers as the most severe within the memory, began in October. We are told that firewood cost three to four shillings a cord, as much as three to four pounds of butter, or 16 to 20 quarts of milk, and represented a day's wages. Chimneys were made of clay and supported by sticks. If the fire burnt to the wood, the whole house could go up in a blaze.

Deep snow was accompanied by temperatures of 45 degrees below zero; the ice was four feet thick on the river. Meat prices escalated because of the scarcity of buffalo, and little grain was available. Many were forced to eat their dogs and horses. The mixed-bloods demanded that the HBC distribute food being held in storage, but the Company refused, doubtless agreeing with the Reverend David Jones that the destitute should have been more diligent.

Despite the severity of the winter, the leadership of the settlement felt optimistic in early 1826. On 6 February, Donald McKenzie wrote to Andrew Colvile that the settlement was prosperous and tranquil at last. A new grain mill had been put into operation, and 1,600 bushels of wheat were in storage. George Simpson was even more enthusiastic in a report penned on 10 February. In it, he argued that flax culture and livestock rearing would be the most profitable aspects of agriculture for the settlement. He projected a scheme for the Company to supply livestock to the settlers, in which the profits "may in my humble opinion be made even to surpass the Fur Trade in value."

The settlers did not share in the official enthusiasm. By early April, there were rumours of plots against the authorities involving the French mixed-bloods, the Canadians, the Swiss settlers, and especially the de Meurons. Some of the rumours involved sacking Fort Garry, others attacking the Scots in Kildonan. The HBC offered grain to those that kept the peace, and importuned the Catholic clergy to keep their people under control. These efforts turned out to be unnecessary as the coming floodwater put an end to all thoughts of mob action.

The Flood of 1826

The spring thaw came suddenly at the end of April. Ice jams occurred on the rivers, and rain fell heavily. By 3 May the water was overflowing the banks of the Red, which rose five feet at the Forks over the next 24 hours. The ice suddenly gave way about 2 p.m. on 5 May, "with an awful rush, carrying away cattle, houses, trees and everything else that came in its way." Forty-seven houses were carried away in the first half-hour, and others soon followed. At the last moment, perishable goods and property were taken to higher ground, or placed on scaffolding in the trees along the banks. One surge followed another as the ice gave way in various places. John Pritchard wrote to his brother, "When the ice broke up in our neighbourhood, it was late in the evening. The night was dark and stormy accompanied with rain. The flood at once rose higher than ever known by man. The crashing of immense masses of ice was loud as thunder; neither the tallest poplar nor the stoutest oak could resist its impetuosity. They were mowed down like grass before the scythe."

According to Francis Heron, clerk of the HBC at Fort Garry, and keeper of a journal that is our best source for the 1826 devastation, before many of the inhabitants could remove their valuables, "their houses and part of their furniture were swept off before their eyes by the icy deluge. The havoc was terrible." The break-up in 1826 produced sudden inundations rather than the gradual rise usually associated with Red River flooding. Donald Gunn wrote that "the water rose so suddenly that, in some cases, its rushing into the houses roused the inmates from their beds. . ." The maximum flow, estimated at 260,000 cubic feet per second, was the highest recorded on the Red, then or since.

The Company's boats were kept busy over the next few days "snatching" people from "watery graves," often off the rooftops of their houses. As the waters continued to rise, the settlers were forced into constant retreat to higher ground. Even Fort Garry, on the highest piece of ground available around the Forks, was under 11 $^1/_2$ feet of water. The heavy loss of buildings was in part attributable to their impermanent construction, but mainly to their location at river's edge. Those not swept away began to collapse. According to Francis Heron, "the pickets and the chimneys of the houses are falling daily, as well as the plastering of the walls, and even the houses themselves begin to totter on their founda-

Trials and Tribulations

tions." Livestock was especially vulnerable and there were heavy losses. One of the few bright spots of the inundation was the destruction of much of the settlement's vermin.

It wasn't until 22 May that the water crested, and then took over a month to recede completely. According to John Pritchard, writing to his brother, "You may form some idea of the extent of this flood by considering the river whose usual breadth may be compared with the Severn at Shrewsbury having expanded itself over a surface of more than seventeen miles, which is the distance between the hills on which the settlers took refuge." When the waters receded, planting was begun in small plots on new ground away from the riverbanks, and continued until early July. Damp ground made it impossible to plant the quantity of land cultivated in 1825. Not surprisingly, the mosquito invasion was severe that summer. Surprisingly, loss of life was slight, in view of the fact that the water rose as much as 40 feet above ice level. Francis Heron recorded five deaths. One de Meuron settler was drowned while hunting for his cattle, and a man and three children were drowned when their canoe overturned.

However, property damage was extensive. Not only were houses, buildings and outbuildings destroyed, but the cattle herds, built up at great expense, were severely depleted. Contemporaries found some small solace in a circumstance John Pritchard observed in his letter to England: "the three churches, the residence of the clergy and the house of our social prayer meeting, with the exception of the windmill," were "the only buildings which have not been carried away or so much injured as not to deserve notice." These structures had been put on higher ground, although Pritchard insisted that the sites had not been deliberately chosen for that reason.

In his first report on the flood, dated 14 June 1826, George Simpson observed, "All former reverses are scarcely worthy of notice compared with the present and this I consider an extinguisher to the hope of Red River ever retaining the name of a Settlement." Not surprisingly, the Swiss and de Meuron settlers, always the most restive and discontented, saw the flood as the final straw, and decided to move en masse to the United States. Simpson refused to advise them to remain, on the grounds that they would demand assistance in the form of free gifts or credit.

About 250 of the Europeans departed, heading first for Darlington, Wisconsin, and eventually ending up in St. Louis. The HBC's Donald McKenzie saw this exodus as "a consummation much to be desired." The departed, he argued, "were composed of idle and turbulent characters who infested the Colony for several years." They also represented a distinct ethnic group in the settlement, and their departure was another step in the emergence of the mixed-bloods as the dominant ethnic element in the community. The elimination of the Swiss and Germans was so total – only one or two people from this entire population remained – that it was hard to believe they had once been so numerous.

One of those who left Red River on 11 July 1826 – and whose presence would be sorely missed in the settlement – was the painter Peter Rindisbacher. Born in Switzerland, in 1806, he had received some instruction in landscape painting in Bern before accompanying his family to Red River. Rindisbacher provided a visual record of the Swiss adventure. He sketched the ships and the ice during the passage, and captured the struggle of the journey to Fort Douglas. In Red River, he sold paintings and sketches of life in the settlement and of its inhabitants (including the Aboriginals) to HBC officials, who collected them as souvenirs. George Barnston of York Factory, and John West both bought paintings from Rindisbacher. West's ended up being reproduced as lithographs in London, in 1826, with himself listed as the artist. Paintings ordered by Andrew Bulger, depicting the acting governor in action, were reproduced for Robert Parker Pelly, who had coloured lithographs made from them with his image in the middle. Rindisbacher's work provides virtually our only visual record of life in the early period in Red River.

The flood, another disaster in a long decade of disasters, provided more evidence for the Selkirk family – if it was needed – of the unlikelihood that the settlement could ever be made profitable. The Selkirk estate would hang on to Red River for another decade, but it displayed less and less interest, and certainly invested no more money in it. By default, Red River became part of the Hudson's Bay Company operations long before the HBC formally assumed that role in 1835.

-3-
From Flood to Full Government

Red River recovered surprisingly quickly from the devastation of 1826, suggesting a vitality unrecognized by most of its residents. However, for the next decade there was nobody who really wanted to provide it with a long-term direction. The Selkirk estate had lost interest in the settlement, and policy, insofar as there was any, was chiefly in the hands of George Simpson. In 1861, one chronicler of Red River observed of this period that, although peace prevailed, the settlement "experienced but the cool and languid care of a stepmother. Everything was attempted, but everything failed – and that through the want of perseverance, good management, and concentrated effort."

For a few years, from 1830 to 1833, while his young British wife was in residence in the settlement, and he obviously intended to make it his home, Simpson did make some attempts at economic development, though he treated the settlement as a personal fiefdom. But with the departure of his wife for England in 1833, after the death of their infant son, Simpson became much less involved in Red River affairs. The establishment of a formal government, in 1835, ought to have enabled Red River to begin to provide its own policies, but there were so many hedges on the political structure that it was never able to operate effectively. It was replaced by a more thoroughly articulated system in 1839. Whether greater formality would improve the situation was another matter.

Expansion

Despite much trepidation on the part of George Simpson, the little settlement sprang quickly back to life after the inundation of 1826. By 5 July, Frances Heron noted, "the people of the settlement employed enclosing their farms, and building new houses, with as much enthusiasm as if no misfortunes had ever befallen them." David Jones and William Cockran rebuilt the school, insulating it with mud. John Pritchard observed in August that, despite the departure of many, "the old residents still remain and are actively employed in re-establishing things as heretofore; so that I expect next summer the remembrance of the flood alone will be retained." Pritchard was not quite accurate in his assessment; people's memories were even shorter than he had predicted. Despite the extent of the devastation in 1826, settlers resumed their occupation of low-lying land, and no serious efforts at flood protection, such as dikes, were undertaken. The inhabitants of the Red River Valley would have to relearn their flood lessons with every return of the high water.

Although the loss of an entire European population was in some ways a serious matter, most residents felt that the Swiss and de Meurons had never fit into Red River. Their departure made it considerably easier for mixed-blood families, displaced by the merger of the great fur-trading companies, to settle permanently at Red River. About 150 individuals arrived in 1826 alone at St. Boniface, most of them the families of Francophone voyageurs from the north. Other arriving families were the products of marriages between Protestant Orkneymen, employed by the HBC, and Aboriginal women. They would settle in a cluster north of the Forks at Grand Rapids, the site of present day St. Andrews.

At Grand Rapids, the newcomers received land grants from the HBC. The size of the grants depended on the Company status of the grantee. Senior officers received up to 200 acres, and the eldest sons of employees 25 acres. The depth of the lots in the grants did not vary. What did vary was the river frontage, which went from 33 feet (or one and one-half chains) to over 250 feet (or 12 chains). As was always the case with new settlement, free land did not necessarily produce a successful farm. Many of these families were extremely poor, lacking the capital to properly furnish and stock a farm. While some eventually made the transition to farming, many continued to work as hired hands, either for their more affluent neighbours, or for the HBC as "boatmen" or "tripmen." Contemporaries – especially the missionaries – often saw the failure to become farmers as evidence of the inability of these mixed-bloods to progress from "barbarism."

The arrival of a new English-speaking population and its movement northwards from the Forks saw the Anglican mission move in tandem. David Jones had opened a church on Image Plain, (now Middlechurch

Trials and Tribulations

on the western side of the Red) in 1825, and William Cockran established a Church Missionary Society church at Grand Rapids in 1829. Construction on the Grand Rapids church had begun in 1830, with wood floated down the river sufficient for a frame building 50 feet long, 22 feet wide, and 11 feet high. It was finished in 1832, and Cockran pointed out to the CMS that it had not provided a "single shilling" towards its construction. An experienced farmer before he joined the church, Cockran attempted to operate a model farm to set a good example for his flock. Cockran was a Scot, born in Northumberland, England. Raised as a Presbyterian, he converted to Anglicanism and came to Red River in 1825. Both Cockran and his wife came from humble origins. She had been a servant maid, and Cockran's speech was "broad and vulgar even as a scotchman." Donald Ross, in 1835, wrote to James Hargrave that Cockran was "as usual murdering the King's English most unmercifully in the flights of pulpit eloquence." He would come to one of Frances Simpson's dinner parties at Lower Fort Garry riding on a cow. Such antics horrified high society but endeared him to his congregation.

The newcomers also encouraged the establishment of other schools. In 1827, a "Female School" was opened, initially managed by Mrs. Cockran. David Jones explained to the CMS that "Experience has taught the Society, the influence which female education is calculated to produce in an uncivilized Country. . . .. The Females in question [the mixed-blood daughters of the officers of the HBC] are never likely to see any Country but this. In the course of time, they will be disposed of in marriage to persons of the Country; and may we not hope, that thus we shall have Female Missionaries by and bye throughout the Indian Territories?" George Simpson questioned Ann Cockran's qualifications for her task. He called her a "Dollymop. . .who ever prays and cooks and looks demure," later adding that her "assumed Puritanism but ill conceals the vixen, shines only when talking of elbow grease and the scouring of pots and pans."

The school did not flourish. William Cockran attributed its problems to the attempt to convert the children of Indian wives into "Accomplished Ladies all at once." He saw more practical skills as important for Red River children. When David Jones' wife arrived at the settlement in 1830, she took over from Mrs. Cockran. At about the same time, Bishop Provencher opened a school for girls at St. Boniface, to accompany the school he had founded in 1818. The schoolmistress was Angélique Nolin, the daughter of Jean-Baptiste Nolin, who had come west from the Sault in 1819 at Lord Selkirk's urging. Provencher had urged Ms. Nolin to open a school as early as 1824, but her father kept her at home until 1829.

J. M. Bumsted

The Catholics and the Anglicans each had three churches in operation by the early 1830s. Despite the presence of a number of Scots, and long-standing promises of a Presbyterian clergyman, no minister had ever been sent. The Scottish made do with the Anglican clerics, some of whom, like William Cockran, were ex-Presbyterians. The Anglican churches were all north of the Forks, at the present site of the Anglican Cathedral, at Image Plain and at Grand Rapids. In 1832, William Cockran succeeded in persuading nine Aboriginal families, headed by Chief Peguis, to settle at Sugar Point, just south of the present town of Selkirk. This became the Indian settlement of St. Peter's. In 1833, a log school was built on the site, as well as nine small houses 24 feet by 16 feet with a cellar in the centre of the room for potatoes. In 1836, a wooden church was constructed. Frances Simpson reported on the two Anglican churches nearest Fort Garry, describing the one at Middlechurch as the larger, and the one at St. John's as small, and attended mainly by those in the Fort itself.

The Catholic churches were at St. Boniface, at Pembina, and at White Horse Plains. In 1832-3, Father George Belcourt began a mission to the Chippewa west of White Horse Plain, at Baie-Saint Paul, called "Wabassimong" in the native tongue, which by 1839 had a village, many of the buildings constructed by the missionary himself, including a church dedicated to Our Lady of Mercy.

William Cockran opened a school for mixed-bloods in his Grand Rapids parish in 1831. Cockran reported that the children "are exceedingly wild. . .and have given us to understand that they know all that is necessary," while his schoolmaster insisted that the pupils learned very quickly to assimilate, having all "cropt their heads." A year later, on 8 May 1832, David Jones wrote George Simpson outlining plans for a "respectable seminary on a large scale in this settlement." From York Factory, Simpson wrote approvingly of the endeavour, and suggested educating daughters as well. Thus the Red River Academy was founded, at the Forks, to provide elitist education to the children of HBC officers. On 27 August 1832, Jones sent Indians down river to collect stones for the school's foundation, and the school opened a short while later.

The curriculum was a mixture of the practical and the classical. It taught "reading, writing, arithmetic, geography, the use of globes, history. . .catechetical information. . .bookkeeping, algebra, mathematics," as well as those essentials of the well-educated, Latin and Greek. A graduate of King's College in Aberdeen, John Macallum, arrived in the settlement the fall of in 1833 to be master of the school, and

61

Trials and Tribulations

Mary Lowman arrived to be the governess. The cost was £35 per year, which covered both tuition and boarding. The school experienced a variety of early problems, including a sex scandal in 1833, involving a daughter of a commissioned HBC officer and an Aboriginal boy who worked in the kitchen of the school. As a result, Simpson insisted that the Indian school be moved to Grand Rapids. A similar academy was operating under Catholic auspices at St. Boniface, with clerical teachers of both sexes, and English instruction as well as French from 1834.

As well as academies, the two principal denominations also had local schools in operation. According to William Cockran in a report to the Church Missionary Society in 1835, Donald Gunn at Grand Rapids was teaching 70 mixed-blood and 25 First Nations children on a regular basis. His attendance averaged between 50 and 55 percent, for during some seasons the older children helped with the farming. There was a day school and Sunday school under Peter Garrioch at the Upper Parish, a school at Frog Plain under John Pritchard, a school at Image Plain, and an Indian school at St. Peter's. Cockran later reported that the schoolhouse at Lower Church was cold and drafty, and in his journal for 19 October 1837 he noted that the children had to wrap themselves in blankets in cold weather and "the ink often congeals in the pen."

If the Anglicans were expanding, so too were the Catholics. In 1829, Bishop Provencher had received an offer from George Simpson to donate £100 to begin a subscription for the construction of a proper stone cathedral. Because of the shortage of skilled stonemasons, and the difficulty of obtaining suitable building material, the foundations of the new cathedral were not actually laid until June of 1833. The building was to be 100 feet long by 45 feet wide, with twin spires overlooking the Red River. As completed in the later 1830s, the cathedral was 100 feet long, 60 feet wide on the exterior, with solid stone walls three feet thick and 60 feet high. The spires were 105 feet high. The building took the form of a cross, with two lateral chapels. The floor of the nave, the balconies, and two rows of columns were made of wood.

The bishop's palace was subsequently attached to the cathedral. The palace was a two-storey structure, 70 feet long, and 40 feet wide, with walls 20 feet high. It had one of the few basements – actually a half-basement – in Red River. The first floor was made of stone and the second storey was covered with plaster inside and out. The roof was shingled. The palace housed the bishop and all the priests of Red River. Most of the

J. M. Bumsted

Catholic clergy in Red River preferred missionary activities among the Aboriginals and spent much of their time upcountry. This suited Bishop Provencher well enough, for he was happy as a sedentary clergyman. In 1838, Bishop Provencher, with the financial assistance of the Hudson's Bay Company, brought two women from eastern Canada to teach weaving. Shortly after its founding, this industrial school was destroyed by fire on 26 March 1839.

The Little Emperor of the Plains

Beginning in 1826, George Simpson began to move the headquarters of the Hudson's Bay Company from the West to Montreal, a process that was fairly far advanced when, in 1829, he went back to Britain, partly for "medical reasons," and partly to find a partner with whom he could found a family dynasty.

In his 18-year-old cousin, Frances Simpson, he decided he had discovered such a mate, and he married her on 24 February 1830. The couple returned to Red River in June 1830 accompanied by Chief Factor John George McTavish and his new bride Catherine Turner. Frances Simpson was violently seasick on the transatlantic voyage, although she appears to have enjoyed the overland passage, especially the receptions given to her at the various posts along the way. Like many physically frail people – the Earl of Selkirk is another example – western travel in the outdoors actually invigorated her.

Simpson and McTavish had both enjoyed long-term relationships with several mixed-blood and Aboriginal women, and had fathered several children whom they supported financially. The practice of taking what were called "country wives" was one of long standing with HBC men. They have been accused of treating women as sexual objects and of callousness towards Native "wives," and this was certainly true, but their behaviour was more sexist than racist. In Simpson's case, there was a Native wife and children whom he had left at Bas de la Rivière in 1829, while McTavish had to settle with Nancy McKenzie, his country wife of long-standing, who had born him seven children. In leaving their country wives, Simpson and McTavish set a precedent that was followed by other senior fur traders, although it is easy to exaggerate the number of HBC men who abandoned their Aboriginal partners. McKenzie would leave the settlement permanently in the autumn of 1832, replaced by Alexander Christie as Governor of Assiniboia, with George Simpson lurking in the background.

Trials and Tribulations

Why Simpson brought his new bride immediately to Red River is not entirely clear, given his move of the HBC headquarters to Lower Canada, and the presence in the West of several of his former country wives. There is undoubtedly some link connecting Simpson's marriage, his desire to settle down with a "proper" family, and his decision to abandon Upper Fort Garry and build a new trading post down river near St. Andrews. Officially, Lower Fort Garry was begun because of the experience of the 1826 flood.

He chose the new site on 11 June 1830, in the presence of Frances, who wrote in her diary that it was "a beautiful spot on a gentle elevation, surrounded by Wood, and commanding a fine view of the River." There was much greater availability of stone and firewood farther down the river, and construction soon began under the supervision of HBC chief mason Pierre LeBlanc, who built a big stone residence facing the river. LeBlanc had married Nancy McKenzie in February of 1831, George Simpson having earlier written McTavish, "I have performed a very important operation by nailing Leblanc for your old woman." Whether the contract for Lower Fort Garry was part of the deal is not known. In any case, the Simpsons moved into Lower Fort Garry in the summer of 1832.

For her part, Frances Simpson brought a new European standard to the settlement, which included not entertaining mixed-blood women in her home. Alexander Ross wrote James Hargrave on 30 December 1830, that Frances provided Red River with "an air of high life and gaity," focused around her "painted house of state, the Piano-forte, and the new fashioned Government Carriole." In her diary, Frances was well disposed if patronizing. "The reception I here met with," she wrote, "convinced me that if the Inhabitants of this remote region were plain & homely in their manners, they did not want for kindness of heart, and the desire of making every thing appear favourable, and pleasing, to the eye & mind of a stranger."

Frances suffered from ill health during her entire residence in Red River, partly caused by her sense of isolation, partly by the attitude of her husband – which was imperious, to say the least – but mostly by a difficult pregnancy and childbirth, which ended with the death of the young heir.

Frances was young and spoiled; George was older and domineering. It was a recipe for disaster. Frances returned to England in 1833, and did not rejoin Simpson until 1838, by which time he had re-established his permanent headquarters at Lachine in Lower Canada. It does not appear overly fanciful to see Simpson settling in as the baron of Red River (or the

"Little Emperor of the Plains" as his enemies called him) had his wife been happy there. Instead, in 1834, he took his big banquets and entertainment budget back to eastern Canada.

Little of political importance happened in Red River in the early 1830s. The first minute book of the Council of Assiniboia only begins on 4 May 1832. It showed Simpson as president. The council meeting dealt with the danger of fires, many arising from "the wilfulness of some ill-disposed persons, and the negligence of others." The main cause was brush and stubble-burning which was inherently dangerous on a wind-swept prairie, and fines were provided for those who lit fires more than 50 yards from their house, or beyond the boundary of their farms. This meeting also dealt with pigs and horses running loose in the settlement, suggesting a greater agricultural maturity than had existed in earlier days. From 1824 onwards, the HBC took a census almost annually, which often counted animals and buildings as well as inhabitants.

While he was still "in residence" in the early 1830s, Simpson organized a series of projects which, like the earlier buffalo wool company, and the introduction of hemp and flax, were designed to provide an export crop for the settlement. One was a sheep scheme, which had a long and chequered history. It had its origins in several earlier projects. One was a plan of Lord Selkirk to drive his Merino sheep (which had been purchased in the United States) from Upper Canada to Red River. This plan was ended by the War of 1812; the American invaders ate the sheep. A second project, in 1821, saw the importation of 15 Merino ewes and five rams from Saxony. This scheme foundered when many of the sheep were drowned on the passage to the settlement. Colin Robertson proposed a third project, called the Assiniboine Sheep and Wool Company, in 1824. Robertson wanted a grant of land from the Selkirk estate and £1000 in capital to obtain sheep and shepherds in the United States. He planned to sell mutton in Red River and export the wool. Simpson did not like Robertson, and he did not support the Company. In 1826, however, Simpson had begun to raise subscriptions to purchase a large flock of sheep in the, but the flood ended the scheme at that point.

Simpson had nevertheless observed that the prairie contained an abundance of good pasture, and in 1832, he raised £1200 to purchase sheep in the United States. Three emissaries, one from the HBC, another from the settlement, and the third an experienced sheep farmer, were sent down to St. Louis. The party departed with carts and horses in early November of 1832. Despite their best efforts, they missed the last

Trials and Tribulations

riverboat of the season at Fort Snelling. They pressed southward on sleighs, in canoes and on foot, and arrived in St. Louis early in 1833. But there were no sheep available for purchase at the prices they wanted to pay, and they were advised to try Kentucky. In the Blue Grass State, they purchased 1,475 sheep, and began herding them back to Red River. About 1,200 were lost on the prairies of Minnesota, mainly to speargrass infections, but, surprisingly, a Sioux war party allowed the remnants of the herd to pass without taking any action, and the party arrived home on September 16, 1833, with about 250 sheep still alive. Many complaints were heard about the management of this venture, and the criticism led Simpson to return the subscription money.

Undaunted, Simpson now tried to organize a Tallow Company, to export tallow and hides from cattle. Capital was raised, with 200 shares sold at £5 each. While the scheme looked a winner on paper, it inexplicably did not take into account the length and extremity of a Red River winter. Many of the newly-purchased cattle died on the prairie, and, we are told, "the ears, horns, hoofs, and tails of many of them froze and fell off and the cows lost their teats." The survivors of this herd were sold at auction, and the HBC paid the difference to investors in 1843.

George Simpson's "man of business" in the settlement from the arrival of Frances had been his kinsman Thomas, who had been born in Dingwall, in 1806, and educated at King's College, University of Aberdeen. When George had visited Dingwall in 1825, he had been quite impressed with young Thomas, and offered him a job as secretary. Thomas declined in 1825, but accepted a renewed offer in 1828. Thomas very quickly established a bit of a reputation as a brigade leader and wilderness traveller, but he spent most of his time looking after the paperwork at Upper Fort Garry. If George thought it was advantageous to have a kinsman working at Red River, he was sadly mistaken, for Thomas did not like George, and his correspondence home emphasized the point. The "Little Emperor" was not a tactful man with subordinates, and according to Thomas, during the early 1830s Simpson became "wavering, capricious and changeable," growing "painfully nervous and crabbed," especially after the relationship with his wife began to deteriorate.

At the same time, Thomas Simpson was no more tactful or patient, and he shared the general contempt of the Scottish fur trader for the mixed-bloods. In late 1834, he became involved in a major dustup with the mixed-bloods of the settlement. When a young tripman named Antoine Laroque entered Simpson's office under the influence of alcohol and demanded a pay advance, Thomas refused. The two men exchanged further words and eventually blows, with Simpson wielding a fireplace poker. It was hardly surprising that Laroque got the worst of the exchange.

The Francophone community confronted the settlement's officials at the gates of the fort, demanding that Thomas be turned over to them for punishment. Father Belcourt settled down the mob with promises of rum and tobacco. The whole affair blew over, although it may not have been entirely forgotten. In 1836, Young Thomas was shipped off to join Peter Debase in an expedition of Arctic exploration under the auspices of the HBC. Characteristically, Simpson travelled from Red River to Fort Simpson over the winter of 1836/7 – a distance of 1,277 miles – in only 62 days.

Thomas Simpson's contretemps with Antoine Laroque was not an isolated event, but part of a growing sense of grievance against the establishment on the part of the younger mixed-bloods. The problem was a combination of social and economic discrimination felt by the mixed-blood community, both Francophone and Anglophone. The mixed-bloods were not allowed employment in the HBC above the most menial ranks; those higher positions were kept for imports like Thomas Simpson. Moreover, the mixed-bloods were held to be socially inferior. Neither the settlement, nor the HBC, had fully adjusted to the change in demographics of Red River, which was no longer the home of large numbers of immigrants from Europe, but rather of large numbers of mixed-blood immigrants from the fur trading country. The social structure of the settlement was now one in which a handful of fur trade officers (mainly from Scotland) allied to a small number of Scottish farmers, and an even smaller number of clergymen (from England and Canada) lorded it over a population mainly composed of mixed-bloods and a few Aboriginals.

William Cockran, in a letter to the CMS in 1833, described the mixed-bloods as "the progeny of the adulterer and the whore." According to Cockran, after exploiting Aboriginal women throughout his career, the fur trader, in old age, "thinks of making an effort to remedy the errors of 30 or 40 years, by one mighty struggle." The missionary continued:

> "Out of his many connections he finds someone that ranks above the rest. He selects her to be the companion of his old age; collects his multifarious Progeny from the ends of the earth (for he has been everywhere through All this Continent) and bends his course to Red River, with a worn-out Constitution, with small means, with a woman that knows

none of the Duties of civilized life, with a dispirited family who know nothing but what the heathen have taught them, who have no interest in each other's welfare, to begin life anew, to learn with his heathen family how to discharge his duty to God, his neighbour, and his own soul."

Given this analysis of the origins of the mixed-blood community in Red River by a clergyman who lived in its midst, it is no wonder that the mixed-bloods were regarded as lesser people. Not only their origins, but also mixed-blood patterns of behaviour were stereotyped and criticized. In a historical account, published in the *Nor'-Wester* in 1861, but describing the settlement in the 1830s, an anonymous writer reported that:

"Canadians and half-breeds are promiscuously settled together, and live much in the same way, although I shall be able to point out some differences. They are not, properly speaking, farmers, hunters, or fishermen; but rather confound the three occupations together, and follow them in turn, as whim or circumstance may dictate. They farm to-day, hunt to-morrow, and fish the next, without anything like system; always at a non-plus, but never disconcerted. They are great in adventuring, but small in performing; and exceedingly plausible in their dealings. . . . In the spring of the year, when the Europeans are busy, late and early, getting their seed into the ground, the Canadian Halfbreed is often stuck up in the end of his canoe fishing goldeyes, and as frequently is he sauntering about idle with his gun in his hand. At the same time, if you ask them to work, they will demand unreasonable wages, or even refuse altogether; preferring indolence to industry, and their own roving habits to agricultural or other pursuits of civilized life. Their own farms, if farms they may be called, point them out as a century behind their European neighbours. Harvest time shows no improvement on sowing time, for they are to be seen anywhere but in the neighbourhood of their proper work. In short, they do all things out of season, and in the multiplicity of their pursuits oftener lose the advantage of all than accomplish one; verifying the old proverb of too many irons in the fire. While they are planning this and that little work, the summer passes by, and winter threatens them often with their crops unsecured, their houses unmudded, and their cattle unprovided for."

The sense of social inferiority probably affected the Anglophone mixed-bloods more than the Francophone ones, although Antoine Laroque certainly exploded at the treatment he received from Thomas Simpson. Problems were often exacerbated by the fact that, as George Simpson once noted, the Europeans invariably chose the prettiest mixed-blood girls in the settlement. In 1834, a lovematch between William Hallett, a young mixed-blood, and the daughter of an HBC chief factor was terminated by her guardian, Alexander Christie, who was also the settlement's governor. Hallett was told that he should not aspire to the best society, and the young lady was subsequently married to a Scot. Hallett and his friends were understandably happy to join the mob against Thomas Simpson.

The reappearance of a sense of mixed-blood consciousness, which had not been evident since 1816, was not the only new development of 1834. For the first time, the settlement was visited by a band of Sioux, the fiercest of the tribes inhabiting the plains to the south of Red River. On this occasion, 36 braves under the leadership of Chief La-Terre-qui-Brule, made their appearance. All would have gone well had not a party of Saulteaux braves arrived at about the same time, perhaps by coincidence, but likely through design. The Saulteaux had suffered heavy losses in recent encounters with the Sioux on the plains, and came to the Forks "breathing fury and revenge." Red River stirred itself to prevent a violent confrontation. One of the mixed-blood leaders named Parisien led a party which escorted the Sioux out of the settlement.

Although this incident passed peacefully, for many years after the residents of Red River felt that they were living on top of a powder keg, where tribal animosities or land claim disputes, might erupt with violence at any time. Particularly worrisome was the continued insistence by the Cree that the Saulteaux had no land rights whatsoever. To add to the complexity of the issue, all the Aboriginal groups maintained that, at best, European property rights included only the land on either side of the rivers immediately around the Forks. No negotiations about land rights, beyond those conducted by Lord Selkirk in 1817, had taken place.

Also in 1834, epidemic disease, which for the most part Red River had managed to avoid, struck with considerable force. It made its first appearance in September, in the form whooping cough, and violent dysentery. Several of the children of James Sinclair died at this time. Thomas Simpson noted in December, that "the Settlement has not been healthy this fall and the hooping cough, followed by a severe intestine

Trials and Tribulations

disorder, has thinned the swarm of children not a little." A number of the elite of the settlement lost children to disease, which carried on into 1835.

In June of that year, another outbreak of disease occurred. William Cockran gave us our most detailed description of the disease of that year, writing, "An epidemic rages of the most alarming nature. It seizes the old the middle aged, the young, and the infant, all are groaning and many are prostrate under its evil influence. . . .. The symptoms all are similar, soreness of throat, excruciating pains in the chest; debility and pains in the limbs; violent headache and earache; a discharge of pus from the ears; deafness; delirium; inflammation of the eyes, intermitting fever; and severe cough and in some accompanied with expectoration of blood." This epidemic had apparently begun in Norway House, and what Cockran described was obviously some strain of viral flu. This outbreak marked the end of isolation from epidemic disease for the settlement, which would thereafter be regularly visited with serious illnesses carried along the river systems

Then, after years of supplying goods on credit at the HBC store, in 1834 the Company introduced a cash system and refused to reconsider this measure. We are told that the supply of goods was deliberately reduced under this regime, and further curtailed by opening the store only on certain days. The new system was particularly hard on the poor, who had little money. Goods remained in short supply for several years, until private traders (who did give credit) were allowed to operate by the Company. It is worth noting that this new policy was introduced just as George Simpson was completing his move to Lachine.

A New Government

In 1835, the Hudson's Bay Company finally purchased the settlement from the Selkirk family. Whatever the cost of Red River to Lord Selkirk and his estate – and the figure of £85,000 was often bandied about by contemporaries – the family received only £35,000 for it, and this sum was probably considerably more than it would have been worth at public auction. The settlement had survived without formal laws, and without any real political structure, yet the population lived with considerably fewer disagreements than one might expect. Indeed, it surprised an anonymous historian of the settlement, writing in 1861 in the *Nor'Wester*, that the population "should in such a case have held together so harmoniously during a period of twenty-four years." A governor, the Council of Assiniboia, which met infrequently, and passed mainly municipal regulations for controlling loose livestock, plus a handful of part-time constables constituted the entire government of Red River before 1835.

George Simpson and the HBC officers constantly complained about the potential for violence, especially given the mixed-blood population, but in truth very little aggressive behaviour – certainly nothing resembling the anarchy constantly predicted – had appeared. The mob actions at the end of 1834 may have helped convince the HBC of the need for a form of government that better represented the existing population, but there was nothing really threatening that demanded immediate action.

Nonetheless, on 12 February 1835, George Simpson presided over a meeting of the Council of Assiniboia held at Fort Garry. To the current list of councillors, five men were added "to assist with their advice" in the deliberations: Bishop Joseph-Norbert Provencher, another Company fur trader (Donald Ross), and three civilians: Alexander Ross, Sheriff of Assiniboia, John Bunn, the chief physician in the settlement (and a mixed-blood), and Andrew McDermot, the major private trader in Red River. Provencher was the first representative of the French interests ever asked to attend the council, and the invitation to three individuals not part of the Company gave evidence of a desire to broaden representation. Simpson opened the meeting by reading a formal address to the council. He noted that the population of the settlement had reached 5,000 souls – an overstatement of official figures by 1,300, although perhaps Simpson had good reason to increase the numbers in the census books – and existing institutions were no longer sufficient to "maintain the tranquility and good government of the settlement." The administration of justice needed to be put on a more regular footing, and Simpson proposed a series of resolutions for the council's consideration.

To raise revenue, he proposed the levy of an import duty of 7 $1/2$% at York Factory, and the appointment of James Bird as Receiver of import and export duties. Simpson also recommended the construction of a public building for a courthouse and a gaol. To oversee this construction, he suggested the appointment of a committee of management for Public Works, to consist of Robert Logan, Alexander Ross, John Bunn, Andrew McDermott, and the head of the HBC as chairman. To help finance it, he announced a grant of £300. Another recommendation was for the dismantling of the present police force, to be replaced by a volunteer corps of 60 officers and privates, to be paid out of the new revenue. Alexander Ross was to be appointed commanding officer of the new corps. The Council ratified these measures.

Trials and Tribulations

The Council thanked Simpson and the Company for its generosity, and then proceeded to divide the settlement into four districts, with a magistrate for each district to hear cases of petty offenses and debt under 40 shillings. The magistrates appointed were James Bird, Robert Logan, James Sutherland, and Cuthbert Grant (who would soon be added to the council). To deal with more serious cases, and to handle appeals from the petty courts, a General Quarterly Court was set up. It was to consist of the Governor and Council, plus the magistrates, and would meet monthly at the governor's house. No rules of procedure were formally adopted at this time, beyond the establishment of court fees to avoid "frivolous and vexatious litigation."

These reforms were certainly a start, although a thorough reorganization of the government of the settlement, and the introduction of a fully articulated judicial system had to wait until 1839. Some of the mixed-bloods protested the new measures, but there were few other public complaints about the new regime. An idyllic view of this period came to flourish, and our anonymous historian of 1861 was moved to report: "In no instance were the decisions of the magistrates questioned or disobeyed. No collision of interests or parties disturbed the place. So much confidence was reposed in the simple and straightforward course pursued, that the good will of the people always strengthened the hands of justice. Thus peace and order were thoroughly maintained in the colony; the laws were respected and life and property were secure."

In truth, the first effort at criminal justice under the new system, by a petty jury impaneled on 28 April 1836, was quite controversial. Louis St. Denis, a Francophone Canadian, was found guilty of theft, and was sentenced to be publicly flogged. The sentence was carried out the next day, and the individual carrying out the flogging was attacked by the crowd, and forced to take refuge at Upper Fort Garry.

In an early example of progressive thinking, the Council of Assiniboia, in 1837, passed resolution stating that "the evidence of an Indian be considered valid, and be admitted as such in all Courts of the Settlement."

An 1835 census, conducted by George Taylor, found 559 households at Red River, cultivating 3,237 acres, an average of 5.7 acres per household. At St. Andrews in that year, 97 farmers cultivated 568 acres, or 5.8 acres each. Also at St. Andrews 17 householders had no cultivated acreage, while 19 had over ten acres. Scots at the Forks cultivated more land than the mixed-bloods at White Horse Plain. The harvest of 1835 was an exceptionally bountiful one. Curiously enough, it did not produce great contentment among all the inhabitants of the settlement.

In the autumn, a number of Scots decided to leave Red River for the United States, claiming "there is nobody there [at the settlement] to purchase their produce." One Scot would write that "few will remain here who can carry themselves away." A series of bad harvests, which succeeded the good one of 1835, probably did not reduce the pressure to remove.

The year 1836 saw yet another attempt by the HBC at creating an experimental farm. George Marcus Carey agreed to become manager of the farm, established not far from the Forks. Carey's background and qualifications for the appointment were obscure. Alexander Ross thought he was "more of a florist than agriculturist." The farm did not succeed. It never managed to hire proper labourers, and the settlers opposed it as undue competition, pointing out that Carey cultivated the same crops and livestock that were being raised and sold by everyone else in Red River. Carey took it over as a private venture upon the expiration of his agreement, cultivating 60 acres next to Upper Fort Garry until 1847. The suspicion in the settlement persisted that the experimental farm had been established by the Company for nefarious motives, partly to reduce the agricultural market available to the colonists, and partly to demonstrate, through its failure, that the country was not useful for agricultural purposes. Whether or not this was really the case, it was true that the HBC was quite ambivalent about the settlement, since its continued growth went contrary to the company's philosophy for the region.

In December of 1836, Red River was visited by the first of a series of unusual strangers, often from the United States. General James Dickson was a soldier of fortune who had attempted to recruit a small army in New York State, to create an independent utopian state for Aboriginals somewhere in California. The remnants of this army – perhaps a dozen men – appeared in Fort Garry at the end of the travelling season. Dickson's plans fizzled out in Red River after he was unable to recruit mixed-bloods to join his "cavalry." Dickson's personal appearance was consonant with his endeavour. George Simpson described his face as "covered with huge whiskers and mustachios and seamed with saber wounds." When he left the settlement early in 1837, he made Cuthbert Grant a present of one of his ceremonial swords.

Less than two months later, a party led by Pierre-Louis Morin d'Equilly, arrived overland from York Factory. This group had been stranded at the Bay, and had decided to trek to the settlement. Their sleds carried tea, sugar, rum, moose meat, slices of buffalo hump meat, grease, biscuits, and flour. In his journal, Morin described his winter clothing: "a

Trials and Tribulations

pair of trousers which came right up to my shoulders, a kind of tunic covering the whole body from the top of the neck to below the knees, a vest of muskrat skins, an otter-skin hat, moccasins, long mittens made in such a way that the thumb is not separated from the fingers, other clothes made of caribou hide and lined with a very thick, soft flannel, a multicolored sash, decorated leggings or mitasses and finally, beautiful snowshoes sturdily fashioned by an Indian named Cadieu."

In January of 1838, George Simpson wrote a confidential letter to Adam Thom in Lower Canada, offering him the post of recorder (judge) in Red River. Thom was, at first glance, a curious choice, to say the least. A Scot educated at King's College, Aberdeen, Thom came to Canada as a journalist, and had been the editor of the Montreal *Herald*. He also wrote a number of pamphlets attacking the French-Canadian party at the time of the Rebellions of 1837-8. Having read law, and been admitted to the bar of Lower Canada in 1837, he became a secretary to Lord Durham, and Assistant Commissioner of Municipal Affairs for Lower Canada. This implicit endorsement from Durham was an important factor in his appointment. In his letter, Simpson added that "I presume you are qualified to express yourself with perfect facility in the French Language of the Country, . . . without which you would not be adapted for the situation." Such a presumption would turn out to be most inaccurate.

The invitation to Thom, who was a close friend of Montreal merchants George Moffat and Peter McGill, may also have been designed to soften the opposition of these gentlemen to Simpson's efforts to get the HBC's license renewed four years ahead of time, in 1838, rather than in 1842. Moffat especially, was well known as an opponent of the HBC charter and monopoly. The major reason for the early application was the rise of American annexationist pressure from the settlers south of the Columbia River in what is now Oregon. The Company wanted evidence of support from the British government as the "Oregon Crisis" began, although it also appears likely that Simpson thought he should act at a time of relative tranquillity in the settlement. In its application for renewal, the HBC pointed out the value of the Company to the First Nations, emphasizing its efforts to Christianize and educate the Aboriginals. The British government routinely renewed the trading license for another 21 years, but insisted that the HBC promote colonization and settlement in the region. In that same year Lower Fort Garry – symbol of the HBC power in the settlement – was completed.

In March of 1839, the HBC General Court further reformed the government of Rupert's Land. George Simpson became Governor-in-

Chief of Rupert's Land and a council was appointed. The Governor of Assiniboia became Duncan Finlayson, and a new Council of Assiniboia was appointed. It consisted mainly of Anglophone HBC employees, and retirees, although it included Bishop Provencher and Cuthbert Grant. Adam Thom was named as Recorder of Rupert's Land, and councillor of both Rupert's Land and Assiniboia, although he would not be formally appointed until 30 June 1839. Upon his arrival in the settlement, Thom began a two-year investigation into the legitimacy of the government, ultimately deciding that the Company had both the right and the power to govern. Thom also proposed that he draft a law code suitable to Red River. He sought to "temper law with equity and reconcile the peculiar circumstances of Repute's Land with the fundamental principles of the Laws of England."

The magistrates approved the draft code in the summer of 1840. The Francophones were not shown the draft, however, and Sheriff Alexander Ross, arguing against the new regime, observed that "the law, as it stood, worked well, and what works well should be let alone." In his draft, Thom noted that he intended to introduce the new law code on 1 November 1838, with "provisions to mitigate the criminal law of England with respect to such offences as are most likely to be committed in Rupert's Land." He eliminated barriers to the giving of testimony, admitting both parties as witnesses in all cases. Thom insisted that the code be sent to the HBC for approval, but noted that it was not necessary for Parliament to approve it. The Company decided against forwarding the code to the British legislature.

Adam Thom was insistent that Red River had evolved to the point where a formal law code was necessary to command the respect of the people. He stated that "to hesitate either to make or to enforce any obviously beneficial regulation from an undefined dread of factious opposition is to abdicate respectively legislative authority or judicial functions." George Simpson would certainly have concurred. But, as Sheriff Ross suspected, the expansion of governmental authority and the introduction of a judicial system only exacerbated the growing conflicts in the settlement. The succeeding decade would not see the settlement's political institutions contributing to stability and tranquility, but to exactly the opposite characteristics.

-4-

Resisting the HBC Monopoly

If the HBC had hoped that its political and judicial reforms of 1839 would stabilize the Red River Settlement through the 1840s, it was doomed to disappointment. Part of the problem was that Red River, unlike individual fur-trading posts in the interior, was not populated solely by HBC employees and their dependents, over whom the HBC had unlimited power. Many Red River residents had lives – and minds – of their own, and were hard to lean on. Another part of the problem was that the HBC could not always control its own officials, particularly Adam Thom and Alexander Christie, who insisted on provocative measures in confronting the forces opposed to the HBC's monopoly in the settlement.

A move to encourage dissidents to depart from the settlement for the Pacific Slope was not pursued aggressively after an initial expedition, probably because of the Oregon Crisis, which briefly brought a military force to Red River. But when the troops departed, the dissidents – who had been silent for several years – re-emerged in full force. Fortunately for the HBC, the spokesman for the dissidents in England – A. K. Isbister – overplayed his hand and allowed the HBC to deflect the settlement's complaints. As a result, the British authorities did not intervene in Red River, and by their lack of action allowed the HBC to resolve its problems in its own way in the landmark Sayer Trial of 1849.

Along the way to the open confrontation of the Sayer Trial, the settlement experienced a number of developments both uplifting and disquieting. In the 1830s there had been a sense of forward movement and economic diversification. In the 1840s, employment with the HBC became restricted to a few, the buffalo hunt declined in importance, and a series of bad harvests and epidemics took their toll. The arrival of new missionaries – both male and female – altered notions of race and class in the settlement. The missionaries reinforced the sense of superiority among the fur traders and retired officers of the HBC, most of them Anglophone. The Anglican newcomers attempted to recreate the social order of rural England complete with an Anglican rector and HBC squire. The missionaries had a clear sense that Anglican education in the settlement had moved backward during the decade.

The Catholic arrivals, especially A-A. Taché, were equally committed to the reproduction of an imported social ideal. The Catholics wanted Red River to be like rural Quebec. Both Anglicans and Catholics increasingly worked against the raucous openness of early Red River society by seeking to control drinking and carousing in the name of respectability. Unlike the Anglicans, the Catholics experienced great strides forward in educational terms during the 1840s. The missionaries of both denominations ceased to be in conflict with the fur traders and became their allies. At the same time, Anglicans and Catholics became less cooperative and more confrontational with each other.

Arrivals and Departures

The new decade opened with a number of important arrivals, and several significant departures. In January of 1840, the HBC and the British Wesleyan Missionary Society agreed that "the Mission shall appoint three of their Missionaries to proceed to the HBC's Territories," with one at Moose Factory, one at Norway House, and a third on the Saskatchewan River. Salaries were to be paid by the society, with transportation, and board and lodging in the country the responsibility of the HBC. In early March, three young Methodist missionaries – George Barnley, William Mason, and Robert Rundle – were ordained in London, and soon after were in their way from Liverpool to Montreal, via New York. In April, the Toronto-based secretary of the British Wesleyan Methodist Society, assigned another young clergyman, James Evans, who had developed syllabic alphabet for Ojibwa, as superintendent of the Methodist missionary thrust to the west.

On one level, the arrival of the Methodists did not directly influence life in the settlement; the first Methodist clergyman did not actually settle in Red River until 1868. But on another level, the new arrivals provided an implicit rebuke to those missionaries who clustered in the settlement and administered mainly to the settlers. They were keen to proselytize to the Aboriginals, and were soon both successful and controversial. The translation and printing efforts of the missionaries had some influence on Red River, although even more on the First Nations of the interior.

Trials and Tribulations

In September of 1840, the annual ship from England brought to the West a party of females consisting of Isobel Finlayson, Laetitia Hargrave, and one "Miss Allen," who was to take charge of the girls' school at the settlement. Laetitia Hargrave would settle for becoming the "Queen of York Factory," but Isobel Finlayson (the sister of Frances Simpson), and married to Assiniboia's Governor Duncan Finlayson, approached the settlement as if it were India and she were a memsahib in exile. At York Factory, the party transferred into two York boats, each containing 15 persons, including a crew of 11. The Finlaysons travelled with a manservant, Crosbie, and a lady's maid, Mary. They put into shore for dinner about two in the afternoon, and the travelling case and basket were quickly brought out of the boat. The travelling case was "lined with baize and divided into several compartments, the upper part containing places for knives, and forks, spoons, glasses, cups and saucers, a cruet stand &c., and the lower part is fitted with large Crystal flaggons, for wine and other liquids, and also contains a tea pot and cases for tea and sugar." Dinner was a "rural repast" of "cold beef, ham, tongues, and venison pie," with port and white wine. Upon arrival at Lower Fort Garry, Isobel was greeted by Mrs. Adam Thom, and travelled in style in a four-wheeled carriage to Upper Fort Garry, where she would become the settlement's social arbiter during the period of her residence.

Finlayson has left us a not very flattering description of the lower Red River and of the settlement. She found the first appearance of the river "a gloomy and wretched prospect" with its thick and muddy waters. But gradually signs of civilization appeared in the form of haystacks, livestock, and log houses. Finlayson was impressed with Upper Fort Garry but not with Red River houses, which were:

> "all built of wood, and either painted or whitewashed, a few of the largest being two stories high, but the greater part only one, seldom containing more than two or three rooms while those belonging to the poorer classes are mere log huts. . . They are invariably situated on the banks of the river, and all have a cold and naked appearance as scarcely a tree or shrub has been left standing near them."

She was also less than enthusiastic about the Canadian and mixed-blood inhabitants, whose poverty she ascribed to their improvidence. She obviously had been influenced by the opinions expressed by the officers of the HBC. At the same time, the visitor was much taken with winter provisioning in the settlement, writing:

J. M. Bumsted

Lord Selkirk

Cuthbert Grant

Trials and Tribulations

George Simpson

Adam Thom

"As soon as the frost sets in, the Winter stock of provisions is laid up in the ice house, the meat being all killed at this Season of the year when it immediately becomes as solid as a block of marble, and lasts in this state fresh till the following Spring. It would astonish some of the thrift economical housekeepers in England, could they see the immense quantity, and strange variety of provisions that are collected in the ice house, at this season: beef, mutton, pork, hams tongues, fowls, turkeys, rabbits, sturgeons, whitefish, and vegetables, all frozen as hard as stone, so that when a joint is required it has to be cut off with an axe, or a saw, and slowly thawed, before it can be dressed for the table."

Finlayson found Red River "infinitely superior to the opinion I had originally entertained of it," because "living is cheap and good, and one can obtain all the necessaries, and many of the comforts of life." Beef was two pence a pound, mutton two pence halfpenny, and eggs were four pence a dozen. But, she confessed, "for many reasons, I should never like Red River as a place of residence." Isobel remained at Upper Fort Garry until 1844, when she joined her husband in his new posting at Lachine.

Meanwhile, George Simpson's cousin Thomas, who had spent several years exploring in the Arctic, had returned to Red River in a state of considerable agitation, apparently brought on by continual controversies with Peter Dease. Thomas was high-strung at the best of times, and a number of witnesses insisted that his words and behaviour "betrayed symptoms of aberration of mind." Thomas and a small party left Red River, and on the third day out, having separated himself from the main party, Simpson laid hold of a double-barrelled gun and without saying a word, shot and killed two mixed-bloods who were putting up his tent.

He told a companion, "I am justified by the laws of England in killing these two men; for they had conspired to kill me this night, and carry off all my papers!" His colleagues headed off on horseback to find the main party, and when they returned the next morning, they claimed that they found Simpson stretched out on the ground, "the body warm, and the butt-end of the gun between his knees, the muzzle in a line with his head where the shot took effect, one barrel empty, and his right hand with the glove off, along the guard: his night-cap blown some yards in a line with the position of the gun."

This "suicide" was always regarded as extremely suspicious, but it was over a year before Dr. John Bunn was sent to the scene of the event

Trials and Tribulations

to disinter the body and examine it. Decomposition made it impossible for him to shed new light on the tragedy, and the dead man was returned to Red River for burial. Thomas's brother, Alexander, refused to accept the account given, which he regarded as inconsistent and improbable. In a series of publications, Alexander suggested that Thomas had been murdered by his mixed-blood companions, and their culpability covered up by the authorities at the settlement, an accusation that has found considerable support from subsequent writers. Although there was insufficient evidence to indict the mixed-bloods for the crime, Simpson's death provided another impetus to the growing racial conflict of the period.

A notable departure, this one collective, occurred in May of 1841. James Sinclair, one of the brightest and most outspoken of the mixed-blood traders in the region, was chosen by George Simpson to lead a party of settlers west to the Oregon territory. Simpson had approached Alexander Ross, but the sheriff claimed to be too old, and recommended Sinclair. The expedition would serve two purposes. First, it would provide a British foothold in the Oregon country to counter the growing American presence. Secondly, it would provide a safety valve for mixed-bloods, like Sinclair, who felt stifled in Red River. The party consisted of 121 souls, including representatives of a number of the leading Anglophone mixed-blood families in Red River.

The cart train assembled at White Horse Plain, intending to travel overland through the Rockies to the Pacific Slope. Although the "Carlton Trail" to Fort Edmonton was neither as well known nor as frequently travelled as the "Pembina Trail," travel on it was hardly very adventurous. The men dressed for the buffalo hunt in buckskin shirts and jackets worn with heavy homespun trousers. Moccasins and capotes completed their attire. Women wore dark homespun dresses and shawls. Each member of party had 50 pounds of pemmican. George Simpson wrote: "Each family had two or three carts, together with bands of horses, cattle, and dogs. ...As they marched in single file their cavalcade extended above a mile long." The emigrants were pictures of good health and left in exceptionally good spirits.

Sinclair's party reached Edmonton House in early August. Here, Sinclair met Mackipictoon, a Wetaskiwin Cree, who offered to lead the party across the Rockies via a pass hitherto unknown to Europeans. This leg of the journey was considerably more dangerous and adventurous than the Carleton trail, but Sinclair and his party reached Fort Vancouver in October of 1841. From the moment of their arrival, there was trouble, and by 1843, most of the party had left the region of the Cowlitz and

Nisqually rivers, north of the Columbia, and headed for the Willamette to the south. Their crops failed in 1842, and they were not treated generously by the HBC.

Not only did the people of Red River regard this expedition as a failure, but also it was not followed up by the HBC. As a result, discontent increased in the settlement. Retired fur trader James Sutherland wrote in the summer of 1842: "I have now four sons at the house with me, the two oldest are now men fit for any duty in this part of the world [but] there is no opportunity for young people to push themselves forward in any way, better than labourers, either as farmers or Boatmen in the Co's service and either way they can barely make a living – my two youngest sons has got a better Education than I had when I came to this country yet it will be of no use to them."

The Growing Presence of Adam Thom

Recorder Adam Thom did not recede into obscurity after instituting his law code in 1840. Instead, his behaviour made clear that he had no objection to taking stands on controversial matters. The first of these was the "Ordination Controversy," which emerged in 1842, when the Anglican Bishop of Montreal proposed a journey to Red River to ordain clergymen – there were several missionaries in the settlement who wanted to be ordained – and to assert his Episcopal authority in the settlement. Thom responded to this news with a document entitled "Observations on the Colonial Ordinations Act, 59 Geo. 3, ch. 60," in which he argued that the Bishop of Montreal could not act in an Episcopal capacity in Red River. Behind this document several local observers detected the hand of George Simpson, who allegedly wanted to use the shortage of ordained clergy as an excuse for asking the Methodist James Evans to move to the settlement and take over the Upper Church. Simpson's attitude towards religion was always utilitarian rather than denominational.

Meanwhile, in 1843, Thom became a defendant in his own court. His former governess, Helen Rothney, sued Thom for back wages, after he had terminated her employment when she was five months pregnant. A jury awarded Rothney her pay until the end of her contract, and her expenses home, which was more than had been claimed. Thom refused to pay, and she eventually agreed to settle for past services only. There was no process for appeal within the law code of Assiniboia, and instead of taking the case to the Council of Assiniboia, Thom wanted the court to overturn the jury's verdict.

Trials and Tribulations

Subsequent to the court action, Rothney married William Drever, but it was speculated that she wanted people (including Thom's wife) to suspect that Thom was the father of the child. This was only the first of several court cases in which Adam Thom became personally involved. In the Rothney case, Thom was probably an innocent victim of a determined servant, but she was certainly able to take advantage of a growing hostility to Thom amongst the people of Red River.

As well as taking advantage of the animosity already building to Adam Thom, Helen Rothney had attempted to utilize the power of rumour and gossip within Red River. Newcomer Robert Clouston described this phenomenon in a letter to his family in August of 1844:

> "... as is usual in small Communities, anything that occurs in one family spreads over the whole Settlement, but by the time it reaches the most distant parts it has been so changed that no one could recognize it – thus – a person was thrown from his horse and broke his collar bone – about 20 miles from this – but by the time the story reached here, he was reported dead. If a bachelor is seen conversing with a young lady, they are pronounced to be on the eve of marriage – and from all such occurrences and phenomena they invariably coin some plausible fictions & give them forth as truths – but in no instance have I known the scandal brought home to its propagator – "they have raised it" is the usual expression, who the respectable persons thus designated may be, is seldom or never clearly established. Thus, you see, the current topics of conversation among the generality of people, spring from such polluted fountains that a person who wishes to adhere strictly to fact cannot repeat those stories he hears without feeling very uncomfortable as to their authenticity nor listen to them with confidence in their correctness."

The power of rumour and gossip continued to be an important ingredient in the history of Red River throughout its early years, and was even the subject of a *Nor'-Wester* feature article in the early 1860s. Major William Caldwell, in 1849, described the community as "a village, rife with gossip and slander, in which every man, whatever his rank, was intimately known and censoriously judged." Understandably, Adam Thom would be one of rumour's principal adversaries, as well as one of its most frequent victims.

Thom also quickly developed a reputation for judicial harshness. As early as 1842, the London authorities of the HBC became fearful that their

Recorder's sentencing practices would inflame resentment. Thom was warned "not to sentence any one to such a harsh judgement as may be called in question but rather to subject the guilty persons to pains and penalties which cannot be censured." Thom had already argued against this attitude at the time of his revisions of the law code in 1840. He had written, "It is only by commanding the respect of the people, that law can practically exist in Red River, and such respect is not more inconsistent with boldness in doing what is believed to be unreasonable and wrong, than with timidity in doing what is admitted to be reasonable and right. In so simple and natural a state of society, there can be no temptation to frame such laws, as may be mischievous or even doubtful, and to hesitate either to make or to enforce any obviously beneficial regulation from an undefined dread of factious opposition is to abdicate respectively legislative authority or judicial functions."

A few years later, Thom openly defied Aboriginal custom as well as the imperial authorities. The case involved a Saulteaux named Capenesseweet, found guilty of murder, despite claims by the Aboriginal community that First Nations people were beyond the judicial authority of Thom's court. The trial was held without giving the defendant the benefit of counsel, although lawyers were often not in evidence in the early days of Red River justice. Use of an interpreter was necessary since the defendant spoke no English. The jury was charged by Thom to find the defendant guilty, and the recorder pronounced sentence of death.

Thom knew perfectly well that imperial law called for him to send such cases to Canada for trial, but he insisted that such an action would cause nothing but trouble for the witnesses. The obvious solution was to send the prisoner far away from the settlement, for he could not be sentenced to long-term incarceration given the limited detention facilities. Thom was nothing if not courageous, however much Red River found the subsequent execution excessive and distasteful.

Thom was never content merely to be a judge. He was also responsible for the recommendation of a series of measures designed to control the trading practices of Red River inhabitants. In June 1845, Thom recommended a substantial import duty on American goods, which was never implemented, but which, according to Alexander Ross, made him an object of "odium" among the mixed-bloods. Thom's negative measures became part of the "free trade" agitation discussed in the next section.

Thom seemed never able to escape controversy. When Anglican missionary Robert James and his wife arrived at the Grand Rapids, in July of 1846, they found the parsonage occupied by Adam Thom and his

Trials and Tribulations

family. Thom had leased the property from John Smithurst, acting for William Cockran. After James' arrival, a dispute arose over occupancy. Thom later claimed that he had expected to share the parsonage with James (as Smithurst had proposed), and James had initially accepted this arrangement, later reneging on it. Thom also insisted that he expected to be supplied with food from Cockran's farm for the winter. For his part, James argued that the lease was automatically cancelled by the arrival of a new incumbent.

Thom found the dispute "painful" and insisted that Mrs. James did nothing "to sweeten or to dignify the nauseous pill" of having to move. In fairness to Thom, the Reverend James made little effort to make himself liked in the settlement. In 1847 He would write to a CMSA correspondent: "The men who brought us to Red River were nearly all members of my future congregation at the Rapids. Only one or two showed any regard for us, others robbed our scanty provisions and generally they acted without affection. The first two days they were all intoxicated and this with their subsequent conduct induced us to regard them nearly all 'heathens.'"

The Reinvigoration of Religion

Apart from the HBC, the most important institutions in Red River were the churches. They ministered to the community's spiritual needs, and also controlled education and health care within the settlement. In 1843, Red River's 5,143 settlers included 2,798 Roman Catholics, with most of the remainder being at least nominally Anglicans. Robert Clouston, a year earlier, had reported four Protestant and three Catholic churches in the settlement. Within a few years, however, both denominations had been reinvigorated. The principal problem – the shortage of clergy – was the result of the colonial status of both the Catholic and Anglican missions at Red River. Neither denomination was able to ordain priests or to finance themselves. The issue of ordination and the financial problems were resolved over the course of the decade of the 1840s.

The Catholic Church

In 1843, Bishop Joseph-Norbert Provencher had only four priests at his disposal to serve both the settlers and the surrounding Aboriginal population. Provencher knew that he needed priests who "must have a liking for the work and be educated men, steadfast in character and not given to rancour, able to restrain themselves and refrain from losing their temper, men who are not at a loss for words and can also sing." In Montreal he managed to persuade the Sisters of Charity of the Hôpital Général in Montreal (the "Grey Nuns") to supply the settlement with four sisters "to assure Christian teaching and the teaching of household arts to the young women."

Sister Marie Louise Valade – a mixed-blood – eventually agreed to lead the group as Superior of the Red River convent. The nuns arrived at Red River on 20 June 1844, after a harrowing canoe journey from Montreal. They moved into an abandoned stone house near the Bishop's palace on the west side of the Red River, and were soon planning a new two-storey residence. They also began visiting the sick and teaching children at the school. The first class for 27 girls was opened on 11 July 1844.

On his trip to Montreal in 1843, Provencher added another accomplishment to his list of credits. He managed to persuade the Canadian authorities to create an autonomous ecclesiastical province in the west. When Rome agreed with the idea, the vicariate apostolic of Hudson Bay and James Bay was created on 16 April 1844. In France, in the spring of 1844, Provencher and the Society for the Propagation of the Faith at Lyons came to an agreement by which the Society provided the Red River mission with an annual payment of 30,000 livres.

Provencher also met with Charles-Joseph-Eugené de Mazenod, Bishop of Marseilles, and founder of the Congregation of the Oblate Missionaries of Mary Immaculate, who agreed to send Oblate fathers to Red River. The first two Oblates, Pierre Aubert and Alexandre-Antonin Taché, arrived at the settlement in the summer of 1845. With the establishment of a properly funded vicariate apostolic, independent of Canada, and the establishment of two religious orders at Red River, the Catholic Church in the settlement was well prepared to move forward.

On his return to Red River in 1844, Bishop Provencher responded to his more secure situation with an organized campaign against the excessive consumption of alcohol. From the first establishment of the Catholic mission in 1818, the good fathers of the mission had worried about the effects of alcohol on the people of the settlement, especially the French mixed-bloods, but had been unable to do much about the matter. Provencher organized a temperance society with over 400 members, who were committed to abstinence, and to not providing liquor to the Aboriginals. This temperance movement had a good deal of success among French mixed-bloods actually residing in the settlement, although it had little influence on those *hivernants* who seldom came into contact with the missionaries.

Trials and Tribulations

By 1852 it was necessary for Provencher to organize a second campaign, and in 1855 his successor Bishop A-A. Taché created still another one. William Ross would report, in 1856 that the Roman Catholic Temperance Society stood at about 900 members at least two-thirds of who "were once drunkards." This introduction of "Victorian" values was part of the changing nature of Red River society that began in the 1840s.

The Anglicans

In the spring of 1844, George Mountain, the Anglican Bishop of Quebec, departed Lachine for an Episcopal visit to western Canada, an occasion that would deny Adam Thom's earlier insistence that Mountain could not ordain clergy in Red River. George Simpson provided the Bishop with a canoe crew, headed by an Iroquois named Jacques. A famous painting of Mountain's canoe heading west hangs in the library of St. John's College, at the University of Manitoba. There were 17 people in the canoe, all depicted in the painting. According to Mountain, the baggage, bedding, and provisions, along with the equipment of canoe and tents, was estimated to weigh one and a half tons.

Mountain's visit to the settlement lasted for 17 days. The Bishop ordained Abraham Cowley and John Macallum as priests, and confirmed 846 Anglicans. At the Lower Church he confirmed 192 women and girls in the morning, and 150 men and boys in the evening. At Middlechurch and Upper Church, 150 candidates were presented at each service. Mountain also confirmed 204 native converts at St. Peter's. The ceremonies, the vestments worn at them, and the talk of the subsequent consecration of the Anglican churches of Red River, all disturbed the Scots in the settlement who had accepted Anglicanism only as a temporary measure. Alexander Ross complained that the whole visit reeked of "popishness," and another petition for the Church of Scotland circulated soon after Mountain had departed.

A number of underlying tensions were exacerbated by the Mountain visit. One was a division within the Anglican clergy over ritual, with William Cockran representing the Low Church element, and John Smithurst and Abraham Cowley the Episcopalians. Cowley and his ritualism were so badly received by the mixed-bloods at Grand Rapids that he informed the Church Missionary Society that new missionaries would have to be able to speak extemporaneously, lest several congregations desert the Anglican church at the first sign of a Presbyterian clergyman. Behind the liturgical issue was the larger question of the resentment of mixed-blood clergymen like Henry Budd and Charles Cook (low churchmen) at the inequities of treatment. As a result of his observations in the settlement, Mountain returned to Montreal to press the English authorities for a permanent bishopric at Red River, and on 29 May 1849, David Anderson was consecrated as Bishop of Rupert's Land.

The decision to create a diocese in Red River was at least partly the result of a windfall sum of money that was released by the Court of Chancery in 1848. Fur trader James Leith, one of the Nor'westers who had opposed Lord Selkirk, had died ten years earlier. Leith left half his estate for the purpose of "establishing propagating and extending the Christian protestant Religion in, & amongst the native Aboriginal Indians in. . .the Hudson's Bay Territory." The sum of £15,000 was set aside to support the new diocese, and it would subsequently be enhanced by further grants.

Like many another colonial bishop, and more than a few English ones as well, David Anderson was a clergyman of little distinction when he was appointed to Red River in 1849. At the time of his ordination, the Church Missionary Society provided a grant of 500 pounds to establish a missionary society in Rupert's Land for the education and training of Native teachers. Unmarried, Anderson was short and balding, and somewhat affected in his dress and manners. He had no sympathy for Presbyterian worship in his diocese, or for the consumption of alcoholic beverages. He was heavily influenced by his strait-laced sister, who accompanied him to Red River on board the *Prince Rupert*. The Andersons would become social leaders of the "respectable" faction of European settlers in the settlement. Anderson would also become a major political figure of Red River as well.

The Buffalo Hunt

One of the most important social and economic institutions of the Red River mixed-bloods was the buffalo hunt, which probably reached its greatest influence and importance in the 1840s. Some aspects of the hunt are quite controversial, as we shall discuss later, but there is substantial descriptive agreement among both contemporaries and later historians. We have lengthy descriptive narratives by three contemporary eyewitnesses, resulting from their participation in different hunts at three different times of the year. Alexander Ross spent much of the summer of 1840 with the main hunt; Father Georges Belcourt travelled with the autumn hunt in 1845; and an observer unnamed in the *Nor'Wester*, but otherwise known to be Viscount William Fitzwilliam Milton, spent some weeks with the summer hunt in 1860.

Trials and Tribulations

In addition, there are a number of briefer descriptions of the hunt in the accounts of virtually every visitor to the region before Confederation. Alexander Ross was quite articulate on the notice shown the hunt by visitors:

> "We are now occasionally visited by men of science as well as men of pleasure. The war road of the savage, and the solitary haunt of the bear, have of late been resorted to by the florist, the botanist, and the geologist; nor is it uncommon now-a-days to see Officers of the Guards, Knights, Baronets, and some of the higher nobility of England, and other countries, coursing their steeds over the boundless plains, and enjoying the pleasures of the chase among the half-breeds and savages of the country. Distinction of rank is, of course, out of the question; and, at the close of the adventurous day, all squat down in merry mood together, enjoying the social freedom of equality round Nature's table, and the novel treat of a fresh buffalo steak served up in the style of the country – that is to say, roasted on a forked stick before the fire."

From Ross's perspective, this romantic picture only helped to retard the "elevation of the savage" in his "progress in civilization." All observers were agreed that the hunt was central to the lifestyle of many of the mixed-bloods.

The Hunt Described

The organized hunt had come into existence around 1820. Before that time the hunt was conducted without large-scale organization. Donald Gunn describes the hunt in his account of the first Red River settlers wintering at Pembina in the winters of 1812-13, and 1813-14. According to him, the settlers had to go out to the hunter's camp, and bring back the frozen meat on sledges. It is clear that even at this early date, the buffalo frequented what came to be the American side of the Red River Valley. Some writers think that the buffalo were more plentiful around the Lower Red River Valley before the arrival of settlers, but others, led by Frank Roe, insist that the buffalo had always been migratory, and that the Lower Red was the outer limit of their range. The creation of a formal hunt probably had to do with the establishment of the Buffalo Wool Company in 1821. As well as the creation of this new market, the presence of hostile Indians in the grazing grounds of the buffalo helps account for the development of an organized, community approach to hunting.

The big hunt was the summer hunt, which began in June, and lasted until August. The summer hunt was chiefly concerned with the production of dried meat and pemmican, and the kill was processed on the spot. A smaller hunt went out in September, and returned to the settlement in late October or early November, eventually driven off the prairies by the arrival of winter. Because the weather was colder, this hunt was able to preserve some of the meat, and did not attempt to process everything at the site. The frozen meat was known as "green meat." The hides were much superior in the autumn, as the buffalo were in the midst of producing their warm, thick, coat. Not as many people went on the autumn hunt, partly because it competed with harvest time in the settlement, but more critically because many of the mixed-bloods, unable to afford to winter in the settlement, had already begun moving to winter quarters and camps where they could survive by hunting.

There were also different parties of French mixed-bloods involved in each of the hunts. One party was based at Pembina. A second consisted of those who lived on the Red to the north of St. Boniface. A third had its centre in St. François Xavier and was known as the "White Horse Plain brigade." By 1860, the latter would separate from the other groups and hunt independently, although still in contact with the main expedition. Through the early years, Cuthbert Grant had led the White Horse Plain group. Jean-Baptiste Wilkie of Pembina usually led the Pembina contingent, and William Hallett was a frequent chief of the Red River party. In view of the frequent association of the buffalo hunt with the Francophone mixed-bloods, it is worth noting that all three of these leaders were English-speaking.

When the parties assembled at the start of the hunt, they held councils that selected their captains and organized the rules of the hunt. The rules were designed to avoid confusion during the actual hunt, and to guarantee safety, especially from marauding parties of Indians, who remained a constant danger. A number of captains were chosen – Ross says ten – with two being designated as senior captains. Each captain was given ten "soldiers," who were expected to follow orders without hesitation. Their job was to keep the expedition orderly. Ross observed that the French mixed-bloods were fond of the number ten, but Milton in 1860, wrote of 12 captains, which suggests that organization was to some extent dependent upon the number of participants. This quasi-military form of organization would be later be adopted by Louis Riel in forming his provisional government in 1869.

Men were also chosen to guide the expedition. They worked on a daily rotating basis, being responsible for raising the flag in the early morning, and for lowering it at night. During the day, their authority was primary, although when actually in camp the captains were in charge. All observers were impressed by the intuitive ability of the guides to

Trials and Tribulations

navigate the seemingly featureless prairies. Viscount Milton wrote, "to avoid marshes, go round lakes, and find a path between precipitous hills, requires a very correct knowledge of the country, and is certainly a very difficult and responsible duty."

The size of these expeditions was substantial. Alexander Ross wrote of an increase from 540 carts in 1820, to 1,210 carts in 1840, and Milton and Cheadle write of "1500 or 1600" carts in 1862. In 1845, Father Belcourt accompanied the smaller autumn expedition, which he reported consisted of 213 carts, 55 hunters, 300 horses and more than 100 oxen. Mr. Flett, in 1849, made a census of the summer White Horse Plain brigade, and found 603 carts, 700 half-breeds, 200 Indians, 600 horses, 200 oxen, and one cat. The *Nor'-Wester*, in 1860, listed the size of the White Horse Plain group as: "154 families, including 210 men able to bear arms (of whom 160 were buffalo "runners"); and 700 'non-combatants' women and children," accompanied by "642 horse, 50 oxen, six cows, 522 dogs, 533 carts, one wagon, 232 guns, ten revolvers, 21,000 bullets and 270 quarts of gunpowder." The newspaper also reported the size of the main hunt, a product of a "close and careful count" of "500 men, 600 women, 680 children, 730 horses, 300 oxen, and 950 carts."

The party camped in what contemporaries described as "lodges" or "tents." In addition, there were a number of larger lodges for council meetings and gatherings. Each hunter required three to four carts, and the entire expedition would sometimes stretch out over several miles of prairie. Each hunter was also accompanied by three to four family members, and the women and children did much of the work. Not even advanced pregnancy kept women at home during the hunt. The result was a large, and not very maneuverable community, difficult to protect from marauders. Ross thought it "the largest of the kind, perhaps, in the world."

Any expedition generated a good deal of noise and was not likely to go undetected for very long. One ox in rawhide harness usually drew each cart, with a collar like a carthorse, although sometimes horses were employed. The sound of the creaking of the wheels and axles of the carts was legendary; in 1868, Charles Mair wrote his brother that the sound "makes your blood run cold." At night, the bellowing of the cattle and the neighing of horses provided a constant background of noise for the barking dogs. Viscount Milton wrote of the dogs that they "seemed to delight in noise, and the bark of one was quite sufficient to get the entire canine population of the camp yelping in full chorus."

The camp usually broke at daybreak, with the daily guide in front, accompanied by parties of armed scouts and soldiers. Other scouts rode on the flanks and to the rear of the caravan. When the caravan stopped, it wheeled into a large two-columned circle, with each cart parked wheel-to-wheel to its neighbour. This configuration contained the livestock. At night, the tents were pitched inside the ring, each beside its owner's cart. Belcourt said that the 1845 autumn hunt was one of 60 lodges.

The fact that the Red River hunts operated mainly in the United States had not escaped the notice of the American authorities, who, beginning in the 1840s, had attempted to force the hunters to become American citizens. Contemporary observers argued that the Americans could cripple Red River by strict policing of the boundary, and most French mixed-bloods were quite prepared to take on American citizenship if required.

All observers were singularly impressed with the skillful way in which the hunters operated. They were able to maneuver their horses by leaning from one side to other, leaving their hands free for handling and reloading their gun. The horses were adept at avoiding fallen animals. Although this was the perfect place for a repeating rifle, most of the hunters used muzzleloaders. They carried up to four additional balls in their mouths, and reloaded on the dead run. This could be a dangerous procedure. In one notorious incident in 1860, the hunter put his powder in too soon after the last discharge, and put his mouth over the muzzle to blow the powder home. The fresh powder ignited, severely burning his mouth and throat, and he died two days later.

The chase not only tested the skill of the hunter, but also challenged his courage, for the work was highly hazardous. A hunt was seldom completed without at least one serious injury or death. Falls were common. The buffalo would often butt the horses, and a fallen rider was liable to be trampled, or even gored by an infuriated animal. Another danger was that the hunter could easily become caught in a stampede. Father Belcourt reported one such incident that he had witnessed in 1845:

> "Having dashed off in pursuit of a numerous herd of cows, they were in full career, in the very midst of the herd, when they arrived suddenly at the brink of a steep, rock-strewn cliff. Over they went, pell-mell – hunters, horses, and buffalo – in such confusion that it is difficult to explain why some were not killed, crushed against the rocks or trampled beneath the hooves of the following horde. Only one man was knocked unconscious, and he soon recovered. . . .. The hunters who had been un-horsed jumped quickly back into their saddles with reassuring cries, and took up the chase once more,

cracking their whips with a will in an endeavour to make up for lost time."

There was also the danger from stray bullets, for "from every direction they whistle through the clouds of dust in a most disconcerting manner." Finally, the hunter who was skinning his kill on the open prairie was sometimes exposed to great risk from lurking Sioux. The dangers of the hunt provided for many a tale around the evening campfire. Alexander Ross was probably correct in his assertion that most of these men were positively drawn by "the mixture of hope and fear – the continual excitement – the very dangers themselves."

After the chase was finished – it consumed no more than an hour or two at the most, and was usually limited by the need to replenish ammunition and powder – the hunters leapt off their horses, and began to field-dress the kill where it lay. Observers were impressed with how each hunter appeared able to distinguish his own kill; there were remarkably few disputes over dead animals, even though they were usually not marked by the individual hunter.

The hunter propped up the dead animal on its knees, spreading its hind legs so that the buffalo was supported on its belly. First the small hump was removed, then the hide was slit down the back and taken away. Then the animal was butchered. Father Belcourt identified sixteen different cuts. The heat from the freshly killed animals was very intense, and the hunter worked up a considerable thirst, which he quenched with water from a small keg, or by chewing on various raw parts of the carcass. The hunter worked backwards through his kill, skinning the last animal first.

The carts collected the meat and carried it to the camp, where the women took over the task of processing. The men were responsible for cracking and boiling the bones to extract the marrow, but the females in the party dealt with the remainder of the work. "The day of a race is as fatiguing for the hunter as the horse," wrote Alexander Ross, "but the meat once in the camp, he enjoys the very luxury of idleness." The women cut the meat into long strips and hung it on wooden frames to dry. The choicer bits were then rolled up and packaged into bundles of jerky weighing 60 to 70 pounds each. The remainder was fried to a crisp over a hot fire, then pounded into a powder to which melted fat, and sometimes dried fruit was added. The mixture was worked with shovels and then packed into rawhide sacks called "taureaux." According to Father Belcourt, one cow's meat supplied only enough pemmican for half a "taureaux" and less than one bundle of jerky. When the hunt was finished, the carts – each filled with 1,000 to 1,500 pounds of meat – would creak their way back to the Red River. This time, the women and children would walk behind.

The Critics of the Hunt

Although contemporary observers were in general agreement about how the hunt operated, the question of its implications were more controversial. Much of the debate originated with Sheriff Alexander Ross, whose views of the hunt were generally negative, because in his view the excitement and adventure of the buffalo chase helped prevent the French mixed-bloods from settling down to a steady agricultural existence. The central feature of Ross's critique was the extent to which the hunt perpetuated the improvidence of the mixed-bloods. He maintained that the "plain hunter's life is truly a dog's life – a feast or a famine," and he wrote movingly of the starvation experienced by the children in the hunt camp before the buffalo were sighted.

As part of the pattern, he pointed out that the hunters often left much of the kill on the ground for the wolves, while in camp, the dogs were allowed to gorge themselves. "There is a manifest conflict of want and waste in all their arrangements," Ross maintained, and as "a proof of the most profligate waste of animals," he insisted that on the hunt he observed, 2,500 animals were killed to provide a quantity of pemmican and dried meat that 750 animals could have supplied. Even allowing for the feasting at the campfire, said Ross, most of the food was wasted. "Scarcely one-third in number of the animals killed is turned to account." Ross felt that this behaviour reflected the mixed-blood's "improvidence and want of forethought" inherited from their "savage" ancestors.

This sort of thinking fit well into the arguments of those who sought to prove that the hunt was in large part responsible for the disappearance of the buffalo from the plains. The first major writer to advance this line of argument was William T. Hornaday, whose *The Extermination of the American Bison, With A Sketch of its Discovery and Life-History*, was published in 1887. Hornaday relied almost exclusively on Ross's testimony to support his conclusion that the "Red River settlers, aided, of course, by the Indians of that region, are responsible for the extermination of the bison throughout northeastern Dakota, as far as the Cheyenne River, northern Minnesota, and the whole of what is now the Province of Manitoba."

However, Frank T. Roe in 1935 pointed out the dangers of extrapolating from a single expedition to the entire hunt, particularly when Father Belcourt's figures suggested a yield per cow of three and

Trials and Tribulations

one-half times that stated by Ross. Nevertheless, he observed that "the legend of Red River wastefulness has become so embedded in popular belief that it is apparently considered to be an indispensable feature in any allusion whatever to the Hunt." In other writings, Roe offered a variety of other explanations for the disappearance of the buffalo.

The question of the range of the buffalo, and its supposed narrowing over time under the pressure of hunting, has been the subject of considerable debate. In the late 1850s, Professor Henry Hind talked about two herds of buffalo known to the Red River hunters, one being the Grand Coteau/Red River herd, and the another in Saskatchewan. Hind wrote of the westward pressure on the buffalo, noting, "The country about the west side of Turtle Mountain in June 1858 was scored with their [French mixed-bloods] tracks at one of the crossing places on the Little Souris, as if deep parallel ruts had been artificially cut down the hill-sides. These ruts, often one foot deep and 16 inches broad, would converge from the prairie for many miles to a favourite crossing or drinking place; and they are often seen in regions in which the buffalo is no longer a visitor." Roe, on the other hand, disputed this conclusion, arguing that the buffalo's appearance had always been irregular.

Beyond the question of mixed-blood profligacy was Alexander Ross's larger socio-economic criticism. The hunt was not only wasteful, but also economically and socially dysfunctional, maintained Ross. To illustrate the economy of the hunt, Ross calculated that the capital outlay required to equip the 1840 expedition he accompanied was 24,000 pounds. Half of this outlay came from credit, Ross insisted, and he described (unfortunately not in detail) a system of truck in Red River in which the French mixed-bloods were caught in an ever-escalating web of debt:

> "before they have paid their debts in part, got their supplies in part (for everything they do is by halves), the whole of their provisions, one way or other, is dribbled off. In less than a month, therefore, they have to start on the second trip, as destitute of supplies, as deeply in debt, and as ill provided as at first. . . .. The writer is not acquainted with a single instance, during the last twenty-five years, of one of these plain-hunters being able to clear his way or liquidate his expenses, far less to save a shilling by the chase; the absence of a proper system, and the want of a market, render it impossible."

Moreover, the hunt was socially disruptive, argued Ross, for it agitated the remainder of the inhabitants of the settlement both before its departure and after its return.

Worst of all concluded Ross, was the blithe persistence in the face of the handwriting on the wall. "The buffalo, the exciting cause, once extinct, the wandering and savage life of the half-breed, as well as the savage himself, must give place to a more genial and interesting order of things; when here, as in other parts of the world, the husbandman and the plough, the sound of the grindstone, and the church-going bell, will alone be heard." This theme would be constantly reiterated in the settlement, not least by Alexander Ross's son James in the pages of the *Nor'-Wester* in the 1860s.

The Free Trade Movement

In 1843, Norman Kittson an American-based fur trader constructed a trading post at Pembina on behalf of the American Fur Company, just south of the international border. The post, on the site of earlier of the NWC and HBC posts, soon drew a number of mixed-blood traders from Red River. Commerce with the Americans quickly began to flourish. The HBC, always sensitive to threats to its trading monopoly, was soon planning counter-strategy. Alexander Christie's appointment as Governor of Assiniboia was intended to provide tougher enforcement of the laws of the Red River Settlement. The Council of Assiniboia began to enforce the customs duties.

As already noted, Recorder Adam Thom recommended a series of "negative" measures, including a land-title deed that, if taken seriously, put its recipients in virtual feudal servitude to the HBC. The deed was not a grant of land in fee simple, but rather a grant of one thousand years tenure, and was based upon a whole series of collateral prohibitions and obligations amounting to a civil contract with the HBC. The holder agreed not to evade the HBC's trading monopoly, or trade in furs or spirits. He also agreed to contribute to the expenses of all public establishments, and to help with roadwork for up to six days per year. He could not alienate any part of his land without the written permission of the HBC. The deed was invalid if not registered within six months, and any violation of its terms abrogated the agreement, and rendered the land subject to forfeit. Not surprisingly, very few grants were accepted under this deed.

Simultaneously, Sir George Simpson began to lobby the British government for a military force, ostensibly to defend the British West against the Americans, but more particularly to enforce the law, mainly the various trade prohibitions in Red River. On 8 December 1844, Alexander Christie issued several proclamations, including one

Trials and Tribulations

requiring all importers to guarantee that they would not use their goods in the fur trade, and another making the mail liable to HBC inspection.

A series of large public meetings and open confrontations with the authorities of the settlement followed, although the Anglican clergy worked very hard to keep their mixed-blood charges away from the gatherings. In one of the earliest, Sheriff Alexander Ross visited the house of trader Alexis Goulet, searching for goods that had been brought into the settlement without a license.

The house, reported Ross, was "surrounded with men, horses, carioles, dogs & a mob of people, [so] that I had some difficulty in getting to the door...the half-breeds filled the front room, the back room, where the goods were, was chock full of canadians." Ross stated his business, noting that Goulet had signed a bond, on which he had now reneged. Ross found the half-breeds reasonable, but the Canadians kept urging them to resist. Eventually Goulet agreed to give up the goods, provided Ross would return them when he proved ownership. Ross maintained that "any subject of this Colony,...may bring goods from the States, from England, from any country under the sun, & trade those goods in this Colony, providing the thing is done openly & fairly – there is no law to prevent it, but no subject from any other State, neither from America, nor from England itself nor from any other country, can bring in goods, or trade goods here legally without a license."

Goulet offered two witnesses to prove his ownership of the goods, which Ross accepted. Ross told the gathering that he hoped there would be no further such meetings to "disgrace Red River." Ross stated that his meeting was unlawful, and that all such meetings or mobs not called by public authority were unlawful. Ross was subsequently apologetic about giving in to the mob, but pointed out that he did disperse it, and had little other choice since he had no armed authority at his back.

Escalating matters, the governor and council of Rupert's Land passed a series of regulations on 10 June 1845, that limited the importing and exporting of goods to traders that the governor of Red River "reasonably believed" had "neither trafficked in furs themselves since the 8th day of December 1844, nor enabled others to do so by illegally or improperly supplying themselves with trading articles of any description." By this point, both sides were ripe for a confrontation. Having chafed for years under HBC restrictions, they sought the highest possible moral and political ground for their opposition.

On 29 August 1845, the mixed-blood James Sinclair, on behalf of 19 other traders, wrote to Governor Christie with a series of 14 hypothetical questions dealing with the fur trade. The letter began by declaring "a very strong belief that we, as natives of this country, and as half-breeds, have the right to hunt furs in the Hudson's Bay HBC's territories whenever we think proper, and again sell those furs to the highest bidder." The subsequent questions dealt with further particulars of this assertion of "Aboriginal Rights." Christie answered swiftly. He denied that the half-breeds had any such privileges. As British subjects, he declared, they had the same rights as anyone born in England or Scotland, but these were limited by the HBC Charter. A few days later, George Simpson warned the HBC in London that "without a military post at Red River, I fear the inhabitants of that settlement will run riot and strike a blow at the Fur trade from which its recovery would be very doubtful." It should be understood that the authorities at the settlement regarded any public opposition to the HBC and its monopoly as riotous.

In September 1845, the HBC opened a post on the Settlement side of the 49th parallel at Pembina, under the command of John Palmer Bourke. Robert Clouston described the post a few months later: "Mr. Bourke has a rough log house, the walls of which, inside and outside are plastered with clay, and the roof covered with earth – it is floored with rough logs: the men live in the same house, with merely a partition between them – a mud chimney in each room and a door opening from Mr. B's apartment to his trading room." The only article of furniture in this hut was a table. Cassettes (light trunks) were used as chairs. The boundary marker was visible from the building. "Some wag had pulled up the post of demarcation," wrote Clouston, "and had placed Uncle Sam's initials towards the British territory." The post was designed to demonstrate that the HBC was determined to actively compete with the Americans at the border.

In February of 1846, the traders met again at the house of Andrew McDermott, in the very shadow of Upper Fort Garry, to draw up a request for relief to the British government. The details of the meeting and its immediate outcome are not very clear. Earlier, in 1845, Andrew McDermott's nephew, the trader John McLaughlin, had generated a petition to the American government purportedly signed by 1,250 "half breeds and Canadian settlers." McLaughlin had subsequently left Red River, according to Sir George Simpson, "for the purpose of laying it before the authorities there." The petition prayed "to be admitted as settlers within the Iowa territory, and to be allowed the priveledge [sic] of hunting."

According to W. L. Morton, the February 1846 meeting of the traders drew up two petitions, one in French and one in English, but waited to dispatch them until they knew the outcome of the McLaughlin initiative.

Trials and Tribulations

This account seems most unlikely, for the results of the McLaughlin petition would not be known for some months, and James Sinclair was already preparing to depart for England to lay petitions before the Crown. Moreover, there never were two petitions. Rather, there was one undated petition in French, and a set of instructions in English "addressed to the Delegate in charge of the Petition." As it transpired, McLaughlin proved a useless emissary. Instead of travelling to Washington to present the petition in person, McLaughlin merely posted it in the mail to the American Secretary of State, James Buchanan, who sent it on to the War Department. There it died an ignominious death, evidence of the Settlement's traitorous willingness to deal with the Americans, but otherwise without effect.

We do have a copy of a petition, in French, signed by 977 "inhabitants of Red River." This was undoubtedly the petition referred to by Morton. It was generated by Father Georges Belcourt, at the behest of a large number of French mixed-bloods, who had initially sought more strenuous action against the authorities in Red River, but had been convinced by the priest to adopt this form of protest. Belcourt had counselled obedience to authority, however evil it was, and recommended legal means of achieving justice. Belcourt would subsequently insist that his action in drafting this petition had prevented a more serious confrontation, and he may well have been correct. This was also the petition that was signed at Andrew McDermot's house in February 1846.

According to Norman Kittson, writing in early March of 1846, "Politics are running high in the Settlement at present more so than usual. The Half breeds held a meeting last Thursday at which the Revd Mr. Belcourt a catholic missionary presided, they are to petition the Queen for Freedom of trade, a Governor independent of the H.B.Co and an elective legislature, and if these are not granted, or if they do not receive any relief from the B. Govt. at home, I am certain it will end in a revolution, there seems to be a feeling of this Kind (and it is general) throughout the whole Colony, they are determined on some change and they cannot have any but for the better."

Kittson's description of the demands of the petitioners was not entirely accurate. The petition was full of rhetorical excess, although at its base was a hard core of strongly felt grievances. It claimed that Lord Selkirk's promises – that the colonists' "commodities, etc., would be sold at a satisfactory price, fixed in the said contracts, and that the toil of the labourer would not be paralyzed by his inability to sell his productions – had been evaded and frustrated. It insisted that the HBC monopoly had "weighed heavily on us for about one hundred and seventy-six years," thus dating the burden to the founding of the HBC in 1670 rather than to the founding of the Settlement.

On the other hand, the Petition did provide a fairly straightforward shopping list of requests. First, the petitioners asked to be governed according to the principles of the British constitution. Secondly, they wanted the liberty of trade that prevailed elsewhere in the Empire, so that they would not continue to be "reduced to a kind of slavery." Finally, they wanted land sold to new immigrants, with the proceeds used to improve transportation. "We are near the boundary line, we can go over to the neighbouring territory," the Petition concluded, "but we admire the wisdom of the British Constitution, and we desire its privileges."

Unfortunately, these requests were never really considered by the Colonial Office. Alexander Kennedy Isbister, who made himself responsible for putting the grievances of the residents of the West in the hands of the British government, treated them as an afterthought, rather than the core of the complaint in the Memorial he forwarded to the British authorities early in 1847. Isbister was a country-born mixed-blood, who had been educated at the University of Aberdeen. Part of the problem was that the Petition did not arrive in Isbister's hands in time for him to use it in the preparation of his Memorial that lumped Aboriginal and mixed-blood grievances together, although they were quite different. Mixed-blood grievances came mainly from Red River, while Aboriginal complaints came from the outlying HBC territories.

The petition was not placed in the hands of the Colonial Office until later in 1847, and while it was translated into English, it received little or no consideration. The HBC concentrated on refuting the Memorial's complaints about treatment of the Aboriginals, and the British authorities never really looked closely at the grievances of the Red River Settlement, which ended up falling through the cracks of the Colonial Office proceedings.

On 24 April 1847, HBC Governor Sir John H. Pelly, wrote the Colonial Office. He stated that the mixed-blood's contention that they had a right to trade with the Indians regardless of the Charter was "quite untenable." He added, "the circumstance of their being born in the country may entitle them to call themselves natives, but it neither conveys to them any privileges belonging or supposed to belong to the Aboriginal inhabitants, nor does it divest them of the character of British subjects, all of whom are precluded by the HBC's charter from trafficking in furs within its limits without a license from the HBC, and the

Trials and Tribulations

Red River settlers are additionally bound, by the covenants under which they hold their lands, to abstain from such traffic."

Although he mostly ignored the content of the petition, he did venture to say that if the people of Red River "have any grievances to complain of, and remedies to propose, due consideration will be given to them." Unfortunately, Isbister's overstatements of the abuse of Aboriginal peoples managed to deflect British attention from accusations of political tyranny by the settlers of Red River. In fairness to Isbister, the Colonial Office had no real sympathy for mixed-bloods. The Colonial Undersecretary, who was assigned to comment on the Isbister Memorial, saw the Red River mixed-bloods through the eyes of their critics – as an undesirable mixture of energy and lack of ambition – who were not entitled to support.

The Deflection of the Free Trade Protest

In the short run, the decision to petition the Crown quieted the free trade protest in the settlement. Even the hotheads had to accept that it would take some considerable time for the requests of Red River to be heard by the British authorities. It was 1848 by the time the Colonial Office finally responded to the Memorial of Alexander Isbister. The process of petitioning seems to have had some effect, however. Governor Christie wrote George Simpson, in April of 1846, that some of the magistrates "have expressed a degree of reluctance amounting...to a fixed determination not to adjudicate in cases arising out of illicit fur trafficking," which must have cooled tempers considerably. Other factors also helped to take the steam out of the political situation.

The Evans Affair

Attention at Red River in the meantime turned to other developments, initially to a series of scandals at Norway House involving Methodist missionary James Evans. In 1844, under confusing and mysterious circumstances, Evans had accidentally shot and killed his Aboriginal assistant, Thomas Hassall, while on a canoe journey to the Athabasca country. Then in 1846 there were rumours of sexual "games" being played with young Aboriginal girls in Evans' home, which led to formal charges against the missionary by his parishioners. Evans was exonerated at Norway House, then went back to England, where the Wesleyan Methodist Missionary Society acquitted him of sexual abuse, while criticizing him for treating young Aboriginal women with the same familiarity he showed his daughter. His activities were understandably the talk of the settlement. Evans died of a heart attack in Lincolnshire in November 1846.

The Flu Epidemic of 1846

In late spring and early summer of 1846, the settlement was hit by another major epidemic. As usual it is difficult to get much of a sense of the nature of the infection. Reverend John Smithurst wrote of "another disease following the measles which is far more fatal. It is a kind of dysentery or bloody flux and has carried off 1/6 of the population at the Roman Catholic Settlement on the White Horse Plain." Descriptions suggest some sort of extremely virulent viral flu strain. Alexander Ross calculated that in June and July there were seven deaths per day, or 321 in total, representing one in every 16 settlers. Ross added dramatically, (and quite erroneously): "In no country, either in Europe or America, in modern times, not under the severest visitation of cholera – has there been so great a mortality as in Red River on the present occasion." The deaths were distributed, Ross wrote, one-sixth among Aboriginals, one-sixth among Europeans, and two-thirds among mixed-bloods and French mixed-bloods.

More recently, Gerhard Ens has calculated the death rate in St. François Xavier at 81:1000 and in St. Andrews at 61:1000. George Simpson wrote to the governor and committee of the HBC, on 28 July, that 300 people, mainly children, had died in June of 1846 alone. The disease spread rapidly with the spring brigades from Red River to York Factory, and to the Athabasca, where it had devastating effects among the Aboriginals. In Red River, Alexander Ross insisted, "Hardly anything to be seen but the dead on their way to their last home; nothing to be heard but the tolling of bells, nothing talked of but the sick, the dying, and the dead." To make matters worse, a summer drought in 1846 was followed by an infestation of Hessian fly and a crop failure.

The Arrival of the Troops

In the midst of the epidemic, 383 men, women, and children from the 6th Royal Regiment of Foot (the Royal Warwickshires) – commanded by Lt. Colonel John ffolliott Crofton, were dispatched to Red River via Hudson's Bay. George Simpson finally had his soldiers, although the Oregon Crisis was now over. Alexander Ross observed, in his *History of Red River*, that the troops resulted from "the unmeaning fuss and gasconnade of the Americans about the Oregon question, for we were not aware of any inducement but the protection of the frontiers, that

Trials and Tribulations

could have moved our government to send out troops to this isolated quarter."

Simpson was not entirely happy about the total number, claiming that 400 newcomers were too many for the settlement to provision. The regiment was stationed at the Lower Fort, where they would consume 150 pounds of bread, and 150 pounds of meat per day. Alexander Ross thought that the presence of the regiment stabilized the community. "Generally speaking, everything is quiet & orderly. The presence of the red coats has made us draw in our horns like so many snails. The laws are respected, no mob-meetings, no plots, no threats, no illicit smugglers, no fur traders. We begin for the first time to look upon the property we possess as our own – protection is written in legible characters."

Certainly the year-long residence of the regiment, combined as it was with drought and food shortages, put additional strains on the economy of the settlement. George Simpson saw the effects of the drought in typically racial terms. He reported to London in July of 1847 that "the improvident Canadian and French half-breed settlers suffered much privation from the failure of the crops last season. The Scotch, Orkney and other more industrious inhabitants were amply provided with the means of subsistence." More to the point, however, the shortages of 1846 marked the beginning of a period when the settlement was quite unable to supply the HBC with enough foodstuffs, instead of one where there was no incentive to extend cultivation. For the next few years, Mother Nature would deal Red River agriculture a series of blows in the form of bad weather.

In 1847 Robert Ballantyne, a young Scotsman who had spent six years in the service of the HBC, published his first book. It was based on his letters and journals, and was entitled *Every-day Life in the Wilds of North America, During Six Years' Residence in the Territories of the Hon. Hudson [sic] Bay HBC*. Ballantyne had not spent much time in the Red River Settlement, and so most of his detailed descriptions were of York Factory, and remote fur trading posts in the interior. But he did include a wonderful description of the fur brigades, which by the 1840s, had become an institution of the settlement:

> "On the day appointed for starting, the boats, to the number of six or seven, were loaded with goods for the interior; and the *voyageurs*, dressed in their new clothes, embarked, after shaking hands with, and in many cases embracing, their comrades on the land; and then, shipping their oars, they shot from the bank and rowed swiftly down Red River, singing one of their beautiful boat-songs, which was every now and then interrupt-

ed by several of the number hallooing a loud farewell, as they passed here and there the cottages of friends." The boats were on their way to Norway House."

Ballantyne's book brought the HBC territories, including Red River, to the attention of the international reading public for the first time. It was joined, in 1849, by Robert Montgomery Martin's *The Hudson's Bay Territories and Vancouver's Island*, which painted a somewhat bleaker picture of the fur trade region, which the author regarded as unfit for settlement.

Another literary event of 1847 was the founding of the Red River Library, opened partly at the behest of the officers of the 6th Royal Regiment, who supported it handsomely while in residence at Red River. Before 1847, there had been a subscription library of about 200 volumes in the settlement. This library apparently included some of the books that Peter Fidler had left to Red River on his death in 1822, and it was under the supervision of Robert Logan. The new library received a grant from the Council of Assiniboia (opposed by Governor Alexander Christie) and additional contributions from private citizens. This fund allowed books to be imported from Great Britain beginning in 1848.

Roderick Sutherland was appointed librarian, and a reading room was set up in his house. The library was open on Saturday, and readers paid a small annual fee (3 shillings 6 pence) for the privilege of borrowing a single book, with increasing amounts for additional volumes. In 1851 the library was removed to the house of W. R. Smith. Although the number of volumes steadily increased interest appeared to have waned. By 1860, the *Nor'-Wester* reported that the library housed between 1,200 and 1,500 volumes, but was used by very few inhabitants, and did not have a single subscriber, or any meetings of the management committee.

In May 1847, the British authorities informed the HBC that the 6th Regiment would be withdrawn as quickly as possible, and not until early in 1848 did the HBC manage to negotiate a replacement in the form of military Pensioners. The HBC would pay all travel expenses, plus a daily allowance to each soldier. They would also get land grants, within two miles of Upper Fort Garry, not to exceed 20 acres for privates, 30 for corporals, 40 for sergeants, and 100 for officers. They would own the land after seven years occupancy. The contingent, commanded by Major William Caldwell, consisting of 56 men, 42 wives, and 57 children, left England on board the *General Palmer* in June 1858. Caldwell was also named Governor of Assiniboia, the first

Trials and Tribulations

non-HBC governor since Andrew Bulger. The first of the Pensioners arrived at Red River on 19 September 1848, grumbling all the way. They threatened to mutiny when given pemmican as rations. One HBC observer noted that they were insubordinate and that their officers (Caldwell and Captain Christopher Foss) were unable to enforce discipline.

The Pensioners were regarded as worse than useless. Major Caldwell, who had been described as "a fine tall athletic man of very commanding appearance" proved on arrival to be "an elderly dull-witted giant, punctilious with respect to his own dignity and comfort, but incapable of maintaining the one or of ensuring the other." He and Foss lived in Upper Fort Garry, a situation that would eventually lead to scandal. The bulk of the new arrivals settled into shacks and hovels along the Assiniboine River to the west of the fort, doing precious little farming, and a good deal of heavy drinking. According to Alexander Ross, "If the people on the arrival of the 6th were ready to chant a *Te Deum*, they were no less ready, on seeing the conduct of the Pensioners, 'to hang their harps on the willows' and sing a requiem."

Our most intimate picture of life in the riverfront shacks of the former soldiers – which were flooded out in 1852 and again in 1861 – came in the pages of the *Nor'-Wester* in 1860, where a report appeared of the trial of pensioner Joseph Gazden in 1853 for the murder of George Lyons, formerly of the 6th Regiment. According to witnesses, Gazden and Lyons spent most of their time drinking, and after a quarrel and some threats, Lyons had disappeared. Gazden was eventually freed by the court, but this incident confirmed the worst suspicions of the settlement about the Pensioners.

The later years of the 1840s proved difficult ones for Red River in many respects, not least because of the hostile environment. Not only did the flu flare up from time to time, but also there was a long spell of bad weather, leading to thin harvests, and to the disappearance of much of the traditional game of the region. The Memorial to the Secretary of State for the Colonies in 1847, blamed the loss of game on the "demands of the fur trade," but whatever the explanation, there was general agreement that in many districts "the animals which supply the food of man have become almost extinct." These conditions were particularly devastating to the Aboriginals.

Agricultural conditions seemed much worse in the Francophone communities than among the Scots and mixed-bloods of St. Andrews. In the 1849 census, 6,392 acres were cultivated by 1,052 households within the settlement, an average of 6.0 acres per household. In

St. Andrews, 185 households cultivated 1,558 acres, or 8.4 acres per household. Wheat was the most important crop in both St. Andrews and Upper Fort Garry. Most wheat grown was of the Prairie de Chien variety, sown in the spring, although two bushels of Black Sea Wheat were purchased in Canada in 1847. One-quarter of the total grain crop was barley. Very little oats was grown. Potatoes were also an important crop. According to H.Y. Hind, writing in the late 1850s, the typical variety was the one known in Canada West as "English white." Almost every household had a vegetable garden. The rate of growth of cultivated acreage increased substantially between 1843-1849, partly because of an increased market created by the military presence, partly because farmers attempted to offset low yields resulting from bad weather with increased acreage.

The per capita population of most livestock declined substantially between 1835 to 1849. The number of pigs in the settlement declined from 3,000 in 1835, to 1,500 in 1849, thanks chiefly to the climate, and sheep virtually disappeared. On the other hand, the number of horses per capita increased, from .89 horses per landholder in 1835, to 1.5 per landholder in 1849. In 1848, the HBC obtained a thoroughbred stallion named "Melbourne," a gray thoroughbred mare, an Ayrshire bull, and two Aryshire cows. The breeding programme for the horses had limited success; the mare died in foal in 1849. "Melbourne" kicked his groom, breaking his arm, and the stallion was eventually sent to Fort Pelly, which became the horse breeding station for the HBC.

The spring and summer of 1849 proved unusually wet and cold, the culmination of nearly half a century of unusual weather that had begun in 1816, the "year without a summer," caused by smoke from a volcanic eruption in Indonesia. According to Reverend Robert James, the end of April was little different from January: "The ice is still upon the River, not the voice of one singing bird is heard." The ice on the rivers did not break up until early May; there were snowstorms later that month, and the rivers remained high throughout the summer. Heavy rains and thundershowers continued throughout the summer. The result would be another year of bad harvests in many parts of the settlement.

The bad weather seemed to have little effect on the ongoing political conflict between the HBC and the Red River inhabitants, which had been set aside in 1846, but which resumed in 1848, with the dismissal of the Isbister Memorial by the Colonial Office. A new ingredient was now added to the conflict, as newspapers in eastern Canada, especially the *Globe* in Toronto, and the *Guelph Advertiser*,

Trials and Tribulations

joined the attack on the HBC's Aboriginal policy. Captain William Kennedy, another mixed-blood fur trader and explorer, who had resigned from the HBC in 1846 over its liquor policy soon emerged as a leading critic of the HBC. He had served as commander of a private expedition financed by Lady Franklin to find her husband, Sir John Franklin.

> Some of the fur traders could see the writing on the wall. Donald Ross of Norway House wrote to Sir George Simpson in August of 1848: "We can no longer hide from ourselves the fact, that free trade notions and the course of events are making such rapid progress, that the day is certainly not far distant, when ours, the last important British monopoly, will necessarily be swept away like all others, by the force of public opinion, or by the still more undesirable but inevitable course of violence and misrule within the country itself – it would therefore in my humble belief be far better to make a merit of necessity than to await the coming storm, for come it will."

The Sayer Trial of 1849

As we have seen, political confrontation in Red River had been deferred by the Colonial Office consideration of the Isbister Memorial, and the presence in the settlement of a large contingent of troops. By the spring of 1849, however, it was quite clear to all parties in the settlement that peaceful petitioning had produced no action on the part of the British authorities. Equally clear, was the fact that the Pensioners were not a strong enough military presence to confront the armed French mixed-bloods. The result was another confrontation between the settlement's authorities and the French mixed-bloods.

In the spring of 1849, a number of traders had been arrested for illegally trafficking in furs with the First Nations. Although most were released, one man, Pierre-Guillaume Sayer, had been detained. The trial of Sayer was obviously intended to be a show piece occasion, of symbolic importance. On 17 May 1849, the date set for Sayer's trial 300 to 400 French mixed-bloods surrounded the little courthouse and issued threats to the authorities. They milled around, reported Ross, with "their powder horns on and their shot pouches also, and gun covers dangled from their belts." There were rumours that the Pensioners would be armed for the occasion, but they proved false.

A declaration was made that the people wanted free trade and "That they are determined to trade in furs, until such time as Her Majesty shall issue a proclamation to the contrary." The demonstrators were almost exclusively Francophones. William Cockran, and the other Anglican clergymen of the settlement decided that the entire free trade crisis was a "popish plot" stirred up by the Catholic clergy, and worked very hard to keep the Anglophone mixed-bloods from joining their compatriots. Unlike Father Belcourt, the Anglican clergy continued to support the HBC within the settlement.

The court, headed by Adam Thom, heard several items of minor business, and then a number of French mixed-bloods were allowed into the courtroom as a deputation to "assist" Sayer during his trial. The deputation was headed by James Sinclair, Louis Riel Sr., a prominent local miller, and Father Georges Belcourt. A jury was empanelled. According to Sheriff Alexander Ross, Sinclair challenged nine of the 12 jurors, and in the end, virtually hand picked the jury. Sayer confessed that he had indeed illicitly traded in furs, but insisted that he had permission to do so. The jury found him guilty, but recommended mercy because he genuinely believed he was entitled to trade. One French mixed-blood yelled at Judge Thom, "You speak too much! We don't understand you." Outside the court house, the French mixed-bloods shouted, "Vive la liberté," and on hearing the verdict, replaced that chant with "le Commerce est libre." They yelled and fired their guns all the way from the courthouse to the river, where they raised three cheers followed by three volleys.

Two weeks later, the Council of Assiniboia discussed the unlawful assemblies of 17 May, and the question of the "restoration of the tranquility of the Settlement." They had been informed that the French mixed-bloods wanted Adam Thom removed, the use of French introduced into the court, the rescinding of existing trade laws, free trade in furs, and finally, the "infusion" of Canadians and French mixed-bloods onto the council. The council determined that Thom would be supported, although he agreed to use French "in all cases involving either Canadian or Halfbreed interests." It was also decided that new appointments would be made to the council, as they were over the next few years.

Correspondence between Bishop Provencher and George Simpson ensued, in the course of which Provencher, after consulting with the French mixed-bloods, suggested a handful of individuals, most of which Simpson regarded as too "ignorant and illiterate" to be placed on the council. It would take half a dozen years for a substantial French mixed-blood membership to be appointed to the council. As for the laws, the council could not act upon free trade, since only the Queen, in

Trials and Tribulations

Parliament, could alter the charter upon which the HBC monopoly was based. At the same time, as everyone in the settlement recognized, the HBC would no longer attempt to enforce the monopoly in the settlement and that it had become necessary to accept the leaders of the French mixed-bloods into the governance of the community.

Obviously, a process by which threats of community violence led to concessions was hardly a very satisfactory way to resolve political disagreements. Yet no attempt was made to develop a more satisfactory mechanism for expressing public opinion in the settlement. On the other hand, the compromise orchestrated between the French mixed-bloods and the authorities was a home grown one, not imposed from without, and it would hold for twenty years.

Conclusion

On 15 September, 1847, an American newspaper, the Wisconsin *Herald*, mentioned Red River. It wrote: "Our readers are aware that there is an isolated settlement of several thousand inhabitants in a high latitude of British North America, known as the 'Selkirk Settlement.' Cut off from the commerce of the world, they rely entirely upon their own resources, their farms, their flocks and fishing for support – being a community, so to speak, of Robinson Crusoes." The notion of Red River as a geographical isolate, while perhaps a bit exaggerated, was not entirely inaccurate, and was in keeping with the R.M. Ballantyne treatment. The *Herald* had added, however, "Their crops having failed the last two seasons, they have been forced to break out of the wilds again, and seek food in the Markets of the great brawling world."

In one sense, Red River was indeed breaking out into the great brawling world. In 1849, at about the same time that Sheriff Alexander Ross was dealing with the Sayer trial, a London publishing house was bringing out the first volume of his memoirs. *Adventures on the Columbia* was the tale of Ross's participation in the attempt by John Jacob Astor to plant a fur trading settlement at the mouth of the Columbia River, in the period just before the War of 1812. It was a no-nonsense narrative that still represents one of the best accounts of that venture. With its publication, Ross had introduced another dimension to the settlement where he made his home – a literary tradition that would survive all the coming trials and tribulations.

Perhaps as important as the Red River quest for connections beyond the settlement would be the outside world's clumsy, but persistent intrusion into the quiet life of the settlement. The result, over the next few years, would be the complete transformation of Red River, as it became increasingly near to the frontiers of the expanding United States and Canada. In the process, the existing tensions would be magnified, and eventually lead to a situation teetering on the brink of anarchy.

-5-

Between the Storms

The outside world was moving inexorably closer to Red River. The settlement's isolation had never been total, but some insulation from the immediate impact of external civilization had existed in the earlier years. No longer was this the case. It might still take weeks to travel from the edge of civilized society to the village at the Forks, but more and more people were making the journey on a regular basis. And residents of Red River were travelling in the reverse direction as well. Behind the scenes, events were unfolding about which the residents of Red River had little intimate knowledge, and over which they had even less control. On 5 July 1849, for example, the British House of Commons addressed the Crown, asking for an inquiry "to ascertain the legality of the powers in respect to territory, trade, taxation, and government claimed or exercised by the Hudson's Bay Company on the continent of North America." This initiative came less in response to the petitions against the HBC from the Red River settlers, than in the context of the parliamentary debate over the colonization of Vancouver Island.

A Scandal and a New Governor

A new governor finally reached Red River on 11 August 1850. Eden Colvile was the son of HBC Deputy-Governor Andrew Colvile. He had been appointed governor of Rupert's Land in January 1849, but did not actually arrive at the settlement until a year later. Colvile had been educated at Eton, and Trinity College, Cambridge, and had come to Lower Canada in 1844 to manage land partly under the control the Ellice family. He had prospered in his new environment, and had been marked by George Simpson for a role in the affairs of the HBC. Colvile, who was a "decent chap" and a proper Victorian gentleman in the 19th century sense of the term, joined William Bletterman Caldwell, the Governor of Assiniboia, at the head of affairs in Red River. Colvile and his wife (the daughter of a distinguished Montreal soldier) would soon move into residence in Lower Fort Garry, at least partly to distance themselves from the hurly-burly at Upper Fort Garry, which was in an uproar over a major scandal.

The Foss-Pelly affair was one of those cases that could erupt only in an isolated location where everybody knew everybody else's business. At the same time, it should not be regarded as a tempest in a teapot. There were some real issues at stake, although they surfaced infrequently in the courtroom. The chief question revolved around social attitudes towards mixed-bloods, and it was a complicated one. There was a sense, in parts of the settlement, that Sarah McLeod Ballenden, the Anglophone mixed-blood wife of the HBC chief factor John Ballenden, had been the victim of a gossiping and rumour-mongering campaign, in which some of the most prominent European women in Red River had been involved.

Sarah Ballenden was a beautiful woman, many years younger than her husband. The couple had not slept in the same room for some time, and Ballenden had often been away in recent months. Also residing in Upper Fort Garry were several junior fur trade officers who had an obvious liking for Mrs. Ballenden, a number of personal servants who did not like her, and various officers of the Pensioners, including the dashing Captain Christopher Foss, who was very attentive to the lady. In the background were the social arbiters of Red River society, Bishop David Anderson and his sister, and the officers of the HBC. Acting as a self-styled avenging angel in the settlement was Adam Thom.

The affair had come to a head when two residents of the fort, junior trader Augustus E. Pelly, and mess steward John Davidson, handed John Ballenden sworn depositions accusing Sarah Ballenden of having carried on an affair with Captain Foss. Upon hearing of these depositions, Sarah Ballenden retreated to the home of Adam Thom. Thom investigated the situation, and recommended to Captain Foss that he sue Pelly and Davidson (and their respective spouses) for defamatory conspiracy, in order to "clear the reputation of a Lady." Alexander Ross reported that writs went "to every hole and corner of the colony, in high and low life: Knights, Squires, Judges, Sheriffs, Counsellors, Medicalmen, all the Nabobs of the Co., the Clergy, Ladies & Gentlemen down to the humblest pauper were summoned, a glorious turnout."

The result was a special general court beginning on 16 July 1850. Those present on the bench included Major Caldwell, along with Adam

Trials and Tribulations

Thom, Alexander Ross, James Bird, John Bunn, Andrew McDermot and Cuthbert Grant. None of these gentlemen was directly associated with the HBC, and none was clergy. Indeed, most were either mixed-bloods or had mixed-blood spouses. The lay of the land was established quite early, when Pelly objected to Thom sitting on the bench in a case in which he was also acting as attorney for the plaintiff. These objections were overruled by the court, and the jury, consisting mainly of prominent Anglophone mixed-blood residents, was impanelled.

There is little evidence that the dynamics involved the HBC versus the settlement. As Robert Clouston, Mrs. Pelly's brother, later claimed, "it seemed to be a strife of blood – for even the Jurymen were all Half-breeds or married to Half-breeds." There was also little evidence of an active French mixed-blood presence. All of the jurymen bore English names. The only French mixed-blood involvement came toward the end of the trial, when Louis Riel Sr. was interrogated under oath by Mr. Pelly, who wanted to know whether the mixed-bloods had been requested to allow Thom to sit as a judge. An answer to this improper question was never received because of the uproar in the court.

The evidence was inconclusive in terms of Mrs. Ballenden's behaviour with Captain Foss. She had certainly been indiscreet with the Captain – they had actually been observed touching one another publicly – something just not done in respectable Victorian society. But there was no smoking gun. The evidence given by the female social leaders of Red River clearly revealed their animosity to Mrs. Ballenden. A good deal of testimony was presented which indicated that the most incriminating evidence should have been provided by Mrs. Ballenden's personal maid servant, Catherine Winegart, who had regaled many in the settlement with stories of strange comings and goings in the fort late at night. According to one witness, Winegart said "that Mrs. Ballenden was in the habit of going down to Capt: Foss' room disguised in her [the German girl's] clothes & sometimes other ways & would remain away about ten minutes or a quarter of an hour & told her should Mr. Ballenden become aware & ask for her to say she was gone down stairs."

Unfortunately, Winegart had left the settlement. Mrs. Ballenden's enemies were convinced that she had been bought off, while her friends were equally persuaded that she had not wanted to face hostile cross-examination in the courtroom. In her absence, these stories were merely hearsay. Mrs. Ballenden appeared on her own behalf, and was a credible, dignified witness. Technically, of course, she was not on trial. The question was whether there had been conspiracy to slander Captain Foss. After a detailed summation of the evidence by Recorder Thom, that worthy argued that no hard evidence existed to support the charges, and further maintained that if Mrs. Ballenden was innocent, then the defendants must be guilty.

The jury retired, deliberated for four hours, and came in with a verdict of guilty, with heavy damages against the defendants. Captain Foss publicly forgave Davidson, while later trying to collect from Pelly. Caldwell was understandably dissatisfied with the outcome, and officially complained to London. One thing was clear. The mixed-bloods had triumphed over the settlement's élite, although the victory would prove more than a bit hollow.

Governor Colvile arrived in the settlement with the trial barely over, but with heavy fallout still occurring. In his introduction to Colvile's correspondence, W. L. Morton makes a good deal of a series of complex political maneuverings in the settlement at the time, but the truth is that very little actually happened, except that Adam Thom was told to stay away from court, and would ultimately have his appointment as recorder revoked by the HBC. Thom remained as clerk of the court until 1853, however. John Ballenden insisted that his wife was innocent, and Colvile attempted to support the Chief Factor by allowing the Ballendens to "visit" he and his wife.

The result was one of those comic situations for which Red River became notorious. One day, while Bishop Anderson and his sister were in the Colville house, a knock on the door revealed the Ballendens. "I had to cram them into another room till the Bishop's visit was over, but as he was then going to see the Pellys he had to pass through this room, so that I had to bolt out & put them in to a third room. It was altogether like a scene in a farce." Colvile was initially persuaded that Mrs. Ballenden was "more sinned against than sinning," since the people of Red River were so obviously fond of scandal. In the end, however, Mrs. Ballenden gave herself away in Colvile's eyes by carrying on with Captain Foss. Red River assumed that this was the resumption of the earlier relationship, although this was never proved. George Simpson wrote to Adam Thom in January of 1851, "I placed no reliance on any whitewashing, however dexterously it might be done."

The Scots and the Presbyterian Church

Whatever the culpability of Sarah Ballenden, the Foss-Pelly affair had once again clearly demonstrated that the settlement was divided into a number of factions that could easily come into conflict. The first was the HBC, its officers and servants, allied with

Trials and Tribulations

the Anglican establishment. The second group was the French mixed-bloods, closely connected with the Roman Catholic Church. The French mixed-bloods might complain about being under-represented in the political life of the settlement, which was true, but they knew who they were, and had some sense of corporate community. The third group were also Anglophones, divided into the Presbyterian Scots of Kildonan, and the mixed-bloods of the Middle and Lower Settlement. The latter two groups were searching for an identity within the settlement.

The Scots were the first to try to re-establish their position in Red River. They did so in approved 19th century fashion, by demanding their own church in the settlement. The Scottish immigrants from Kildonan and Sutherlandshire, recruited by Lord Selkirk beginning in 1813, had been promised their own clergyman from the outset. Selkirk had even hired one, although that worthy had subsequently refused to come to North America. Selkirk promised again, in 1817, when he visited the settlement, but the commitment was lost in the conflict with the NWC, and died with his lordship in 1820.

The HBC had attempted to meet the demands of the Scottish community by sending John West, a Church of England clergyman, to Red River, demonstrating that whatever Scottish influence there had been in the HBC was now pretty much dissipated. As for George Simpson, he was not a religious man. He saw churches in purely practical terms, and from his perspective, one denomination was as good (or bad) as another. After the arrival of West, and the establishment of the Church of England in the settlement, the Scots had reluctantly accepted the need for ecumenical compromise on financial grounds. A modus vivendi had been achieved in the 1820s, by which the Anglicans kept the ritual of their church (such as kneeling, genuflecting, and spreading incense) to a minimum in return for the support of the Scots in the pews.

The uneasy alliance of Anglicans and Presbyterians was first openly challenged in 1841, when some of the newly arrived Church of England missionaries strenuously complained of the liturgical concessions which had informally been made to the Scots. In turn, the Scots were able to take advantage of outside influences upon Red River. In 1843, a Presbyterian missionary from Michigan visited the settlement. This visit led a committee of Scots (Alexander Ross, Robert Logan, and James Sinclair) to petition the HBC to supply them with a clergyman of their own persuasion, pointing out the earlier promises that had been made in this regard.

The Scottish community had constructed a church in 1833 on a lot by given to them by Lord Selkirk. This church had been the joint effort of the

Anglican Church Missionary Society and the Scots, who bought pews in the expectation that a clergyman would soon appear. The burial ground at Kildonan, like the burial ground at the Upper Church, was shared by both denominations. The 1844 petition for a clergyman came at a bad time – in the early stages of the free trade controversy – and it may have been seen as political. Be that as it may, the governor and council denied that they had any obligation to the Scots, and forwarded the petition to George Simpson, who did not act upon it.

The Scots then turned to the Free Kirk of Scotland for assistance. The Free Church had come into existence after a bitter separation from the Church of Scotland, one of the chief issues being the absence of colonial missionary activity. The Free Kirk was unable to help, but called on the Presbyterian Church of Canada for assistance. The result was the dispatch of John Black to Red River.

The ecclesiastical situation in 1850 was somewhat anomalous, to say the least. The Kildonan church was clearly a Presbyterian one, in which Anglican clergy officiated according to modified Anglican rites. The church in the Upper Settlement, now intended to be the cathedral of the Anglican diocese, was similarly a joint Presbyterian-Anglican effort, with a burial ground in which more Scots (447) than English were interred, and in which the Presbyterians had clearly stated burial rights. The only church unquestionably belonging to the Church of England was in the Lower Settlement at St. Andrew's.

Unfortunately, when Bishop Anderson had arrived in Red River in 1849, the church in need of a new minister was the Upper Church, and Anderson had taken over there. In the knowledge that the Presbyterians were looking for a clergyman, Governor Eden Colvile attempted to avoid trouble. In the autumn of 1850 Colvile offered land at Frog Plain (in Kildonan), and £150 to the Presbyterians to construct a new church. Colvile and Alexander Ross negotiated long and hard, and the Presbyterians eventually accepted the deal in May of 1851, apparently because their newly-appointed minister, John Black, wanted the matter settled. So far so good.

The obstacle was Bishop Anderson, who wrote to Colvile on 20 September 1851, "I feel it impossible to give up the Upper Church for any other worship than that of the Church of England." Anderson was willing to buy out pew-holders, but not to give up the burial ground or permit it to be shared. Taking a position that only an obtuse and insensitive Anglican clergyman could adopt, Anderson insisted that he would consecrate the Upper Church burial ground, after which all interments would be with the full service of the Church of England.

Trials and Tribulations

Governor Colvile insisted that Anderson had earlier agreed that the Scots had a right to burial in the Upper Church ground. The agreement involved had been read to the Bishop and he had accepted it.

Anderson admitted that he may have accepted the agreement that Presbyterians would continue to have the right of burial, but insisted that his understanding was that such burials would be under Church of England auspices. "As to their burying in the Churchyard with a Minister of their own, it never entered into my mind nor did I dream of it," wrote Anderson. The bishop continued, "My coming out here was on a mere delusion, if I can have a Church but no Churchyard – a Cathedral but not a foot of ground upon it." Colvile was unable to convince the bishop to bend, either by building a new cathedral, or by moving its site to St. Andrew's. In the end, Colvile had to turn the question over to the London committee of the HBC, which decided to take over the burial ground, thus leaving Bishop Anderson without his churchyard. Donald Ross wrote from the settlement that the bishop was "obstinate as a mule and for all his meekness and learning is very deficient in charity and common sense." The fallout from the loss of the burial ground was a blow from which Anderson – and his relations with the Presbyterians – never recovered.

As for the Presbyterians, they welcomed their new pastor, John Black, in the autumn of 1851. Black was not initially keen on his assignment, writing his brother, "Nobody else would go, and so I am called to go." But within a few years he had wooed and won Henrietta Ross the daughter of Alexander Ross, and settled down at Frog Plain to raise a large family. The creation of the Kildonan Presbyterian Church probably divided the ranks of the establishment in Red River, although it also enabled the Scottish residents of the settlement to assert their own identity. After 1851, only the Scottish-Orcadian mixed-bloods of the middle and upper settlements lacked any sense of community.

In 1851, Red River was visited by two Americans, H. Wesley Bond, and the Governor of the Minnesota Territory, Alexander Ramsey. They had come to Pembina to negotiate a treaty with the Saulteaux, who they had induced to surrender over five million acres of Red River land south of the border, fifty miles on either side of the Red River, from Pembina to the country of the Sioux, in return for a payment of $230,000. A down payment of $30,000 would be followed, on Senate ratification, by an annuity of $10,000 for twenty years. Under the table, most of the down payment of $30,000 was to go to 141 half-breeds. Even the United States senate was shocked by this chicanery, and refused to ratify the treaty.

Ramsey would later describe thirty miles of continuous village along the river, adding that "each of these narrow farms having their dwellings and the farm out buildings spread along the river front, with lawns sloping to the water's edge and shrubbery and vines liberally trained around them, and trees intermingled – the whole presenting the appearance of a long suburban village – such as you might see near our eastern seaboard, or such as you find exhibited in pictures of English country villages." Both men were equally impressed with "the numerous windmills, some in motion whirling around their giant arms, while others motionless are waiting for 'a grist.'" From this time, Alexander Ramsey became convinced that the country north of the border should become part of the United States, and he would be one of the chief advocates of annexation over the next twenty years.

The Flood of 1852

Bishop David Anderson had not shown to very good advantage in either the Foss-Pelly affair, or in the church controversy. He came off somewhat better in the next crisis he faced, one which struck the entire colony in the spring of 1852, when the banks of the Red River once again overflowed. The 1852 flood did not crest quite as high, or remain quite as long as in the 1826 flood. Modern engineers later calculated the maximum discharge of the 1852 flood at 165,000 cubic feet per second, the maximum elevation at the Forks at 762.5 feet, and the elevation above datum at James Avenue at 35.2 feet, with a probable frequency (again understated) at once every 150 years.

Large areas of the settlement, especially well below the confluence of the Red and Assiniboine Rivers, were completely spared. At the same time, the colony was far better established and prosperous than in 1826, and property damage was, in relative terms, more extensive. Dislocation was felt far more acutely, particularly among the less prosperous elements of the population, who tended to cluster in the low-lying areas. The disaster of 1826 had affected everyone in the colony relatively equally; that of 1852 was far more selective.

Weather conditions had been building toward a major inundation for years. Summer and autumn rainfall had been heavy since 1848, and the rivers had overflowed in 1850, and 1851. In 1852 a heavy March snowfall was followed by a cold April which delayed the break-up of the ice until the end of the month. Unlike 1826, the water rose gradually, beginning on 25 April. Then, on 9-10 May, there was a sudden rise, due to the cresting of the Assiniboine. In his journal of this

Trials and Tribulations

flood, Bishop David Anderson reported on 9 May, the eerie sound of "the pouring of water over the plains." It sounded like a distant waterfall, he wrote.

Mgr. Provencher reported a somewhat different sound: "Day and night, I could hear the waves, whipped by a strong wind, beat against the walls of my house." On 12 May, a ceremony in the Catholic chapel was punctuated by the noise of water under the floorboards. According to Governor Colvile, the rise of the river was gradual, varying from five to eleven inches per day. The waters began receding around 20 May, allowing the fields in many places to dry by early June. For most inhabitants there had been more than sufficient warning to remove valuables and livestock to higher ground. In Pembina, the postmaster, George Setter, began living from 30 April on a boat "with all his trading goods on board."

Bishop Anderson's journal, subsequently published in London, provides a poignant account of his tribulations. Water began trickling into the manse on 12 May, soaking his papers, which were supposed to have been stored safely. A day later, the family said prayers in the kitchen in three inches of water. A boat was unable to remove the piano because the waves were too high. Anderson and his sister remained on the second storey of the house until 14 May, initially refusing evacuation because of the property of others stored there. The bishop was reunited with his children on his six-year-old's birthday. "He said his little presents were not to be given to him until he returned home, as he called the old house, now almost a wreck."

While many buildings had their main floors covered with water, few were actually swept away. The major property damage in most areas – apart from houses which had to be dried and cleaned after having their floors covered with 6 to 12 inches of muddy slime – was to fencing and outbuildings. The loss of fencing was particularly severe, since it was difficult to keep livestock out of planted fields without it. Also, a shortage of timber made it expensive to replace. That fencing was a substantial item of damage distinguishes 1852 from 1826; in the earlier flood there was little mention made of lost fences. Agricultural practices had changed and progress made over the years.

Some planting was delayed or prevented, but the settlement experienced only one death – David Lowe, a servant of Bishop Anderson, was drowned. While estimates of property damage ran as high as 25,000 pounds sterling – Bishop Anderson reported trees throughout the settlement littered with "a motley assemblage of wheels, hay-carts, tables, doors, chairs, &c." – the flood was taken in stride. As one old

French mixed-blood who had lost his home commented, "C'est le bon Dieu qui afflige."

According to Bishop Anderson, who had obtained a copy of a report to the Church Missionary Society of the 1826 flood before attempting the comparison, the inundation of 1852 was simultaneously more, and less, serious than the earlier devastation. The total value of property losses was higher in 1852, admitted Anderson, but the settlement's resources were not so totally destroyed as in 1826. Losses to livestock, in particular, were proportionately much lower. People were able to carry off their property in boats rather than on their persons. "Instead of a few solitary settlers, unknown and almost forgotten by their fellow-men, they are now parts of a mighty system, linked more closely by sympathy and interest to other lands."

Perhaps the most serious aspect of the 1852 flood was the geographical distribution of the damage. The areas which experienced the greatest flooding were along the Red, just south of the Forks on both sides of the river, and along the lower part of the Assiniboine. In addition, the land north of the Forks around St. John's Cathedral was also inundated. Most buildings removed from their foundations were in these areas. The most affected sections were those in St. Boniface inhabited by French mixed-bloods, and around Fort Garry, occupied by the British army Pensioners. According to Alexander Ross, 3,500 inhabitants were forced to flee their homes. Most settlers went to either Stony Mountain or Little Mountain, where tents were set up by the military.

The Scots and mixed-blood settlers in St. James and St. Andrew's districts were virtually unaffected. Their ground was high enough to escape the water entirely. The Scots were reported to have saved all their wheat on hand, up to a three-year reserve. According to Governor Colvile, the wheat reserve was 16,000 bushels. Thus, this flood – and a later one in 1861 – helped confirm the division between French and English mixed-bloods in the settlement. Governor Eden Colvile commented that the improvident "will have in great measure to trust to the produce of the gun and the net."

In choosing the sites for their homesteads, the French mixed-bloods had simply replicated earlier eastern Canadian patterns of settlement, ignoring the fact that in Red River, those areas were susceptible to spring flooding. The Pensioners had clustered around the low-lying land near Fort Garry because no one else had much wanted it. They were forced to evacuate their homes en masse, and were of course disheartened by the experience. Even among the Pensioners, however, only three houses were actually lost. Although most dwellings required some repair, Colvile did not regard the repairs as extensive, at least to render them habitable. Bishop Anderson insisted that several of the residents of the flooded houses or shacks sold them for a pittance while they were under water. Colvile reported that most of the people settled on unusually low ground they had purchased from a settler rather than the HBC. Better construction than in 1826 was credited for the survival rate of the dwellings.

Food prices were temporarily raised by the flood, although the 1852 harvest was less a disaster than had been predicted. As usual, a warm summer followed a flood. So did the mosquitoes. By 23 May, Dr. William Cowan reported in his diary that the "mossies" had "become very troublesome." Seed wheat was distributed to those who had no 1852 crop. As expected, those without capital resources – the "improvident" – increased their reliance on hunting and fishing. By early September, Governor Colvile reported "that no apprehension need be entertained as to scarcity." The 1852 flood, even more quickly than the 1826 one, receded into memory.

By the end of November 1852, the school near the Cathedral (which had been taken over by Bishop Anderson after the death of John McCallum in 1849 and renamed the St. John's Collegiate School) had been repaired. The Anglican missionary William Taylor observed, "We want help – mechanics, artisans, labourers. I often think the surest and best way of improving the colony is to favor immigration, particularly of honest, industrious and sober labourers. This class of people introduced from England would do more than anything else for this colony." Despite his exemplary behaviour during the flood, Bishop Anderson permitted old hostilities to re-emerge in its aftermath, and he refused to accept any help from the Presbyterians, whose settlement had not been flooded.

More Religious Adjustments

The bishop's open battles with the Presbyterians resumed early in 1853, when several proprietors of Middle Church complained of its consecration without their consent. The bishop insisted that proprietors' rights were not affected by consecration, while the proprietors maintained that they were not merely pew-holders but part owners of the entire structure. Anderson responded that he had no problem with a Presbyterian Church at Frog Plain. "But if in addition to this you seek to introduce disorder and confusion into every Church of the Settlement and to thwart the proceedings of those who are not of your own communion, it is indeed the sad requital for the gratuitous services of thirty years." The proprietors acknowledged they could not enforce their claims, but insisted that more openness in the consecration proceedings would have been appropriate. For his part, the Bishop wrote that he would turn over the correspondence to the HBC, "that it may be seen to what a system of continued annoyance I am subjected here." As this exchange suggested, neither side was really prepared to call the hostilities off, and the controversy continued to simmer.

On 7 June 1853, Bishop Joseph-Norbert Provencher died. His lengthy tenure as head of the Catholic Church, and leader of the French mixed-bloods had seen his church firmly established in the settlement. There were two parishes, one at St Boniface and the other at White Horse Plain. The former had a cathedral and a hospital, and both had highly successful schools taught by the various religious orders. Two new parishes, at St. Charles and St. Norbert, would be established by his successor. Provencher had also been successful in establishing three major missions in the interior of Hudson's Bay lands. Despite these spiritual successes, Provencher had been unable to convince the authorities to allow his people to be represented in government commensurate with their importance in the settlement. Father Louis-François Lafleche had been appointed a councillor in 1850, and François-Jacques Bruneau (a French mixed-blood born at Lac Vert) was put on the council in 1853 as a "man of sound standing in the settlement & of fair education." But George Simpson admitted that the "Canadian Half-breeds... feel that they are not put on a footing of equality with the other classes in the community."

Provencher's successor was Alexandre-Antonin Taché, an Oblate missionary born in Boucherville in Lower Canada in 1823. Taché had been handpicked by Bishop Provencher despite his youth, and many of his order in France were suspicious of him, a hostility that persisted for many years. Taché would remain in office until his death in 1894, thus serving for over forty critical years. He proved adept at raising money, and especially good on getting on with the HBC's officer class. In fact, Governor Alexander Dallas once commented that Taché's Catholics supported the HBC better than the Protestants. Soon after he assumed the bishopric, Taché managed to obtain a number of new French mixed-blood appointments to the Council of Assiniboia, which meant that the French were well-represented on the Council for the fifteen years before the Rebellion of 1869/70. As a result of a sense of political satisfaction among the French mixed-bloods, and the ability of Taché to deal with the local authorities, the years before the Rebellion were indeed a golden

Trials and Tribulations

period for the French mixed-bloods, one which they would not easily give up.

In October of 1853, Bishop Anderson insisted to Alexander Ross that he would consecrate the burial ground at the cathedral regardless of the London committee ruling, "reserving especially on my own part. . a right for all the Presbyterians. . .to bury in it after their own manner in that use. . . prescribed by our Church." Ross replied that the Presbyterians had no objection to consecration if it could be done without affecting their rights. A few days later, Ross's son William, wrote to his brother James in Toronto, "His Lordship (Bp. R. Land) again tried to seduce the people to consent to allow him to consecrate the burial ground – he wrote a very flattering letter to Father – but he was sadly mistaken – if he thought that we were to be turned with every wind that blew – he has consecrated the church and I hope that holy writ has imparted strength to the dilapidated walls." William added that the Presbyterian church at Frog Plain was nearly finished.

Red River and the External World

Having completed his studies at St. John Collegiate School, James Ross had went east to university in Toronto in the late spring of 1853. He travelled overland to St. Paul, arriving on 7 July, and left the next day aboard the steamer *West Newton*, arriving at Galena, Illinois, 27 hours later. Ross left Galena on 11 July, travelling by coach 80 miles to Rockford, Illinois, whence he travelled by train to Chicago. This was his first train-ride, and he was absolutely awestruck by the scenery and the speed of transit – 25 miles per hour. Ross spent four hours in Chicago, and then headed on by rail to Detroit and Buffalo. At Buffalo he boarded the steamer *Chipewa* to Niagara, then took a coach to Queenston, where he sailed on the *Peerless*, a vessel he described as the best boat on Lake Ontario.

Ross was impressed with Toronto, mainly for its facilities for drinking, a not surprising observation from a man who would become Red River's most distinguished alcoholic. "There is every change, every inducement – plenty of liquors of every kind, plenty barrooms and plenty people too ready to offer a glass."

The complete journey from Red River to Toronto had consumed the entire summer, and could not yet be executed entirely on the railway; the Canadian end was obviously still not connected, and there were some gaps in Illinois. Ross was fully aware, however, that the part traversed by train had gone very quickly indeed. He realized that once the railways were completed, Red River would be truly connected with the world.

While Red River waited for the completion of its Presbyterian Church, and for the railway from the south, the settlement sought to become less isolated by opening regular postal links through the United States. Some of the local free traders arranged with the Pembina post office to make five trips a year to St. Paul to collect the mail. James Sinclair was the first postmaster in Red River, Charles Cavalier in Pembina. Pembina would soon become a county, possessing its own local government and a customhouse designed to prevent British traders from entering the United States.

In November 1854 Adam Klyne was hired to carry winter mail between Red River and St. Paul. Three months later, in February 1855, the Council of Assiniboia appointed William Ross as postmaster. A monthly courier service was established between Red River and Pembina, increased to twice monthly in the summer of 1856. Rates were set at 3d per single letter, and 1d per newspaper. Ross subsequently reported to the council in February 1856, that between March 1855, and February 1856, the post office had handled 2,437 papers, 2,821 letters, and 580 parcels. Henry Youle Hind reported meeting the mail south of Pembina being carried on the back of a mixed-blood, in "a large leather bag by means of a strap passing round his head." The carrier had been 15 days coming from Crow Wing. The system, it should be noted, bypassed Canada and British North America entirely.

By the mid-1850s, it was increasingly clear that great changes were rapidly taking place on the open plains of the United States. The buffalo were moving further west, or disappearing. The Sioux were feeling increasing pressure from encroaching settlement. The Sioux treaties of 1851 opened much land in the southern part of the territory, and over the next years, hundreds of settlers arrived, pushing the Sioux into the northern areas. A number of French mixed-bloods were migrating south of the border, attracted by the buffalo hunt and the mission run by Father Georges Belcourt at St. Joseph, which had a population of over 1,000 people by the mid-1850s.

Constant conflict with the Sioux led the Dakota territorial government to petition Congress for protection through the establishment of a military garrison on the border, but nothing was done immediately. The year 1855 was filled with reports of potential trouble, but the French mixed-bloods went off on the hunt as usual. About sixty miles from Pembina, the party was surprised by a band of Sioux. In the ensuing fight, seven mixed-bloods were killed, and a number of families had to return to Red River on foot, having lost horses and carts.

Trials and Tribulations

In 1856, the Americans decided to build a military post in the Red River Valley, and Fort Abercrombie, at Graham's Point was constructed in 1857. Late in the summer of 1856, Sir George Simpson returned to that oldest of HBC themes, the fear that "an unpopular measure or accidental collision might lead to a general rising against the HBC and the destruction of their establishments." Simpson was able to seize upon the dispatch of American cavalry to the frontier as a pretext for military protection. The HBC knew full well that the American troops were designed to protect American citizens against the Sioux, but insisted that the Yankee garrison made necessary a British regiment "to serve as a counterpoise to the growing influence of the United States in the North West Territory."

While the American troops may not have represented a threat, the arrival of land speculators did. Claim jumpers had moved into the Red River Valley in 1855, and town sites were surveyed in many parts of unceded Indian territory. Evidence of settlement began to spread in the Red River Valley, and by 1857 St. Cloud already contained over 500 people. Everyone on the British side recognized the symptoms. Soon an American population would creep north of the border, demanding the rights of Americans, and Manifest Destiny would claim more British territory.

At the same time that American interest in Red River was picking up, so too was the interest of Canadians. In 1850 John McLean, (the author of *Twenty-five Years Service in the Hudson's Bay Territories*, published in 1848, and highly critical of the HBC) wrote to George Brown, the editor of the *Globe* in Toronto, that "the interior of Rupert's Land belongs to the people of Canada both by right of discovery and settlement and it is therefore our business more than that of the people of England to claim the r*estoration* of rights of which we have been so unjustly deprived."

These arguments had little effect at the time, but by the middle of the 1850s a small cadre of about fifteen individuals had joined McLean to spearhead the movement for Canadian control of the western region. Many were of Highlander descent and had some historic association with Red River. The group included Allan Macdonell – whose father had been employed by Lord Selkirk – as well as William Macdonell Dawson and his two brothers Aeneas Macdonell Dawson and Simon James Dawson. They were joined by Captain William Kennedy, George Brown, the editor of the Toronto *Globe*, and William McDougall, the editor of the newspaper *North American*. Both Brown and McDougall were reformers who quickly brought their party around to support for western expansionism.

J. M. Bumsted

The movement for Canadian expansion was predicated on the construction of railways, which were the popular fancy of the 1850s in Canada, as well as on a sense in Canada that good "waste" or "wild" land was ripe for development. Adding impetus was the British withdrawal from the old mercantile system, and the institution of free trade, a process completed by the end of the 1840s. Canadian businesses no longer operated within a protected imperial market, but were forced to seek new markets. Toronto and the Ottawa Valley were both hotbeds of western expansionism. As if on some master schedule, eastern Canada became interested in the West at the same time as the Americans.

The Canadian claim to the West was based on a resurrection of the arguments employed against Lord Selkirk in the courts of Upper Canada. According to this line of thinking, the French had controlled all of North America beyond the English colonies, and Canada had inherited these lands after the conquest. The HBC could thus be styled as interlopers into the territory already possessed by Canada.

In 1856 Alexander Ross published the final volume of his western trilogy, entitled *The Red River Settlement*. In this work, Ross found a major theme in the conflict between the indigenous cultures of the West and European civilization. His narrative was a study in the vagaries of human nature studded with picturesque settings and fascinating personalities. Ross's thematic emphasis on the conflict between wilderness "savagery" and civilization, was a dichotomy familiar to many of his contemporaries. Unlike many observers of Red River, Ross characterized the clash in human rather than environmental terms. But the result was a similar sort of conclusion. For Bishop David Anderson, Red River was "the centre of light, the little oasis in the wilderness," totally surrounded by darkness. For both Anderson and his Catholic counterpart Bishop Taché, a failure to introduce Christianity into the surrounding darkness would be a total disaster. Only a year after Ross's book, Bishop Anderson would tell the Parliamentary Committee of 1857, that the more civilized man always conquered "the less civilized man." Pushed to its logical conclusion, this would mean that the First Nations would disappear in the face of the expansion, a prediction often made by those who advocated the Canadian annexation of the West.

Alexander Ross's eye for telling detail, presented in ironically, combined with a compelling story told in plain style, all marked a major accomplishment. Ross was scathing in his criticism of the "half-breeds." This hostility greatly upset his son James, who protested strenuously. Part of the problem was the paucity of contemporary terminology for mixed-bloods, which in Ross's work equated French mixed-bloods and

Trials and Tribulations

English mixed-bloods under the generic term "half-breed." Despite this conflation, most of the hostility of the HBC officers was directed at the French mixed-bloods. But it was an Anglophone mixed-blood, a relative of Alexander Kennedy Isbister, rather than the French mixed-bloods, that resumed the attack on the HBC. The new critic was Captain William Kennedy.

Born at Cumberland House, to the Cree wife of an HBC chief factor, Willam Kennedy had been educated in the Orkney Islands of Scotland before joining the HBC in 1833. He spent some years in Labrador before quitting the HBC over its policy of selling liquor to the Aboriginals. Kennedy subsequently served as commander of Lady Franklin's second privately-financed expedition to find her husband. He insisted on proper equipment, including Aboriginal outer garments, and although he failed to find Franklin, he returned his crew to England without loss of life. He published an account of this expedition in 1853 as *A Short Narrative of the Second Voyage of the Prince Albert, in Search of Sir John Franklin*. He led a second expedition on behalf of Lady Franklin, but this one foundered in Chile after a mutiny.

In 1856, Kennedy was back in Canada, and he joined the Canadian lobby to annex the West. In December he told the Toronto Board of Trade that Canadians "now saw that the comparatively small fragment of the continent which they occupied would soon be both too narrow and too short for them, to small a field on which to exercise and develop their new born energies." Kennedy insisted on this occasion that "it was the most notable work for the Canadians of the present day to undertake to bring within the page of civilization the larger half of the North American continent, a country containing 270 million of acres." He would become employed by the North West Trading and Colonization HBC – established in Toronto in January 1857 – and it was on behalf of this HBC that Kennedy and his brother Roderick travelled overland from Toronto to Red River in February 1857 to prove that overland transportation in the region was feasible.

At Red River, William Kennedy attempted to stir up support for annexation by circulating a petition calling for the extension of Canadian laws and political institutions to the region. It was printed in the *Globe,* 12 June 1857. The usual reading of this agitation is that it was a failure. Certainly it did not attract the interest of the French mixed-bloods. They had already gone the petition route, and they had recently achieved a major political ambition when it had been announced that a number of French mixed-bloods would be appointed to the Council of Assiniboia. As a result, George Simpson could smugly report to the governor and committee that the French mixed-bloods and their clergy "warmly supported the constituted authorities during the...agitation by Kennedy's party."

But Kennedy did attract considerable support from the remainder of the settlement, particularly among the Anglophone mixed-bloods. He organized meetings in mixed-blood parishes from March to May of 1857, calling for the election of members to serve in the Canadian House of Assembly. The meetings did result in the signing of the petition by a large number of residents. The version reprinted in the report of the House of Commons Select Committee of 1857, gives 575 names. In April 1857, while Kennedy was still agitating, Anglican missionary James Hunter reported to the Church Missionary Society; "The fact is, the people are tired of the present government and are anxious for any change that will open up the country to colonization...People have suffered so long from the HBC that they are now determined to make a great struggle for emancipation." Kennedy had clearly planted the seed of a political alternative to the HBC.

A Parliamentary Enquiry, New Arrivals, and New Initiatives

In the year 1857, a number of currents that had been swirling around for some time came together. The result was a year of great importance for the settlement at Red River. In February, of 1857, a parliamentary select committee began holding hearings and collecting testimony into the license held by the HBC. This enquiry was the logical consequence of the impending expiration of the HBC's monopoly, but it recognized other factors, including the ambitions of Canada to extend settlement into the region of the monopoly, the need to deal with Vancouver Island, and "the present condition of the settlement which has been formed on the Red River." These hearings would lead to two expeditions, one British, one Canadian, being sent into the West.

The British Parliamentary committee began its hearings on 20 February, and completed its report on 31 July 1857. Testimony was heard from all interested parties, including a number of official representatives of the Canadian government. George Simpson and other HBC officials insisted that the territory involved was totally unsuitable for agriculture, chiefly because of the uncertainties of its northern climate. Edward Ellice told the enquiry "I have no doubt that gentlemen who go out in the summer and look at the border of these rivers and see the fine pastures

Trials and Tribulations

which they find for the buffalo, say, 'These will make admirable farms,' but they have not been there during the winter, and they have not considered the circumstances of the country with respect to fuel."

During the hearings, several of the witnesses demonstrated their contempt for the "half-castes" of Red River. Bishop Anderson testified that they were not equal in intelligence and thrift to white people. The committee eventually concluded that although the HBC had, on the whole, administered the territory well, the "growing desire of our Canadian fellow-subjects that the means of extension and regular settlement should be afforded to them over a portion of this territory." Canada should be allowed to annex such portions of the West as she could open and control, opined the committee. Apart from this territory, the HBC should continue its administration, in order to protect the "Indian population from a system of open competition in the fur trade, and the consequent introduction of spirits in a far greater degree than is the case at present." The British committee also argued for continuing the HBC monopoly to protect the "more valuable fur-bearing animals."

While the British Parliament was considering the future of the West, the two scientific expeditions set out for the region. One expedition was led by Captain John Palliser (1817-87), an Irish landlord and adventurer, who had spent a lifetime seeking excitement around the world. He had travelled in the American West in 1847 and 1848, bringing home a menagerie of wild animals, including three buffalo, an antelope, a bear, two Virginia deer, and a half-wolf Indian dog.* Such a "splendid chap," in the Victorian context, could hardly be denied when he proposed to the Royal Geographical Society, in 1856, to survey a large portion of North America. The Society persuaded the Colonial Office to contribute £5000 for an expedition.

The British understandably wanted to know more about their western possessions, especially since the Americans were researching their own prairie region. Lorin Blodgett, an American scientist, had published data in 1856 and 1857 suggesting that the prairies were hardly as barren as most people imagined. Blodgett pointed out that it was not so much the northern latitude as it was the isotherms that influenced the climate, and insisted that much of the region was "perfectly adapted to the fullest occupation by cultivated nations."

Palliser consulted eminent scientists, including Charles Darwin, and a team of experts, including geologist James Hector, and botanist Eugène Bourgeau, were recruited for the expedition. The only amateur was Palliser, who formally received his commission during the parliamentary

---

*While in New Orleans, when a professional musician had failed to appear, Palliser had sung both male parts in a charity performance of a Handel oratorio.

enquiry of 1857. They left England on 16 May, on the Royal Mail Steamer *Arabia*, docking in New York, and then heading west via American railway and steamer. At Sault Ste. Marie they picked up two canoes, and their *voyageur* crews, made their way by steamer across Lake Superior, and paddled to Lower Fort Garry, where the explorers spent a few days before journeying across the plains. The expedition would continue to travel the west in 1858 and 1859. The maps and reports of this expedition provided basic information about the southern prairie and Rocky Mountain regions of Canada.

On 23 July of 1857, the same year that Captain Palliser departed for North America, the Canadian Exploring Expedition, under the titular command of retired HBC trader George Gladman, left Toronto for the West. Gladman was accompanied by Simon James Dawson, an engineer, and Henry Youle Hind, an English-born, and Cambridge-educated professor of chemistry and geology at Trinity College, Toronto, who acted as geologist and naturalist. The Canadian sponsored party consisted of 44 persons. It sailed from Toronto to Collingwood, then by steamer to Fort William, where the party took canoes via Rainy River and Lake of the Woods to the Winnipeg River and then to the Red River. The journey took 27 days and six hours. Hind managed to make some geological observations in 1857, and, in 1858, to do quick surveys of the Assiniboine, Souris, Qu'Appelle and South Saskatchewan river valleys. Hind was not much of a geologist, but his account of his journeys in the region was very colourful and extremely popular.

The findings of these two expeditions, which were published fairly quickly, served their purpose in expanding geographical knowledge of the West and in helping to end the public perception of this vast region as unfit for human habitation. The final reports from Hind and Palliser, besides containing much scientific observation, acknowledged the great potential of the West. Indeed, the aura of "impartial science" that surrounded their bulky and stodgy documents gave their findings, in the eyes of enthusiasts for western expansion, greater cachet.

Hind, for example, in his *Reports of Progress; Together with a Preliminary and General Report on the Assiniboine and Sasktatchewan Exploration Expedition* (Toronto, 1859), waxed lyrical over the "truly fertile valleys of the West," calculating that between Red River and the south branch of the Saskatchewan, there were over eleven million acres of fertile and arable land. Palliser's *Papers Relative to the Exploration* were also published in 1859, and after three more expeditions between 1858 and 1868, Her Majesty's Stationary Office published his *Journals, Detailed reports, and Observations Relative to the Exploration* (1863)

Trials and Tribulations

in an edition of less than 100 copies. Palliser made the same point as Hind, that millions of acres of the west were prime agricultural land, although he also identified what came to be known as "Palliser's Triangle" – a drybelt area of the west, that even today, is the graveyard of farmers' hopes.

Palliser also recognized how much easier it was to get into the British West via the United States, and he advocated a "railway on the British side of the line to the northward and westward, through the southern portion of 'the fertile belt' to the Rocky Mountains; at all events as soon as the country showed symptoms of becoming sufficiently populated to warrant such an effort." Both sets of reports identified sub-regions and reported differences of soil and climate from one place to another.

Those in Canada who were interested in expansion found enough support in the work of these expeditions to advance their cause. Science had now confirmed what continental expansionists had long known instinctively: the Northwest could not only be settled, but as the Canadian government would insist in 1864, was "capable of sustaining a vast population."

In between the departure of these two expeditions, on 23 June, a contingent of Royal Canadian Rifles sailed from Montreal on the *Great Britain*, heading north along the Labrador coast. They would arrive in York Factory on 1 September 1857, where they found their Enfield rifles so badly packed that many were damaged. Tents were in short supply as well. Within a few days the Rifles and their families were on their way south to Fort Garry in York boats, which were in many cases manned by soldiers rather than experienced boatmen. The journey was a hard one. Medical supplies were ruined, and worse still, all the regiment's wine was lost. The Rifles arrived at Fort Garry on 22 October 1857, and George Simpson was soon reporting that "the peace of the Settlement has remained unbroken since the arrival of the troops."

Before the British regiment made its way to Fort Garry in 1857, some considerably less welcome visitors had reappeared. The missionary William Taylor reported that grasshoppers had returned, and "miles and miles of the plains are quite blacked with devastations and that at Pembina they were, in places, 3 inches thick." When Taylor visited Headingley in August, he found the grasshoppers heavy on the ground: "being a strong west wind they rose up from the crop and literally pelted us as we went on, getting among our clothes etc. We found them in the houses, holding onto the outside walls and ravaging all before them." Even if Blodgett's observations about climate were correct, these new arrivals – had they been much known outside Red River – might well have cast a pall on the newly-found enthusiasm for Red River agriculture.

Despite his testimony to the Parliamentary Committee on the limits of agricultural potential in the West, and the reappearance of grasshoppers, Sir George Simpson decided to open an experimental farm at Lower Fort Garry in the spring of 1858, under the supervision of Alexander Lillie. It was located on the west side of the fort, extending to over 100 acres, and included extensive fields of wheat, barley, peas, and vegetables, as well as a large herd of cattle. In 1868, 5,000 pounds of pork and 10,000 of beef were slaughtered. Most of these provisions were sent north for the fur trade. Local farmers resented the competition, and the farm was never profitable.

New Communication and Transportation Initiatives

In the late 1850s, a number of signs foretold the rapid approach of outside civilization from several directions into Red River. One of these was the maiden voyage in 1858 of the HBC's steamer *Rescue*, from Collingwood, in Canada West, to Fort William. The steamer carried Captain William Kennedy and some mail for Red River. Captain Thomas Dick of Toronto subsequently received a contract to carry summer mail to the settlement. The rate from Fort William or Red River to anywhere in British North America was 3d per half ounce, with letters for the U.S. 6d per half ounce, and those bound for the United Kingdom 7 $^1/_2$d per half ounce. This service was irregular, and did not flourish. The Canadians would try again in 1859, with another summer mail service, via the steamer *Ploughboy*, and a winter service along the "Timber Route" from Penetanguishene to the Sault to Fort William to Red River. This one was also a money-loser, but there was a large surplus carried over from a legislative grant, which the Canadians used to try to improve roads on the Red River route.

In the spring of 1858, news of the discovery of gold in the Fraser River in British Columbia, spread like wildfire across North America, and Red River became a staging area as fortune-seekers sought an overland route to the goldfields. On the 20 July, a party of nine men left St. Paul for Fort Garry, intending to carry on overland to British Columbia. The party had its origins in the Faribault District of Minnesota, and was intended to serve as a pilot project. The Faribault party was organized into two messes, one of five men, and the other of

Trials and Tribulations

four. It arrived at Fort Garry on 18 August. Its members found a small village with a few stores outside Upper Fort Garry which housed two companies of the Royal Canadian Rifles. They thought the settlement quaint, purchased some equipment at great expense, and headed on to British Columbia. Other overland expeditions would arrive at Red River after the further discovery of gold in the interior of British Columbia in 1862.

The Americans continued to contemplate the improvement of transportation links to the settlement. Captain Russell Blakeley, and John R. Irvine, toured Red River in October of 1858, reporting to St. Paul that steamboat navigation was possible on the Red River during the summer months. About that time, the American merchant Anson Northup bought the steamboat *North Star* in Minneapolis, and had her transported to Crow Wing, where she was dismantled. In March of 1859, 60 men and 34 ox teams carried the machinery, cabin, and furniture of the *North Star*, as well as cut and frame timber for the hull, from Crow Wing to Lafayette, opposite the mouth of the Sheyenne River, three miles from Georgetown, Minnesota. The steamer was reassembled at Lafayette for an early summer run to Red River. James W. Taylor, an American enthusiast for Red River annexation, believed that this demonstrated that a steamer beginning on the Red River could follow the lakes and rivers all the way to the Rocky Mountains.

The Search for a Mixed-blood Identity

Late in 1858, a new movement sprang up in the settlement. It was sparked by several developments. One was the increasing sense on the part of Canada that acquisition of Red River and the West was its ultimate destiny. As the Orange leader Ogle Cowan told a meeting at Toronto's St. Lawrence Hall, in late August of 1857, what Canada needed was "a specific and pacific boundary," adding, "I go for the territory and the whole territory." A second was the continued hostility to the HBC on the part of many in the settlement, especially among the Anglophone mixed-bloods. The animator of the new movement was the Reverend G.O. Corbett, an Anglican clergyman who returned to Red River in the spring of 1858. Corbett, an Englishman of somewhat mysterious origins, had first appeared in the settlement in 1852, after being refused ordination by the Bishop of Montreal for unknown reasons.

He had established a new mission at Headingley, west of the Forks on the road to Portage la Prairie, where most of his parishioners were young mixed-bloods moving up the Assiniboine River in search of new land. The mission failed for financial reasons, and Corbett returned to Britain in 1855. There he apparently studied medicine at King's College. At the time of the parliamentary investigation, Corbett testified that the HBC prevented settlement at places like Headingley, and routinely opened mail before it left Red River, but he was unable to provide any concrete evidence for his charges. He also insisted that residents of the settlement were eager for representative government.

When he returned to Red River later in 1857, Corbett brought with him a small hand-set printing press. He used the press to print a broadside entitled *A Few Reasons for a Crown Colony*, that supported a petition for Crown Colony status, circulated by himself and fellow missionary Rev. John Chapman of St. Andrew's parish. For Red River to become a Crown Colony, wrote Corbett, would mean that it would acquire its own elected assembly and take its rightful place as the centre of British North America's western empire. The absence of law and order in the settlement, the result of the HBC's failures, would be swiftly ended by the appearance of proper British justice.

The notion of Crown Colony status for Red River was an interesting one, particularly as an alternative to annexation to Canada. It had been implicit in the petitions to the Crown of the 1840s, but had never before been articulately advocated. The last thing the British Colonial Office wanted to do, of course, was to recognize Red River as a formal colony. Such a recognition would leave the financial burden of Red River in the hands of the British government, whereas annexation would shift it to Canada. A number of Anglophone leaders, including Donald Gunn, William Kennedy, and James Ross, responded to the Corbett petition with one of their own, calling for Canadian annexation.

The two petitions were sent to the Colonial Office. Corbett was supported by many of the Anglophone mixed-bloods, who had clearly found an issue to unite them. This identity would increasingly take shape over the ensuing few years and then be discouraged by Corbett's involvement in a major scandal. But for the first time, the English mixed-blood population in Red River was asserting itself as a distinct element of Red River society clearly differentiated by religion and language.

Despite the interest of the Reverend Corbett in the mixed-bloods, his concern apparently did not extend into the arena of higher education. After 1849, St. John's College had begun producing Native clergymen. Four men ordained between 1849 and 1864 – Henry Budd, James Settee, Henry Cochrane, and Henry Budd, Jr., were First Nations people, and another four – Thomas Cook, Robert MacDonald, Thomas Vincent, and

Trials and Tribulations

John A Mackay, were mixed-bloods. Despite this record, the college was allowed to run down in the later 1850s, and was finally closed in 1859 by Bishop Anderson.

To some extent, the college's success with Natives worked to its detriment, for many of the elite in the settlement became reluctant to send their children there. For many of the Presbyterian community, moreover, the college's Anglican emphasis was undesirable. In 1860 Bishop Anderson himself, in a piece in the *Nor'-Wester*, blamed the college's problems on the declining interest in classical studies, writing "Parents continually requested that their sons might not learn Latin and Greek, and so far from finding any demand for the higher education the effort [of keeping the college running] was sustained for some years at heavy pecuniary loss." Lack of employment opportunities in the settlement and a lessening number of inhabitants interested in higher education (for which read "elite Europeans") may have also contributed to the demise of the college.

-6-

The External World Intrudes

Two events occurred in 1859 that would epitomize the new directions taken by Red River in the early 1860s. The first was the arrival of the steamship *Anson Northup* at a wharf in Red River on 9 June 1859. The steamship had been launched at Lafayette, Minnesota, earlier in the spring. The *Anson Northup* was a sternwheeler with a capacity of 50 to 75 tons, and engines delivering 100 horsepower. The vessel was 90 feet long and 22 feet wide. "She drew fourteen inches of water light," reported the Toronto *Globe* on 9 July 1859. The shallow draft was necessary because the Red River contained precious little water on some stretches in the summer. One of her captains labelled the steamship "a lumbering old pine-basket, which you have to handle as gingerly as a hamper of eggs." Joseph Hargrave described the accommodations on board the steamship in 1861: "She was provided with four staterooms, each containing two berths. Passengers, over and above the number of those who could be accommodated in these, slept in a series of open berths extending along the main saloon, from which they were separated only by their curtains."

The St. Paul Chamber of Commerce was reputed to have paid builder Anson Northup $2,000 to open the Red River of the North to steam navigation. According to the Earl of Southesk, who arrived in Red River about the same time as the steamer, crowds of First Nations stood on the shore in wonder, little recognizing how ominous was the arrival of this "small, shabby" vessel. "Each turn of the engine," wrote Bishop Taché in 1870, "appeared to bring us nearer by so much to the civilized world."

New Events

The *Anson Northup* was given a great welcome at Fort Garry. The Detroit *Free Press* reported, "The commander of the British force ordered the firing of the cannon in honor of the event. The British

Trials and Tribulations

flag was hoisted alongside the 'stars and stripes' waving at the head of the *Anson Northup*. The great bells of the Catholic Cathedral chimed merrily and the vast throngs of people that pressed all around cheered and waved caps most energetically." The steamship ran down to the Lower Fort "with plenty of people on board," arriving on 13 June. One of the passengers, Charles Cavalier, observed, "it was a perfect circus all the way down, to see the surprise of the Indians." The steamer left for Fort Abercrombie on 17 June with 25 passengers aboard, including James Ross. The return trip took eight days. The boat was subsequently purchased for $8,000 by a syndicate, which included George Simpson acting on behalf of the Hudson's Bay Company.

Only a few months after the arrival of the *Anson Northup*, two young Canadians named William Buckingham and William Coldwell departed from St. Paul, Minnesota by ox team for the Red River Settlement. The two were both experienced Toronto journalists, and had been encouraged by Toronto *Globe* editor George Brown to head west to start a newspaper. In their wagon, Cunningham and Coldwell were carrying a Hoe Washington Super-Royal Model press, which they had purchased at St. Paul. Their departure was not uneventful; the team of oxen bolted, scattering type all over the street.

Less than five weeks later, on 1 November 1859, Buckingham and Coldwell reached Red River, barely ahead of the year's first major snowfall. They set up shop in a small building at the corner of Main and Water Street, in a village which would later be called Winnipeg. On 7 December, 1859, the Council of Assiniboia passed a resolution "That all newspapers direct from the publishers at Red River be free from all postage and also all exchange papers." The young editors brought out the first issue of their newspaper – called the *Nor'-Wester* – on 28 December, 1859, to take advantage of the outgoing mail heading for Pembina. The newspaper measured 22 inches by 15 inches, and contained four pages, with five columns to the page. Most of the issues Buckingham and Coldwell sent out were addressed to other newspapers in the United States and eastern Canada, and soon a constant return flow of newspapers was heading to their tiny office, which was used to provide "international" coverage by the *Nor'-Wester*.

The newspaper would not only help to connect Red River to the world, it would also provide both a record of events and an active effort to influence them. Especially in its earlier years the *Nor'-Wester* sought to be a paper of record for the settlement. The Earl of Southesk observed that the settlement was not only the centre of justice for the region, but also the seat of two bishoprics, which certainly justified the ambition to print a paper of record. For some years, in the early 1860s, James Ross, who had newspaper experience in eastern Canada, was also associated with the *Nor'-Wester*. Joseph Hargrave admitted that the newspaper was useful as "a detailed record of local events," but added that "had the influence of the *'Nor'-Wester'* been at all commensurate with its ambition, it would have frequently so exercised it as to bring the settlement into a state of anarchy."

Later historians have frequently accused the the *Nor'-Wester* of writing what most Canadians wanted to hear. In his 1869 survey of the Northwest, Bishop Taché described the newspaper as "almost entirely supported by the English-speaking population." He also admitted – and the point acquires more force given its source – "whatever other faults may be attributed to it, we must in justice say that all those who have filled its editorial chair have had the good sense to avoid all questions likely to provoke unfortunate disputes involving nationality." On 24 February 1866, the *Nor'-Wester* masthead would include, for the first time, the name "Winnipeg." Under Buckingham and Coldwell, it was a well run operation until 1865. The main factor in its eventual loss of prestige was the editorial stance taken when the newspaper was purchased and edited by John Christian Schultz, and Walter Bown, respectively. Neither had any journalistic experience – Bown was a local dentist – both were ardent supporters of annexation to Canada.

The Unresolved Question of Aboriginal Title

The *Nor'-Wester* made its presence felt very quickly, and made clear that it was not only going to be the newspaper of record, but was quite prepared to publish sensational material if such came to its attention. In its 14 January 1860, issue, it carried a story about a Red River resident who became lost in a blinding snowstorm, and died of hunger and fatigue, his body giving "indications of having undergone intense suffering." The following issue provided a lengthy report of the Joseph Gazden murder trial. The newspaper summarized all the depositions in the case, including that of John Green, pensioner, who testified that in the winter of 1853, Gazden had offered him £12 if he would take away a cloth-covered object from which a human foot protruded. Gazden was eventually found innocent, but the *Nor'-Wester* had brought the trial into the parlours of Red River.

More importantly, on 14 February 1860, the *Nor'-Wester* carried a story copied from *The Aborigines' Friend and the Colonial Intelligencer*

Trials and Tribulations

(published in London), under the headline "Native Title to Indian Lands." Chief Peguis, in a statement given 21 March 1859 (which followed up on one given in 1857, discussed in the Hind report, and noted in the 1857 parliamentary report) insisted that the HBC had never made formal arrangements in respect of Aboriginal lands. "We never sold our lands to the Company, nor to the Earl of Selkirk; and yet the said Company mark out and sell our lands without our permission," stated Peguis. In the newspaper's issue of 28 February, Andrew McDermot attempted to refute Peguis' claims, which he insisted were issued "at the urgent and frequent request of parties who took particular care to misinform him, and to assure him that by so doing he would receive back the lands and be allowed to dispose of them again as he pleased." McDermot referred to the treaty made by Selkirk with the Aboriginals in 1817, noting that those chiefs who had made it did not necessarily possess the land that they had transferred.

On 14 March 1860, the newspaper carried an account of a large meeting held at the Royal Hotel near Fort Garry, in which the mixed-bloods asserted their claim to the country as the "immediate representatives" of the Native tribes, and insisted that the HBC had not lived up to its end of the bargain made by Lord Selkirk in 1817. This was a more precise statement of the claims made by the mixed-bloods in the 1840s. This meeting was adjourned until May. Donald Gunn soon weighed in with a letter to the press defending Peguis, and criticizing Andrew McDermot. Gunn emphasized that although they had not been born on it, Peguis and his fellow chiefs had as much right to the land as any other Natives, since they were in occupation at the time of the treaty.

He also supported Peguis's contention that the treaty of 1817 was not a final bargain for the land, but merely an interim arrangement. Moreover, Gunn insisted, Peguis had not consented to a measured amount of land on either side of the rivers, but merely land "as far back from the river bank as a man standing on the bank could see under the belly of a horse out into the plains."

Andrew McDermot replied that while he agreed that Peguis had been complaining about the deal with Lord Selkirk for many years, it was only recently that he had denied selling the land. At the May meeting of the mixed-bloods, old André Truttier, who claimed to have been present at the treatymaking in 1817, testified under oath that the arrangement was that Selkirk was to have the use of the land for twenty years, and Peguis (aka Paketay-Hoond) had made an affidavit to that effect on 15 June. Peguis also asserted that "There are at this place three Indians who were present when the treaty was made with Lord Selkirk, and they all affirm that no final bargain was made; but that it was simply a loan. The lands were never sold to the money master. I have not two mouths. There is no sugar in my mouth to sweeten my words. And I say positively, "*the lands were never sold.*" There were subsequent complaints that the mixed-blood meeting had not been sufficiently well publicized, but its convenor Pascal Breland countered by stating that the only point of the gathering was to witness the evidence presented by Peguis and Truttier.

There were two quite separate issues at stake here, which everyone in the settlement acknowledged. One was the question of whether the mixed-bloods shared in the Aboriginal title to the land with the Aboriginals. The mixed-bloods had been making this claim sporadically since 1815. And A. K. Isbister had raised the issue before the Colonial Office in the later 1840s. The other issue related to the nature of the arrangement made in 1817 by the Aboriginals with Lord Selkirk.

An anonymous writer, in the *Nor'-Wester* in 1861, after accurately summarizing the treaty of 1817, asked "Where is the proof? I am not indisposed to allow the fact, but give me the proof. We all know of the document. . . which duly attested, signed and delivered, tells us as distinctly as possible that the Indians sold the land. The document was never held secret – how comes it that only now new light is dawning on the matter?" This writer offered a connection between the "half-breed" claim and the Selkirk treaty, maintaining "that the half-breeds" had "trumped up" a case that "no arrangements had been made with the Cree, who were the real owners of the soil in Lord Selkirk's days, and that their representatives, the Cree half-breeds who are now on the soil, are at this moment the rightful owners." The writer dismissed this claim out of hand, partly because many "half-breeds" did not descend from the Cree at all. This point of view was followed up in other issues of the *Nor'-Wester*, was clearly based on Alexander Ross's work, and has been attributed to his son.

These arguments were moot, as the treaty itself stated that the land was sold to George III (not to Selkirk) by both Saulteaux and Cree chiefs alike. The land was to extend for two miles on each bank of the river, except at Fort Douglas, Fort Daer (Pembina), and the Grand Rapids, where a circle six miles in circumference was drawn from these central points. In 1860, most of the chiefs, and all of the legal witnesses were deceased. There is no evidence that Mr. Truttier had been present. The treaty text itself made quite clear that measurable amounts had been involved. Peguis may have been right in saying that he wanted the amounts put in terms of what could be seen from under the belly of a horse, but this had been translated into miles.

Trials and Tribulations

As for Peguis' claim that he had only rented the land for 20 years, it is quite possible that such an arrangement was what he thought he was signing – although it is interesting that this interpretation was advanced by him only after almost all the other official witnesses to the deal were deceased – but this is as unprovable today as it was in 1860. The document itself survives and is relatively clear in its meaning.

Part of the motivation for bringing the controversy to the fore was the attempt by the HBC to force those settled on lands along the Assiniboine River beyond the scope of the 1817 treaty to pay for their land. At an meeting held in Headingley late in 1861, a large number of indignant settlers declared they would not pay one cent. "The principal reasons urged against compliance with the late claims are," reported the *Nor'-Wester*, "that the Company have no rights to the land themselves, never having purchased it, and that the Half-breeds have a very palpable right, being the descendants of the original lords of the soil." A handful of settlers of European origin dissented from this position," offering to pay for the land "as they were able."

In March of 1861, the Aborigines Protection Society addressed a memorial to the Duke of Newcastle on the subject of Indian title in those parts of Rupert's Land "likely to be included within the limits of the new colony at Red River." This memorial presumed that the agitation for Crown Colony status would be successful. It pointed out that the recognition of native rights had occurred in British Columbia. It added that the First Nations were obviously quite aware of their rights in the Red River territory, and noted that "the full and speedy recognition" of the rights of the mixed-bloods would be eminently useful "simultaneously with the constitution of the new colony." Nothing was ever done by the Colonial Office about this memorial or the issues it raised.

Quite apart from the mixed-blood claim and the evidence of the Selkirk treaty itself, there were some other interesting questions about Aboriginal title being raised in 1860 and 1861. One was whether the appropriate Aboriginals had been dealt with by Selkirk in 1817. This is the sort of question which might keep a land claim court tied up for years, and only an *ex cathedra* court decision could possibly settle the issue. Selkirk had dealt with the Aboriginals in possession in 1817. Whether they were the entitled owners is another matter. A second question was the claim of Peguis and other aboriginal leaders that the terms of the Selkirk treaty had not been carefully observed by the HBC over the years. That is entirely possible, although Andrew McDermot insisted otherwise. The HBC records are not clear in the matter. Finally, there was the question of the title beyond the limits of the treaty, known as the "hay privilege." All these discussions clearly demonstrated was that Aboriginal land title was a live issue in Red River that would fester until it was resolved.

Two Disasters

The early 1860s witnessed two major new disasters for the settlement. The first was the destruction of the Catholic Cathedral, the second the flood of 1861.

The Cathedral Fire

The largest, most impressive, and most famous building in British North America west of Fort William was the Catholic Cathedral of St. Boniface. The cathedral was part of a complex of ecclesiastical buildings on the east side of the Red River. There was a college, a convent for the Grey Nuns, and the bishop's palace. The library therein contained a magnificent collection of 5,000 books, and also stored all the records of the diocese, and all the deeds of mission land, including the deed from Lord Selkirk.

Five stone masons had worked on the construction with such speed that the Bishop could not keep them supplied with stone. The main part of the building was finished in 1837, and the final exterior touches applied in 1839. The resulting structure was immortalized by the American poet John Greenleaf Whittier – who had never actually seen it – in his well-known poem "The Red River Voyageur." Whittier wrote: "The voyageur smiles as he listens/to the sound that grows apace/Well he knows the vesper ringing/Of the bells of St. Boniface./The bells of the Roman Mission/That call from their turrets twain/To the boatman on the river/To the hunter on the plain." That Whittier had not actually seen the building probably accounts for his use of the term "turrets;" the surviving illustrations of the structure clearly show spires. Three bells imported from Europe, and collectively weighing 1,600 pounds, chimed from the belfries.

As the Whittier poem suggests, the new cathedral quickly became a local landmark and more than a bit of a tourist attraction. In 1845, a visiting party of Sioux had come to Upper Fort Garry and decided to cross the river to examine the cathedral. When they returned, shots were exchanged with a group of Saulteaux, and one of the Sioux was killed. A Saulteaux was subsequently apprehended and hanged, the last such execution in Red River. The Canadian scientist Henry Youle Hind, who

Trials and Tribulations

visited the settlement in 1857, described the cathedral's external appearance as "neither pleasing nor tasteful." But he allowed that "the two twinned spires, 100 feet high, glistening in the sunlight, give an imposing aspect to the building" and could be seen from a great distance.

The real beauty of the cathedral was on the inside. Over the years, much work had been done on the interior of the building, particularly by the legendary Sister Eulalie La Grave a member of the Order of the Sisters of Charity, who had come to Red River from France. Sister La Grave and her assistants worked on scaffolding to paint flowers and other decorations on the walls, and later on the ceiling. One observer later recalled that Sister La Grave sat on a chair placed on the crossplanks of the scaffold while she painted. This artistic nun also prepared the plaster of Paris moulds for the interior ornamentation, and even constructed a nativity scene for Christmas. The cathedral's first organ, really a melodeon, was reputedly handmade by a medical officer with the troops stationed in Red River in 1846. Sister La Grave, who was also an accomplished musician, played the organ every Sunday until her death in 1859. The *Nor'-Wester* commented, "We have seen St. Michael's Cathedral, Toronto, and we must pronounce that of St. Boniface to have been vastly superior in symmetry and elegant finish."

This splendid edifice, the pride of all residents of Red River, was destroyed in a devastating fire on 14 December 1860. The Red River Settlement possessed no proper firefighting equipment, and the cathedral never had a chance, particularly as the temperature was minus 30 degrees Fahrenheit. The fire began at about 10 o'clock in the morning, and had completed its destruction by lunchtime. As well as a detailed report in the newspaper, the disaster was described in a lengthy letter written by Father Mestre, O.M.I. The two reports were in general agreement, although Father Mestre's contained more particulars. Another letter, written by Sara Riel, to her brother Louis, studying in Quebec, also survives. It is simply headed "Incendie," dated 14 December 1860, and gives an example of the shocked reactions of the pious to the calamity.

The newspaper wrote that the fire had begun in the basement of the palace, where two mixed-blood girls making Christmas candles put 60 pounds of tallow in an immense kettle on the stove. The kettle boiled over, and the candlemakers attempted to douse the resulting grease fire with water, and of course only made it worse. A number of recently-cut boards were being kept over the stove to dry out, and they soon caught fire and spread the blaze upward. Only a handful of people were actually present at the time. The able-bodied among them were so busy saving the disabled that they had no chance to fight the fire, or salvage any of the valuables in the palace. Losses included books, papers, clothing, and furnishings, and a large store of provisions. The food lost included 60 cubic-weight of flour, 1,600 pounds of pork, 600 pounds of butter, and 100 bushels of potatoes.

One of the priests, Father Goiffin, was incapacitated in an upstairs bedroom, having had a leg amputated a few days earlier. He was carried outside on his mattress by two of his fellow priests. Ironically enough, Goiffin had not been recovering well from his operation, but exposure of the leg to the cold outside air cauterized the wound, and he lived well into the twentieth century. Handyman Magloire Morin attempted to reach an old blind man named Antoine Ducharme who had taken shelter behind the stove. Morin was unable to get through the flames. The blind man tried to escape but could not find his way out. His charred body was found well away from the kitchen area. He became the only human casualty of the conflagration.

The flames quickly spread from the palace to the cathedral itself through a half-basement room which extended under the sacristy. By this time, many residents led by students of the college and the soldiers of the Royal Canadian Rifles had gathered. The main doors to the cathedral were locked, and entrance had to be made through a window. Dozens of local people helped to carry precious furnishings out of the building. They managed to save most of the pews, the organ, the holy vessels, and the altar. Sister Gosselin rushed into the vestry three times to save vestments. On the third occasion her clothing caught fire, and she had to be thrown into the snow to extinguish the flames. The two side altars and the pulpit could not be removed in time, and perished.

The fire travelled up the pillars supporting the side-galleries, and soon the entire roof was ablaze, fanned by a strong south wind. Then the roof collapsed with a tremendous crash. This may have been aided by the explosion of a small barrel of gunpowder stored under the cathedral. Eventually the steeples themselves tottered and fell to the ground, and the bells melted completely. The ruins smoked for two weeks. The residents of the settlement rallied round to house the homeless clerics. The HBC sent twelve wool comforters, and merchant Henry McKenney, a Protestant, offered to take some priests into his home until other accommodation could be arranged.

Bishop Alexandre-Antonin Taché was visiting the interior missions at the time of the fire. He returned on 23 February 1861. Legend has it that the bishop knelt in the ashes of his cathedral, and recited the words of Job 1- 21: "The Lord gave, and the Lord hath taken way: as it hath

Trials and Tribulations

pleased the Lord so be it done. Blessed be the name of the Lord." Within months Taché and his clergy would be fighting water instead of fire.

The Flood of 1861

As usual in flood years, a heavy winter snow cover, increased by April snowstorms, was followed by a late and sudden thaw. There was an ice jam at the Forks, which, by this time, residents had come to expect. According to the *Nor'-Wester*, "at last came the winter *finale*. With a loud crash the ice was rent; and driving it before them in wild confusion, the liberated waters rushed down." The water continued rising, as much as a foot between sundown and sunrise. Many along the rivers were forced to evacuate their homes.

The crest was lower than in 1852, although the waters drove all the settlers along the Red north of Upper Fort Garry from their homes. As Henry Youle Hind had recognized in 1858, "Above Mill Creek, on Red River, there does not appear to be any rise of land sufficient to afford security against extraordinary floods, such as those of 1826 and 1852."

Flooding in 1861 ultimately forced many as far as Middlechurch to evacuate. Many residents moved all their possessions to their second storeys, and toughed out the high water there. Point Douglas was under water and St. Boniface surrounded by it, but districts to the south of the Forks appear to have been less affected than in 1852.

The 1861 inundation was also experienced south of the border. According to "G.W.N." in the *St. Cloud Democrat*, "from the mouth of the Sheyenne to Lake Winnipeg – the valley at one time resembled an immense sea, to which, looking from any point on Red River, no boundary could be defined, excepting perhaps to the eastward, in which direction the heights of the Mississippi could be faintly discerned."

No lives were lost in 1861, and few houses were seriously damaged, apart from the usual layer of muddy slime on the floors and walls. Aside from fencing, the most serious damage was to the various mills located along the rivers. Despite the initial inability of the mail-carrier to navigate the swollen rivers, the *Nor'-Wester* reported with some satisfaction that "even during the flood the mails have come and gone with all regularity." As in 1852, those with no grain stocks on hand, or those who had been unable to move their grain to higher ground suffered more severely. Many refugees, mostly mixed-bloods, retreated to Pembina Mountain and St. Joseph. But loss of livestock was low, at least in the settlement. Reports further south suggested that a great many cattle had perished. Because of the freshness of the 1852 experience, most settlers took evasive measures when it first became clear that the water was rising.

As in 1826 and 1852, planting was delayed. "G.W.N." reported that "farming in the Red River valley below [i.e., to the north of] the Red Lake River is utterly impossible this season." Nevertheless, S. P. Matheson observed, in the autumn of 1861, that "nature seemed to adjust itself to our needs and mishaps, with the result that both grain and vegetables matured in time to supply adequately our wants." American observers were nevertheless convinced that "buffalo hunting will be more profitable than cultivating Red River mud." This return to hunting was fueled by reports of immense herds of buffalo heading onto the eastern plains of Dakota, and a rise in the price of pemmican. In any case, Red River would experience a famine only a few years later (in 1868), caused by drought rather than excessive water, demonstrating the vagaries of prairie weather.

Transportation in the 1860s

Despite the arrival of the steamship in Red River, and the increasing extent of railways in both the United States and Canada, travelling to and from the settlement in the early 1860s was still a major adventure. The case of James J. Hargrave, who travelled from England to Red River in 1861, is a useful reminder of the difficulties – and the time involved. Hargrave described his journey at length in his 1870 book entitled *Red River*. He boarded the steam ship *Hibernian*, on her maiden voyage from Liverpool to Montreal, departing on her Majesty's birthday. First-class passengers on the *Hibernian* were conveyed in considerable luxury. Providing one was not sea sick, the dining was superb. Wines and cigars were available at low prices. The vessel arrived at Quebec on 5 June, after a slow passage of nearly two weeks. The passengers actually went so far as to sign a testimonial to the captain, exculpating him from responsibility for the delay. Hargrave then got on a special train run by the Grand Trunk for Montreal; he was pleasantly surprised at the low fare.

After staying for some weeks in Montreal, Hargrave reboarded the Grand Trunk, passing Toronto on his way west. He travelled in a carriage which turned seats into rows of cushioned benches for sleeping. At Sarnia, the Grand Trunk passengers crossed the St. Clair River in a steamboat, then continued by railway to Detroit, and via the Michigan Central Railroad, to Chicago, which they reached at 8 p.m. on 2 July. On 3, July Hargrave started west via the Chicago and North Western

Trials and Tribulations

Railroad to Lacrosse, then the western terminus of the railway. At Lacrosse he picked up a steamer to St. Paul.

At the Winslow House hotel in St. Paul, Hargrave encountered a collection of Red River merchants on the veranda, smoking and reading the evening papers. He went by stage coach to Georgetown, then shifted to a steamer owned by the HBC. It took five days by stage from St. Paul to Georgetown. Georgetown was "a mere village, consisting of a few dwelling houses and stores erected by or for the Hudson's Bay Company."

Hargrave had to wait for some time at Georgetown, arriving on 12 July and not departing till 28 July. It took seven days to get to Pembina, a "small isolated settlement of Americans and mixed-bloods." The following morning they reached the Red River Settlement. The first houses seen were "generally mere huts, consisting of one chamber each, lighted by a single window." A final sharp turn on the river brought the passengers into sight of the stone bastions of Fort Garry on the left and the "fire-blackened ruins" of the cathedral on the right. With a three-week stopover in Montreal, it took Hargrave from 23 May, to 5 August, to travel from Liverpool to the settlement.

As the journey of James Hargrave suggests, despite the advances in transportation in the wider world, transportation in the west was still quite primitive. Within the settlement, the York Boat, Red River Cart, and the dog sledge were local technologies, developed to suit the topography and the climate of the region. Both boat and cart travel reached a high point of organization in the early 1860s, at the very moment they were on the verge of obsolescence.

The Fur Trade Brigades

Trade out of Red River to the north still was still being carried out in York Boats organized into brigades. The York Boat had been developed by the Hudson's Bay Company over the last years of the 18th century, and the first years of the 19th, as the company sought a means of transport that was more cost-effective than the canoe, a swifter vessel but far less capacious. The York Boat remained essential as long as the settlement continued to serve as the breadbasket of the northern fur trade posts. On 3 June 1863, William Cornwallis King left Lower Fort Garry with the Red River brigade for Fort Simpson. Guns banged and cannon were fired, while three to four hundred people cheered the departure. There were three boats departing on 3 June, each containing 75 to 100 packages of 100 pounds each. The total brigade would consist of nine boats. Each boat had a crew of eight men: a steersman, a bowsman, and six middlemen. The boats used sail as well as oars. They were of native spruce, with a 33 foot keel and an eight-foot beam.

Each man was allowed three pounds of food. The boats carried a tool chest and a medicine chest. Each boat also carried three eight-gallon kettles, a two-quart bailing pan, extra sail and oars, and a bundle of portage straps. J. J. Hargrave reported that "the tripmen who man these boats are Indians or mixed-blood engaged at the place where the brigade is organized, and paid a stipulated sum for the performance of the trip." The brigades were organized by both the HBC and private traders. They carried furs and country produce north, and imported goods south. A return voyage took about nine weeks, and steersmen were paid £8, bowsmen £7, and middlemen £6 for the journey.

According to Hargrave, the most important brigade was the Portage La Loche Brigade, which conveyed trading goods into the Athabasca and Mackenzie River country. It carried agricultural produce to Norway House, met the boats from York Factory with trade goods, and then headed west across Lake Winnipeg to the Saskatchewan River. It also carried the summer "packet." It took around 36 days to get to Portage la Loche, but only 21 days back, because the return journey was with the current.

The Red River Carts

Most heavy traffic from the settlement to the south, and some to the north as well, travelled by Red River cart. The carts used on the American route, J. J. Hargrave wrote, were "constructed entirely of wood, without any iron whatever, the axles and rims of the wheels forming no exception to the rule." They could be mended with no tools but "an axe, a saw, a screw-auger and a draw-knife." The cart was little more than a light box frame on an axle connecting two wooden wheels, and cost about £2 sterling in the settlement. Carts were drawn by oxen or horses, usually Indian ponies. Depending on the load, they could make 20 miles a day, travelling for ten hours.

According to Walter Traill, the Swan River cart brigade took ten days to organize; it consisted of 50 carts, each carrying about 400 lbs. and drawn by a horse. Using oxen would double the load but halve the distance. There were three drivers to each ten carts, and a guide in charge of the brigade. Traill described the carts: "the wood being native oak while the leather used in the bindings and harness is raw-hide from buffalo or ox skins. There are only two wheels, seven and a half feet in diameter with hubs ten inches across and space in them for the axles bored out by hand, lined with bushings and bound on the outside with

Trials and Tribulations

raw-hide. The rims, or fellowes, are three inches wide and made of segments of oak joined together with oak pins. The axles are fashioned from split oak so as to have the strength of a straight grain. Repairs to the wheels are made with 'shaganappi' which is raw-hide. The body of the cart is six feet long and three feet wide and is open back and front. The bottom is of inch boards and the sides of round, upright poles capped with a split pole. The trams or shafts taper in width from six to four inches but are three inches thick throughout their nine and a half feet length. The collars, too, are of raw-hide, usually buffalo, and stuffed with hay. They are attached to the trams by iron pins fastened through holes in the wood. This and the iron used in the bushings in the wheel caps is the only metal used, though formerly, I am told, the carts were made entirely of wood."

Joseph Hargrave estimated that in 1870, 1,500 carts worked between Red River and St. Paul, giving employment to about 450 men. This meant that the cart traffic was by far the largest employer in the settlement. Some large merchants operated substantial fleets of carts, although it was possible for individual entrepreneurs to set up in operation as well. A cart carrying 800 lbs weight was worth £7. The cart, harness, and ox cost £15. Wages of a driver for three carts averaged £4 per month. There were also caravans travelling as far west as Fort Carlton, a round trip consuming 70-80 days.

The Northern Packet

In early December a northern packet left Red River to contact every post in the Northern Department. The means of transportation on this occasion were sledges drawn by dogs. Each sledge had two wooden boxes, three feet by 18 inches by 14 inches. Much of the contents of the packets were newspapers addressed to particular recipients. The dogs trotted from daylight to dusk. The teams often made 40 miles a day, and ran from Fort Garry to Norway House, a distance of 350 miles, in eight days.

At Norway House the packet was separated into material going north and west, from that going east. The dogs and sledges returned to Red River with the packet from York Factory, while a new set of bearers headed off from Norway House to Carlton House, travelling 650 miles in 22 days. The return packet from Carlton went through Swan River, reaching Fort Garry at the end of February. The contents of this return packet, consisted mainly of correspondence, and was eagerly awaited at Fort Garry where it arrival was one of the chief events of the winter season.

J. M. Bumsted

Robert Parker Pelly

Andrew McDermot

Trials and Tribulations

Bishop Alexandre-Antonin Taché

Louis Riel

J. M. Bumsted

The Expansion of Amenities

By the 1860s the advance of "civilization" brought new amenities, many of which were duly reported in the *Nor'-Wester*. Most members of the establishment could agree that the regularity of postal delivery, usually via Pembina, meant that newspapers and magazines could be obtained on a dependable – if delayed – basis. James Hargrave complained that his papers often arrived well perused and covered with thumb-marks, but they did eventually arrive.

In 1860, Messrs. Ross and Coldwell opened the Red River Book Establishment, in their printing shop on Main Street. According to an advertisement in the *Nor'-Wester,* reference books, children's books, and both historical works and recent novels could all be obtained. The history shelf included Gibbons' *Decline and Fall of the Roman Empire,* and there was fiction by Dickens, Thackery, Disraeli, E. B. Lytton, and Thomas Chandler Haliburton. The Red River reader could even buy a copy of David Livingstone's travels in Africa.

Public musical performances also began. The St. Paul's Choral Society, founded two years earlier, held a concert and evening supper, "consisting of roast beef and plum pudding, tea and coffee." Musical instruction was by now common in the settlement, and the Earl of Southesk reported on a concert he had attended at the convent of the Grey Nuns, where children performed for him on a piano-forte (which, he wrote, "I confess, it surprised me to see in this remote and inaccessible land." And as a portend of the region's future.

As with books, music, and sports, so too the seasonal round of holidays took on a firmer shape. The Easter Lenten season was always carefully observed by the French, and the Anglicans had begun special services as well. In the autumn came the annual goose hunt, during which many families left the settlement and headed off for a few weeks at a neighbouring lake. The Ross family went to Shoal Lake, north of Woodlands, every year for the goose hunt, which was an important time in their life. Christmas was a busy season, with the snow providing for easy sleigh travel. Hargrave reported "The amusements are of course chiefly of a private and home kind, theatres and Christmas pantomimes not being yet known at Red River." But there was much visiting and dancing.

A high point of Christmas was midnight mass at the cathedral of St. Boniface. The church was brightly lit with hundreds of candles, and music was performed by those nuns and clerics who had musical skills. For many in Red River, the really big holiday was Hogmaney, the

Trials and Tribulations

Scottish New Year's Eve celebration. This was a holdover from the fur trade period, when New Year's Eve was the occasion for merriment at almost every trading post. According to one mixed-blood memoir, "At New Year's we had a big time. Each man put up a feast. One day I would put up a big feast and invite my friends to come. We would dance the old-time dances and the Red River Jig – reel of four, reel of eight, double jig, strip the willow, rabbit chase, Tucker circle, drops of brandy, and all the dances. There were always lots of fiddlers. Nearly every man could play the fiddle."

The Goldseekers

In 1861 a renewal of interest occurred in the overland route to the British Columbia gold fields. By early June of that year, a number of goldseekers, headed by Dr. Alexander Reid of London, Canada West, were in Red River, where they hoped to obtain provisions for the western journey. The steamship *Pioneer*, carrying the provisions, was delayed until the river receded, and most of the prospective miners gave up, but Reid and a party of six headed west along the Carlton Trail in mid-June. The normally well-marked trail was obscured by the remnants of high water, and the little group got lost several times on their way to Fort Ellice. A journey that normally took ten days consumed the better part of a month.

By early 1862, another gold strike had been made in the Cariboo region of British Columbia, and talk of gold was afoot everywhere in North America. One of the major questions was the best route to take. Timoleon Love, an experienced American goldseeker, and George Flett, a resident of Headingley, had letters published in the *Nor'-Wester* proposing overland expeditions. James Ross commented in the *Nor'-Wester*, "Who will take the lead and who are to follow? We are such a staid plodding people that we dislike such a novelty as gold digging. Mining is not our way of thinking – it is an outlandish business, fit only for Yankees and other desperate speculators – a wild goose chase – a thing to be sternly frowned down by paterfamilias when thoughtless, ardent sons speak about it! Yes! this is the light in which nine-tenths of the people of Red River regard the gold business. Mr. Love will, next month, at the latest, go through to St. Paul to form a party for actual operations. Mr. George Flett, Mr. George Gunn, and others will endeavour to organize a party of Red Riverites to anticipate Mr. Love. Very good so far. The rivalry is generous – carry it out, gentlemen, and the results will amply reward your efforts and benefit the country."

Flett insisted that Red River people were ideally suited for the journey, for they could deal with the Aboriginals, and were experienced at wilderness survival. He wanted to lead 25 to 30 tough men – "half gents – bread and butter heroes – who cannot toe the mark – will not do" – and wanted to leave around 20 May. Three meetings were subsequently held in March, at John Macdonald's in St. Andrew's, at the Kildonan Schoolhouse, and at Pascal Bréland's at White Horse Plain. James Ross complained that the Hudson's Bay Company sought to throw cold water on the scheme.

In late May, the *International* sailed from Georgetown for Fort Garry, taking seven days. She brought 200 passengers, including a number of American and Canadian goldseekers, some of whom had begun in the east and followed the route west taken by J. J. Hargrave in 1861. A party being organized by Thomas McMicking hired Charles Racette (Rossette) as a guide. He had deserted the Jones party in 1858, and his brother, George "Shaman." Racette, was described as "a remarkable man, monstrous in size, strength, and appearance, supplying the middle link between man and gorilla, physically." The newcomers' demand for supplies virtually cleaned out the settlement.

Not surprisingly, the *Nor'-Wester* reported an inflation in prices. Flour which had been selling at 14-16 shillings per cwt, jumped to 20-25 shillings per cwt. The HBC offered to provide supplies at lower prices, although, as Ross noted, "they would not have done this under Sir George Simpson. He would have haughtily kept them at their distance and rejoiced if for want of supplies they had been obliged to return to their native hearths." More than 250 people were looking for supplies, a substantial population shopping the little collection of huts at the Forks.

Three parties were formed out of the large group of temporary visitors to the settlement. Because it seemed to be well organized, many of the incoming adventurers joined the McMicking group. It departed from White Horse Plain on 5 June, travelling westward by Red River cart. The American group had as its nucleus nine men who had come to Red River from St. Peter's, in what is now Minnesota, arriving in Fort Garry in early June. They travelled in mule-drawn wagons and brought most of their supplies with them. They left the settlement on 7 June, and arrived at Fort Edmonton on 31 July. George Flett's Saskatchewan Gold Expedition mustered at Portage la Prairie on 15 June 1862. It consisted of 64 men, three women, one boy, one girl, 43 oxen, 23 horses, four cows, and one calf. A number of Red River men were included in this party, the organization of which was based on the buffalo hunt.

Trials and Tribulations

The Founding of Winnipeg

The main impact of the gold expeditions was the establishment of a number of new businesses in the settlement, which laid the foundation for the economy of the future city of Winnipeg. The name "Winnipeg," we are told, is an Aboriginal word meaning "foul water," and by all accounts the rivers were never very clear and pristine, even in the early days. Commercial development did not begin until the early 1860s, when the first houses and buildings of the village were constructed about a quarter mile from Upper Fort Garry, on the west side of the Red. Even before the Red River Rebellion, most contemporaries called the village Winnipeg, although the official postal address was Fort Garry until 1876.

The site of early Winnipeg was dominated by the structure of Upper Fort Garry, a walled enclosure covering about a modern city block in the middle of what is now Main Street. The original fort, about half the eventual size, was flanked on each corner by a round tower, 20 feet in height. Inside the walls, a wooden gallery encircled the fort, with stairways at intervals. It was thus possible to ascend to the gallery and gain a view of the surrounding countryside, and equally possible to perambulate the walls for exercise and avoid the necessity of walking in the mud. A newer addition was built of walled in logs on the outer side. The historic gateway which still stands on Main Street was put in the centre of this wall; it was never a public entrance to the fort, but merely a private gate leading to the houses and gardens within. The major walls were constructed of Tyndall stone. The main gate faced southward, and a small postern gate existed in the eastern wall.

Within the enclosure were a number of yellow and white clapboarded buildings – the houses and stores of the HBC. In the centre of the enclosure were two houses facing southward. Surviving photographs indicate that these houses were substantial, and well-kept. The largest of these was the residence of the officer in charge of the fort. It contained a large mess hall for the officers and their wives. A wing on the eastern side of this large house provided accommodation for other families, and the rooms in the upper storey were reserved for guests. The other central house in the enclosure was Bachelor's Hall, occupied by the single officers on the first floor, and the clerks on the second floor. Along the west wall were large warehouses, and at the southeastern corner, a large sales shop, which provided most of the goods and liquor for the entire settlement, until it met competition from Winnipeg merchants.

J. M. Bumsted

In 1846 the fort had been expanded to accommodate the officers of the British regular troops stationed at Red River, and it was added onto again in the 1850s. In the grasshopper infestation of 1868, the bodies of the dead grasshoppers were piled four feet high against the sides of the walls, and in 1869, newly-arrived A. W. Graham noted that one could still see the discoloration on the walls where the grasshoppers had been stacked. The walls had begun crumbling even before Louis Riel occupied the fort in 1869-70, and the entire structure was razed in 1882, to allow for the southward extension of Main Street.

Beyond the gate of Upper Fort Garry, just east of the present Main Street bridge, was the St. Boniface ferry landing. There were no bridges in the settlement before Confederation. A cable spanned the river, and a scow roped to the cable was pulled across. The cable and ropes frequently broke, often depositing the cargo in the river. Understandably, most horsemen preferred to swim their mounts across the river. Not far from the ferry was the dock where the flat-bottomed steamboats landed two or three times a summer. The arrival of the steamboat was an event eagerly awaited, and the sound of the steamer whistle could quickly empty a church on a Sunday morning.

The first to build below Fort Garry was Henry McKenney. Born in Amherstburg, Upper Canada, McKenney had come to Red River in 1859 (the same year that the first steamboat and the first printing press arrived in the settlement) to open the Royal Hotel, the first in Manitoba, in a building rented from Andrew McDermot. McKenney, with his wife and eldest son disembarked at Fort Garry from the maiden voyage of the *Anson Northup* on 10 June 1859. In 1861, McKenney erected a sawmill on the east side of Lake Winnipeg, employing a schooner to haul lumber to the settlement, and in 1862 he selected a spot for a depot on the edge of the HBC land reserve at the point where the trails along the Red and Assiniboine Rivers intersected. This would become the fabled corner of Portage and Main.

The Red River track was the one which brought farmers and their crops from down the river into the settlement, and the Assiniboine track was the one travelled by the mixed-blood buffalo hunters on their way to the plains. The location was obviously strategically critical for trade. It was also extremely low land, which according to oldtimers, turned into a marsh every spring, and was inundated in every flood.

Before freezeup, in 1862, McKenney constructed a long narrow wooden building, fitted the lower storey as a shop, and the upper storey as a dwelling place. The building had a steep roof and looked, said one observer, like Noah's Ark without the hull. What would have become of

Trials and Tribulations

McKenney and his business venture had there been a flood in 1863, or one of the immediately succeeding years, is an interesting question. The intersection was eventually improved with landfill, and McKenney's success at attracting trade soon brought others to join him, and before long there was a little land boom with greatly inflated prices. Increased prices led buyers to insist on indisputable title, not easy to provide in Red River.

McKenney soon discovered that he had no flare for hotel-keeping, and in 1862 he sold the hotel to another newcomer, George Emmerling, always known as "Dutch George." Emmerling, who had reportedly arrived in Winnipeg with a barrel of whiskey and two barrels of apples, understood something about being a successful hotelier. He imported two pool tables around 1867, and served liquor from a substantial and varied supply. The bar at the "George" was always the place to drink in Red River.

A number of the other houses and huts of the village dispensed alcoholic beverages, and some provided a few rooms for lodgers. There was one small eating establishment run by an old Pensioner. Tradesmen also operated out of buildings which served as their homes. There was a watchmender, a harness-maker, a cutter (sleigh) builder, a tailor, two butchers, a baker, and a shoemaker, among others. Walter Bown had a dental office from 1866. One house was used as a school by the Sisters of Charity. Andrew McDermot put up a steam-mill, which served both as gristmill and sawmill. Three of the buildings served as "churches" on Sunday. Methodist missionary George Young and his family used their home for services. Another, called Knox Church, at the corner of present Portage and Fort streets, was used by the Presbyterians. The Anglicans employed Red River Hall, the first building put up by Andrew McDermot.

In appearance, the early village was hardly a prepossessing spectacle for visitors and newcomers. Methodist missionary George Young wrote of Winnipeg on his arrival in July 1868:

> "What a sorry sight was presented...on the day we entered it! What A mass of soft, black, slippery and sticky Red River mud was everywhere Spread out before us! Streets with neither sidewalks nor crossings, with now And again a good sized pit of mire for the traveller to avoid or flounder Through as best he could; a few small stores with poor goods and high Prices; one little tavern where "Dutch George" was "monarch of all his Survey"; a few passable dwellings with no "rooms to let," nor space for Boarders; neither

church nor school in sight or in prospect; population about One hundred...."

In 1869, newcomer Charles Mair was struck by the extent of swampy marsh to the south of the Forks, chiefly in present-day St. Norbert and St. Vital.

The Corbett Affair

Despite its modest appearance, and boggy underpinnings, the village of Winnipeg was frequently the scene of considerable excitement. Just outside the walls of Upper Fort Garry was the settlement's court house, located on about the present site of the Fort Garry Hotel. The court house was a small wooden structure, half devoted to a court room, the other half to the jail. In the jail, prisoners shared space with liquor confiscated for non-payment of duty. In the court room, quarters were cramped. The elevated box that served as the dock for the prisoner was very small. The raised bench for the justices was extremely narrow, and a portly judge could barely squeeze into his place behind the chairs of his colleagues.

There was a little table covered with green cloth in the centre of the room, where the clerk of the court sat with his Bible, his record book, and a jug of cold water. Around the clerk clustered the various "agents" in the case at trial: the prosecutors, the defence counsel, and the interpreters. To the left of the judge were two rows of benches for the jury: six Anglophones and six Francophones, according to standard Red River practice. Only a small space existed for the accommodation of spectators. "The very imperfect ventilation of the courthouse," noted one contemporary, "has long been a subject of remark." The proceedings in the courthouse were viewed as a spectator sport in Red River. Any number of juicy cases had filled, and at times overflowed the tiny spectator area of the building over the years, but none provided more excitement than the trial of the Reverend Griffiths Owen Corbett, charged with five counts of attempting to procure an abortion.

Corbett had returned from England to Red River in 1857. He had undertaken some medical study while in the mother country, and he now added medical practice to his work among the mixed-bloods. Corbett also continued as an avowed enemy of the Hudson's Bay Company and of the Roman Catholic Church, oppositions he managed to unite in 1861 when he accused Governor William MacTavish of selling out Protestantism by marrying Mary Sarah McDermot, the mixed-blood

Trials and Tribulations

Catholic daughter of Andrew McDermot. These sorts of public stances made him extremely popular with the Anglophone mixed-bloods of the settlement, among whom he ministered in the frontier parish of Headingley. As we have already seen, the settlers of Headingley were aggrieved that the HBC was attempting to collect purchase money for their lands.

In the autumn of 1862, Corbett again became involved in settlement politics. The Council of Assiniboia had petitioned the British government for the reposting of troops to Red River, this time to protect them from wandering bands of Sioux who had been driven out of the United States. In response to this petition, James Ross in the *Nor'-Wester*, began a counter-petition, which called for "such changes in the system and administration of the local government as will remove the present discontent and dissatisfaction," notably the establishment of Crown Colony status.

Nearly 1,800 names were collected on a petition to the Colonial Office, but Ross refused to publish it in the newspaper. As a result, by unanimous vote of the Council, Ross was dismissed from his various official appointments, including those as postmaster, as sheriff, and as governor of the jail. The leading officials of the HBC also ostentatiously cancelled their subscriptions to the newspaper.

This was the classic behaviour of an entrenched oligarchy to populist criticism, as Ross fully recognized. He seized the moment, and called a number of public meetings to protest both his treatment, and the administration of the settlement, as well as to solicit signatures for his counter-petition. At several of these meetings, the Reverend Corbett – who was already on record as being in favour of political reform, including Crown Colony status, and the establishment of a legislative assembly – spoke in favour of the Ross petition.

Not all the people of Red River were reformers. At least one public meeting heard the elder Louis Riel declare, "I wish to show and prove that Mr. Ross is a deceiver, misleading the people, for he says that the dissatisfaction with the Company and the Council is 'universal,' whereas the truth is, that among my people, the French Half-breeds, there is no such dissatisfaction. Thus I have proved that he is imposing upon you, and is therefore, an imposter." This was not the elder Riel's first attack on Ross. In 1861, when the *Nor'-Wester* published an article suggesting that other mixed-bloods were better than French mixed-bloods, Riel had threatened Ross and sung to him "la chanson du juge Thom." Bishop Taché would later point with pride to the support provided to the HBC by the Francophone community in 1862 and 1863.

Just prior to these public meetings, it became known that Corbett's young mixed-blood servant girl, Maria Thomas, was pregnant, and rumours had begun circulating throughout the settlement that Corbett was the father. Corbett had attempted to staunch these reports by attempting to have the girl swear an oath, which he drafted, denying his sexual involvement with her. On 2 August, 1862, Thomas and her mother, along with Corbett and his wife, appeared before Headingley magistrate John Taylor, but the girl refused to sign.

In the autumn, Corbett's supporters circulated a petition of support for him as a clergyman and as a medical practitioner. This was presented to him as a "testimonial" on 5 November. A number of those who signed this paper later disowned their signatures, claiming that they had not realized that they were doing anything more than acknowledging Corbett's medical services.

Eventually, Maria Thomas's father, Simon Thomas, a Hudson's Bay Company tripman, complained to the Anglican bishop about Corbett's behaviour, and David Anderson sent his archdeacon, James Hunter, to investigate charges of seduction. While Hunter did conduct an investigation, he did so in a manner that offered no legal safeguards for the accused, and was quite inappropriate by ecclesiastical law. Corbett was probably erroneous in his charge that the Hudson's Bay Company had paid Simon Thomas to issue his complaint, but quite accurate in his belief that the settlement's oligarchy was quite happy to pursue the complaint, particularly in the existing climate of public agitation. Even J. J. Hargrave, no friend of Corbett, observed that the "result of the Archdeacon's inquest was a conviction, which he did not scruple to state in public, that Mr. Corbett was guilty as libelled."

The subsequent official investigation decided to not to charge Corbett with "criminal conversation" or "carnal connection" with the girl, but with attempting to procure an abortion on five occasions. There were several probable reasons for this decision. One was that there appeared to be little corroborating evidence for charges of sexual transgression, but considerable collateral evidence that Corbett had indeed attempted to induce the girl to abort. Moreover, Judge John Black insisted that attempting to procure an abortion was a non-bailable offence, which meant that Corbett could be held in jail until his trial.

Naturally his mixed-blood supporters wanted Corbett released on bail. Over 150 mixed-bloods from all over the settlement congregated at the jail on 6 December 1862. The *Nor'-Wester* denied that they had any intention of using violence to release the prisoner. The Governor of Assiniboia, Alexander Dallas, met the crowd, allowed Corbett to address

Trials and Tribulations

them, and only with difficulty retired from the scene. One mixed-blood commented to the governor before he left, "My father bought 14 chains from the Company and they pocketed the money, although they never paid the Indians for their lands." At this point, Corbett refused to allow himself to be taken back to the jail. The authorities responded by mustering the local constabulary, recruiting mainly from among the French mixed-bloods.

The situation was extremely volatile, and the possibility of an armed confrontation was very real. Corbett was eventually allowed to post bail on 16 December, amidst continuing rumours that the HBC had set him up. Corbett himself certainly encouraged such an interpretation, as he wrapped himself in the mantle of a champion of "British liberty." He sent a stirring letter from "Red River Prison," accusing the HBC of "an attack upon our social, political, and religious freedom."

The entire settlement chose sides in the affair. The accused and his lawyers did their best to speed the legal process by demanding a special session of the court, which, understandably, insisted on waiting until Maria Thomas – who gave birth to a baby girl in early January – could travel from her home in Mapleton to the courthouse at Fort Garry. Meanwhile, one John Tait, a Corbett supporter, made such extravagant statements around the settlement about Archdeacon Hunter that the clergyman brought suit for defamation of character. This case was settled out of court in early February.

The trial itself was covered by successive installments in the *Nor'-Wester* with co-editor William Coldwell using his stenographic skills, honed in Toronto police courts, to great effect. Publisher James Ross, who also served as Corbett's defence attorney, chose to publish a complete transcript of the trial. Joseph James Hargrave wrote that "the fact that the *Nor'-Wester*, as a family magazine, survived the publication of the details of that trial, has always here been considered surprising." On the other hand, the newspaper had, since its inception, attempted to act as a paper of record. Moreover, it is possible that Ross, fearing the case might go against Corbett, sought to appeal to the entire community as jury. The full record was the best way of showing just how complicated the case really was, as well as how much was based on the unsubstantiated statements of the victim.

The full transcript certainly demonstrated that the court had not attempted to restrict the testimony to the abortion charges, but had allowed both prosecution and defence to range widely over the alleged history of the relationship between the girl and the clergyman. The defence did its best to put Maria Thomas on trial, and with the publication of the transcript, probably succeeded. James Ross attempted to convince the jury that Maria was both a flighty young girl, and a member of a distinctly lower-class mixed-blood family whose evidence was not to be taken seriously. Neither the Crown, nor the defence, made any serious effort to distinguish between abortion and the action of carnal connection. The prosecution, confirmed by the final charge of the judge, emphasized that while it was not bringing carnal connection charges, the girl's accusation of sexual intercourse provided the context for the attempted abortions.

An experienced prosecutor would have realized that Maria's character would be challenged by the defence, and that the whole case might well collapse, if her seduction account was not taken seriously by the jury. On the other hand, Archdeacon Hunter was allowed to describe, in detail, a "confession" of culpability made by Corbett to John Taylor, which Taylor recounted to Hunter. This hearsay evidence should have been thrown out of court. In any event, the defence was unable to shake Maria Thomas on the witness stand, a point which both the judge and most observers found extremely telling. The jury found Corbett guilty as charged, but recommended mercy. This recommendation may have been because of the political implications of the trial, but also because the jury was not thoroughly convinced that Corbett was indeed the father.

The clergyman was sentenced to six months in prison. A band of his supporters, claiming that his health had broken down during incarceration, soon broke him out of jail and refused to allow him to be returned. The court, faced with the possibility of open civil war if it chose to enforce the sentence, allowed him to remain free. Instead, Judge John Black read to a subsequent grand jury excerpts from a private letter written by Corbett from jail to his bishop. The excerpts seemed to confirm the clergyman's guilt, although in a subsequent letter to the newspaper, Corbett insisted that the excerpts had been taken out of context.

The ultimate effect of the Corbett affair on the English mixed-blood community of Red River was never entirely clear. A good deal depended on the extent to which individual mixed-bloods continued to believe in the clergyman's innocence, which he maintained until his departure from the settlement later in 1863. In any case, Corbett's position as leader of the mixed-bloods was not assumed by any other clergyman, or by any other individual in the settlement, including James Ross.

A few of his supporters talked briefly about establishing a new government in the mixed-blood parishes of the Assiniboine River, but nothing much came of this idea until some years later, when Thomas

Trials and Tribulations

Spence briefly established the "Republic of Manitobah." The English mixed-bloods did not completely lose the identity which Corbett had helped generate for them, but they were somewhat disoriented after 1863. One of the problems, of course, was the realization that if Maria Thomas's story was true, the chief victim of the clerical abuse had been a young mixed-blood girl.

What the Corbett affair had certainly done was to call into question two major institutions of Red River. One institution brought under scrutiny was the system of justice, which was revealed to be haphazard and unable to enforce its decisions. The other institution compromised by the Corbett case was the Church of England, not only in the sense that one of its clergymen had been involved in scandal, but in its equivocal response to the entire business. It had allowed its own quite casual and legally improper investigation of the charges – despite frequent assertions to the contrary, Corbett was never found guilty by a duly constituted ecclesiastical court – to become part of the prosecution case. Even more damaging, Bishop David Anderson had actually encouraged Corbett to flee rather than expose himself (and the Church) to public obloquy. Equally important, however, the case revealed once again the many unresolved tensions present in the settlement. The population was obviously badly divided, and there seemed few institutional ways of resolving these divisions.

-7-
The Morbid Symptoms of Pre-Confederation

On 3 July 1863, a prospectus for a reorganized Hudson's Bay Company was issued to the public in London, with capital fixed at two million pounds. The stock was promoted as an opportunity to participate in the construction of a transcontinental telegraph line across Hudson's Bay Company territory. Shortly thereafter, the Government of Canada refused to have anything to do with the telegraph scheme, and the venture – which had been promoted by English businessman Edward Watkin – came to nought beyond the acquisition of the assets of the great fur trade company by a new set of British businessmen. At the time of this promotion, Watkin was president of the Canadian Grand Trunk, which he was attempting to salvage from financial difficulties on behalf of its principal English creditors, the Baring brothers.

Watkin had been involved with railroads in Britain since 1845, and had acted successfully on behalf of British investors when the Erie Railway in the United States went bankrupt, so his appointment as president of the Grand Trunk in 1861 was a natural one. Even before his arrival in Canada that same year, he had been attracted to the argument that "nothing would serve the Grand Trunk Company so much as the opening of the western prairies." Watkin soon became involved in negotiations for an eastern railway extension called the Intercolonial Railway, which was intended to increase British American railroad traffic. He was also cognizant of the ambitions of the Canadian government to open telegraph and postal routes to British Columbia, as part of its plan to make the West available for settlement.

In 1862, Watkin had sounded out the HBC about purchasing a controlling interest, and he pressed ahead on behalf of a syndicate. All these schemes were part of the overall need, perceived necessary by

Trials and Tribulations

Watkin and other businessmen of the time, to make under-capitalized central-Canadian railways profitable by tying them into larger transportation and communication systems. As Watkin put it, "some effort *westward*" was required, for "Intercolonial is . . . absolutely essential to Grand Trunk: and Intercolonial is, under present circs in Canada, dependent upon this other movement." Prospective investors in speculative ventures reacted well to impressive-sounding schemes, and British investors were easily persuaded to support Watkin.

The financial troubles of one railway in eastern British North America, which led to the acquisition of the great fur trade company that controlled British North America would have profound effects on Red River. In the short run, of course, the major effect was that the men in charge in London were, after 1863, no longer experienced in the fur trade, but businessmen who regarded the settlement as merely a part of a portfolio of investments. George Simpson, who had died in 1861, was no longer available to advise them, and not surprisingly, the management of the HBC no longer operated with a sure hand. If ever there was a time for creative and imaginative leadership on behalf of the HBC, it was the decade of the later 1860s. Instead, everyone in authority simply went through the motions while waiting for the inevitable transfer to Canada. In spite of this neglect, life had to carry on in Red River, and the dynamic of ongoing development was once again clouded by the unresolved issues of land claims.

The First Nations

Beginning in the early 1860s, the First Nations inhabiting the northern American plains became more aggressive, understandably concerned with the increased traffic passing through their territories, and with the obvious encroachment on the settlement. In 1861, the Red Lake and Pembina tribes in the United States began demanding tolls from those crossing their lands, and they also began to menace the steamships on the Red River. A band stopped the *Pioneer* in the autumn of 1861, demanding $40,000. They took $300, and released the vessel. The Dakota Sioux had been forced to surrender large amounts of territory and were being squeezed into a relatively small area. Annuity payments were late in 1862, and the starving Sioux were not allowed provisions in advance, one trader commenting bluntly, "So far as I am concerned, if they are hungry, let them eat grass."

Not surprisingly, a band of young malcontents went on a rampage. Several hundred settlers died as the Dakota offensive continued into

September. The Americans responded with military force, and eventually forced the Dakotas to surrender. A military commission tried the offenders, convicted 323, and sentenced 303 to death by hanging. Most had their sentences commuted by President Lincoln, but 38 were hanged on 28 December 1862. In the short run, the brief conflagration had little effect on Red River, beyond preventing its residents from travelling south in the autumn of 1862.

In the long run, however, the Sioux War did have considerable impact on the settlement, for it forced many Sioux into exile north of the 49th parallel. The presence of small bands of demoralized Sioux was probably more of an aggravation than a serious threat to the settlement. The HBC, of course, used the occasion to request another contingent of troops for Red River, adding that the Americans were massing militarily on the border, but this request was denied by the Duke of Newcastle, who wrote, "His Grace cannot for a moment admit that the Company is not responsible for providing funds for the protection of a Territory of which they claim to be the sole and absolute proprietors." This terse response was due largely to the Duke's understanding that Red River would soon disappear into Canada, but also by his appreciation that the HBC asked for military assistance at every possible opportunity.

In March of 1863, a number of Red River residents petitioned the governor and Council of Assiniboia for the enrollment of 200 to 400 men in cavalry companies to protect the settlement from marauders. Since this petition coincided with the end of the Corbett affair, the authorities may well have been uncertain about the use to which armed parties would be put. The magistrates of the settlement wrote to Governor Dallas in April of 1863 that "it has become too evident that Military protection is as much required to keep down internal tumult, as to guard against Indian disturbances."

Despite the suppression of the main uprising, the Americans continued to organize volunteers to fight the Sioux. One such effort to organize an independent battalion, by a man named Edwin Hatch, would include a company of Red River people, some of whom had enlisted as "Mounted Rangers." A subsequent "Red River Company" was recruited by Captain Hugh S. Donaldson, and joined the Americans. Major Hatch moved northward to Pembina with his battalion, demanding that his forces be allowed to cross the border to "pursue, subdue and disperse" the Sioux. On this occasion he would be denied by Governor Dallas, but he later allowed such an intrusion.

Certainly, by 1863 the Sioux had become an annoyance to the settlement. Samuel Taylor of St. Andrew's recorded in his diary that

Trials and Tribulations

"there is a great number of Sioux in this settlement now this good while back, they annoy people very much." In January of 1864 a party of Red River settlers, led by A.G.B. Bannatyne, lured several Indian chiefs (notably Little Six and Medicine Bottle) to his house and plied them with liquor spiked with laudenum. They were then drugged with chloroform, manacled to a toboggan, and dragged across the border into the United States. The *Nor'-Wester* would subsequently defend this kidnapping against heavy criticism from Canadian newspapers, led by the Montreal *Telegraph*.

The Environmental Troubles of the 1860s

The Prairie West was a region of wet and dry weather cycles, and the 1860s saw the beginning of a protracted dry period, perhaps the most serious water shortage in the nineteenth century, and the most serious of the period before the Dust Bowl of the 1920s and 1930s. As early as 1862, symptoms of the drought had begun to appear. The restiveness of the First Nations in that year was caused in part by the dry weather and its impact on food supplies. Crops did not develop properly, fish and game became scarce, and native fruit and berries became scarce. Samuel Taylor recorded that by 1864, "Dry, dry, the weather was never seen, people Say, so long without rain, it Thunders often and yet no rain, sometimes it is very hot, but it gets very rainlike sometimes but it clears off and there is no rain." Drought also brought several other undesirable features in its wake. One was the prairie fire, and the other was the grasshopper.

Prairie fire was commonplace in the nineteenth century. Although many fires were caused by lightning, observers attributed most fires to human agency, sometimes to brush burning, occasionally to fires set to turn the buffalo aside, often to campfires not properly extinguished, and even to malice or stupidity. One fourteen-year-old boy was blamed for setting two fires in an attempt to force a squirrel from a hole. In 1859, The Earl of Southesk recorded that he had carelessly dropped a match while lighting his meerschaum, and "in an instant the prairie was in a blaze." Few if any human lives were lost to fire, although livestock was at constant risk. Alexander Ross insisted that fire could advance with such speed that "it has been known to overtake and destroy the fleetest horse." During the Sioux troubles there were frequent attributions of fire to Sioux malice.

Many of the fires were a product of changing climactic conditions. In 1864, the *Nor'-Wester* wrote: "The oldest inhabitant does not remember a summer of such extraordinary, long continued heat, as we have experienced this year. . ... One day of sultry, scorching, hot weather follows another... The case will readily be believed when we say that the thermometers have indicated 87 to 90, 97 and even 100 degrees in the shade!" From St. Andrew's, Samuel Taylor reported "the fire is burning the hay in all directions the very earth is burning the like is never been known." And J.J. Hargrave observed that prairie fires sometimes covered the entire country with smoke.

The relationship between grasshoppers and dry conditions was not in the nineteenth century – or today – clearly understood. One common theory was that the insects flourished only when the prairie sod was broken, either by wandering bison or by the plow, which enabled the eggs to be laid. But most contemporaries associated the periodic infestation of the grasshopper with drought. One modern researcher claims that over a thousand different varieties of grasshopper nest in the prairie grass. We still do not have a really good picture of the dynamics of grasshoppers in Manitoba. According to the *Nor'-Wester*, the menace was very limited between 1821 and 1864, when "they made their appearance from the south-west in clouds – they quickly overspread the settlement, but did little damage, as the crops were too nearly ripe to be affected by them." This sparing of the crops would not continue to be the case.

The Reform of the Anglican Church in Red River

The Anglican Church moved into a new phase in 1865. Archdeacon James Hunter insisted that his actions in the Corbett affair cost him the bishopric when David Anderson retired. Hunter wrote the Church Missionary Society, "the storm is pitiless, *a systematic blackening of the characters of all*. No one can live in this land with this adversary, and my prophecy is that in two years there will not be four clergymen on the two rivers." He continued, "Is Archdeacon Hunter to be the Bishop of Rupert's Land? The answer is an emphatic 'No, there is something against it,' mentioned with 'bated breath' as being private. . .. It would have been. . .a wiser and more judicious course. . .to have allowed the tittle tattle and scandal of Red River, for which it is alas! too famous, to have remained in its grave, rather than have given it the slightest shadow of any weight by resuscitating and transferring it across the Atlantic."

Trials and Tribulations

The truth was, and Hunter should have known it, that the Archbishop of Canterbury seldom appointed obscure colonial clergymen to bishoprics, especially when major policy changes were afoot. The Archbishop knew perfectly well that Red River would eventually become part of Canada, and that the diocese could not continue much longer as a missionary church supported by evangelical enthusiasm in England. It would have to pay its own way. The appointment of Robert Machray as bishop in 1865 was a classic British solution to a problem.

Assuming that Lambeth Palace actually knew something about the history of the diocese of Rupert's Land, Machray was a curious choice, given his background. Born in Aberdeen in 1831, he was raised a Presbyterian, but decided to convert to the Episcopal Church of Scotland because of his disenchantment with the continual schisms within the Church of England. Machray found considerable satisfaction in the immutability of the Anglican ritual, and the Book of Common Prayer. He studied mathematics at King's College, Aberdeen, and then attended Sidney Sussex College at Cambridge, where he was appointed dean in 1859. At the time of his appointment to Rupert's Land, he had both administrative experience and some recognition as a scholar. Interviews with the Church Missionary Society immediately before his departure for North America had emphasized both the need for a self-supporting diocese, and for increased training for a home-grown clergy.

He arrived at the settlement on 13 October 1865, already persuaded that his first step was going to be the resuscitation of an Anglican college. Less than a month later, he wrote the Society for the Propagation of the Gospel, "I believe that the whole of my efforts here will depend, under God, upon the success of what I propose – to establish a College for the training of those who wish a better education, in the fear of God, in useful learning, and in conscientious attachment to the Church." Several good reasons existed for a college. The absence of proper observation of Anglican ritual in his diocese was a constant concern, and orthodoxy could be encouraged by an appropriate institution of higher learning, which would not only train clergy, but proper Anglican clergy. "The hearts of the clergy here are almost fainting within them from the discouragement with which they meet, and I am confident there will be no health and life till some such institution as I have indicated shall be established."

As part of his new broom, Machray also sought to extirpate the remains of Presbyterianism in the Anglican churches. Almost immediately after his arrival in Red River, he ordered that the Book of

Common Prayer become the basis of diocesan ritual. He also introduced regular communion at his Cathedral – at least once a month. Furthermore, he ordered that services should be held on the Festival Days of the Church, and he encouraged the use of choirs, chant, music, and musical instruments in the liturgy.

In 1866, Machray managed to attract a hard-nosed subordinate in the person of John McLean, a fellow graduate of King's College Aberdeen, who also had been raised a Presbyterian but converted to the Church of England. McLean had been in Canada West since 1858, and he was summoned to Red River in 1866 as Warden of the Cathedral, ostensibly to assist in the revival of St. John's College. Short and stout, McLean made a nice physical contrast with the bishop, who was tall and thin.

Machray called a conference in May of 1866. Ten clergy and 18 laymen attended. The conference began with a full morning service and the celebration of Holy Communion. In the afternoon the bishop told those present that he wanted the conference to be the full step toward a synod, and then advanced his ideas for a college. Machray's address and various documents were collected and subsequently published in England as a pamphlet. Those attending voted unanimously for the re-establishment of the college, and began to raise money on the spot for a college scholarship to be named after Archdeacon Cochrane. The CMS agreed to pay McLean's salary and to support several students at the college, and annual grants were received from several organizations, including the HBC and the New England Company.

To avoid any technical problems, Machray convened the two remaining members of the collegiate board of the old St. John's College, and they turned over to him any authority still possessed by the board. The old school house near the Cathedral was dusted off, and several other buildings were acquired. The new St. John's College opened its doors on 1 November 1866, with over twenty students and three instructors, including Machray (Ecclesiastical history and Mathematics), Warden McLean (Theology and Greek) and Samuel Pritchard – who had instructed in the old college school, and had been running a school of his own.

A new constitution enumerated the aims of the college. The two principal ones were to train fit persons for the ministry, and to promote instruction at the university level. The constitution also emphasized the close connection of the college and the cathedral, and was clearly intended to be part of the bishop's anti-Presbyterian purification

Trials and Tribulations

procedure. The college was modelled on an English public school, similar to the one at Westminster.

By 1867 the Anglican Church was well on its way to becoming an autonomous force in the West, well equipped to deal with the new age of Canadian expansion. Not only the Anglicans, but the Presbyterians and the Methodists were gearing up for the arrival of substantial new Canadian settlement. There is no evidence, however, that the Catholic Church in Red River experienced a similar reorientation process. It appears, instead, that the Church was largely unprepared for the future.

Canada Acts on Acquiring the West

On the 4th of December 1867, only a few months after the new Dominion of Canada had begun its life as a nation, a handsome, well-built man in his mid-40s rose in the House of Commons to begin the most important speech of his political career. The coalition government of Sir John A. Macdonald had assigned to William McDougall, member from Lanark North, and the Minister of Public Works, the task of introducing into Parliament a series of seven resolutions designed to set the stage for expanding the fledgling nation across the prairies and on to the Pacific Ocean.

McDougall was in some ways a natural choice for the task. He had begun his political career as a Clear Grit supporter of George Brown, and had edited a semi-weekly newspaper, the *North American*, which emphasized progress towards "higher civilization." Like most Grits, McDougall believed that the westward expansion of Canada, by which he meant Upper Canada, was both desirable, and inevitable. In 1864, He had joined Brown in forming the "Great Coalition" with Macdonald's Tories that had created the new Dominion. Unlike Brown, and most other Grits, he had remained in the coalition after it had reached its goal.

McDougall was under a bit of a cloud for his refusal to abandon the coalition, and he also had an reputation for political unreliability; his critics called him "Wandering Willie." This reputation for fickleness joined a rather less savoury one for jobbery, personal ambition, and insensitivity to racial minorities. As Commissioner of Crown Lands in a Canadian Reform Ministry headed by John Sandfield Macdonald and Louis-Victor Sicotte, McDougall had attempted, with some success, to take back land previously reserved for native peoples on Manitoulin Island. There were rumours, never substantiated, that he had personally benefited from the policy he had introduced. McDougall genuinely believed in westward expansion, but not everyone in Canada agreed that his championing of the cause was purely altruistic.

A first-rate orator of the Victorian bombastic school, McDougall introduced his resolutions in a lengthy speech setting forth their background, and then explicating them in some detail. He began by expounding the view that continental expansion was the natural outcome of Confederation, fuelled by the same "dream of the patriot and the speculation of the political philosopher" about the "destiny that should unite" the British people inhabiting the northern portion of North America "in one nationality from one ocean to another."

In his only reference to the resident population of the region, McDougall saw the 10,000 inhabitants of the Valley of the Red River as evidence of the viability of expansion. The HBC could govern Indians successfully, he maintained, but not a colonial territory. He spent a lot of time explaining why it would be advantageous to extinguish the charter claims of the HBC with a cash payment. He also argued the necessity of dealing with Aboriginal rights in the region. He announced the government's intention to build a road connecting Lake Superior with Red River, provided the House voted for the acquisition of the western territory. Only quick action would keep out the Americans, McDougall insisted, who "were fast pushing their way up to the British frontier."

The parliamentary debate that followed McDougall's able opening speech lasted until 11 December. Its content helps explain why the Canadian government would have so much trouble in assuming control over the West two years later. The discussion in the House of Commons exhibited both profound ignorance of the region, and also extreme partisanship. Government supporters were boldly optimistic, opposition spokesmen were coldly hostile. As Mr. O'Connor, the member for Essex pointed out in a lengthy speech supporting the resolutions on the final day, opposition had come from two separate and distinct quarters. These, "though acting in concert, regarded the resolutions from different standpoints, and opposed them for totally different reasons, and with a view to different results."

The opposition proper, the remnants of George Brown's supporters, were few in number. They saw the coalition government as opportunistic and "politically immoral." Their critique of expansion made doleful predictions of its cost. On the other hand, the group led by Joseph Howe, made up of most of the Nova Scotia members, and a number from New Brunswick, wanted the question of the relationship of the Maritime provinces to the federal government sorted out before embarking on

Trials and Tribulations

continental growth. This group recognized that expansion would make secession more difficult.

Both groups agreed on the ultimate desirability of a continental nation, but both sought delay. As O'Connor summarized the objections, they related mainly to the cost of acquisition and maintenance of the new territory. They also included the refusal of many members of the House to allow the HBC any compensation whatsoever. One speaker noted the opposition to expansion within French Canada, which saw westward growth benefitting the Anglophone population at the expense of the French, but he implied that this problem had been resolved by union. No other speaker took up this theme seriously.

The debate did not completely ignore the existence of a local population in Red River. The specific comments made clear, however, that Canada's politicians did not have a very firm grasp of the western situation. A number of the early supporters of the resolutions insisted that the local inhabitants were entitled to liberation from HBC opposition. Like many other Canadians, these speakers were obviously familiar with the editorial thundering of Red River's only newspaper, the *Nor'Wester*. Since its founding in 1859 this paper had combined bashing the HBC with an advocacy of annexation to Canada. Canadian newspapers had often reprinted *Nor'Wester* editorials over the years.

Some speakers may have also known of petitions circulated among the English-speaking population in the settlement requesting annexation to Canada. Only two speakers, however, queried the present opinions of the local inhabitants. Mr. Chipman, from New Brunswick, asked rhetorically, "were all the inhabitants of this territory willing to come into the Union, or were they to be dragged in against their will also?" Chipman's reference was, of course, to the dragooning of the Maritime provinces into Confederation. His comment said less about his intimate knowledge of Red River than about his political opinions about Confederation. Mr. Joly of Quebec said that he "did not believe the Red River people want annexation with us." He provided no evidence for this view. Instead he quickly hared off into a disquisition on the cost of expansion.

Dr. Parker, in a long rambling speech, disagreed with the government. He wanted to take possession of the territory upon the sole principle of the "right of a settler's spade" to cultivate the earth. The Indians (whom he thought had far more rights to the land than the HBC) were driven out of eastern Canada upon such a principle. He saw no reason to treat the "white savage" with more consideration than the "red" one. Parker had some qualms about purchasing the HBC charter "divorcing half a continent, condemned by it to sterility, unchristianity and barbarism." despite these pockets of opposition, on 11 December a motion on an opposition amendment was defeated by a vote of 104 to, 41, and the resolutions were adopted by parliament.

Canada's Members of Parliament had simultaneously managed to endorse continental expansion, enhance William McDougall's reputation, and demonstrate how ignorant they were of the realities of life in the West. The familiarity of the Canadian government with the territory it was proposing to annex did not appreciably improve over the ensuing years. As late as September of 1869, the Privy Council drafted instructions to the newly-appointed lieutenant-governor of the Northwest Territory, who just happened to be William McDougall, calling upon him to supply Ottawa with a vast array of information about the way in which the region was inhabited and governed.

The extent of the material that McDougall was to generate after his arrival in Red River suggests that virtually nothing had happened in Ottawa since 1867 to improve its detailed knowledge of the West. On his visit to Red River, in mid-October 1869, Joseph Howe would claim that he was the first Canadian to examine the extensive official records of the settlement, including the minutes of the Council of Assiniboia. Because the HBC territory belonged to Canada by right of what amounted to "manifest destiny," Ottawa truly believed that it could improvise its way into governing the region.

The Breakdown of Justice

In 1871 Joseph Hargrave published a book entitled simply *Red River*, which was an attempt to bring the story of the settlement from where Alexander Ross had left it in 1856, up to the founding of Manitoba. Hargrave produced an enormous quantity of first-hand information on the settlement, and his presentation of legal events in the 1860s has been extremely influential on subsequent historians. Hargrave saw the problems of the courts as evidence of the breakdown of the traditional government of Red River. Certainly, it was true that after the passage of the Canadian resolutions for western annexation, the pro-Canadian party in Red River became more outspoken and critical of the existing government. At the same time, the will to change with the times was seriously limited in the settlement by the realization that the Canadians would soon be taking over.

Early in 1868, the Canadian party's leader, John Christian Schultz, seriously challenged local authority. As a young man who had expanded

Trials and Tribulations

his business operations extremely rapidly, Schultz had been constantly before the courts of Assiniboia. In 1865 he took his brother-in-law Henry McKenney to court over the dissolution of their partnership. As was common at the time, the court appointed arbitrators to resolve the differences between the partners. But matters moved too slowly for Schultz, and in May of 1866 he complained publicly that the court "had permitted itself to be bullied and browbeaten" by his brother-in-law, and possessed "neither the will nor the power to do justice." When admonished by the court he refused to retract his statements, and Recorder Black in effect found Schultz in contempt of court by refusing to permit him to appear personally until he had retracted or apologized.

Schultz pointedly allowed several cases in which he was plaintiff to remain unheard, and then complained about the travesty of justice in the pages of the *Nor'-Wester*. The plot thickened in 1868 when a creditor of McKenney and Company, Frederick Kew of London, obtained judgement in the Quarterly Court against Shultz in absentia for an old debt of the partnership. The attempt to enforce the judgement by the Court was resisted by Schultz, and he was committed to gaol. In the early hours of 18 January 1868, Schultz was forcibly freed from the gaol by a large party led by his young wife. The freed prisoner wrote in the *Nor'-Wester* that there were "no disreputable characters among the party," that "no violence was used, but the breaking of the door," and that "the marks of a clenched fist on one of the special constable's face would not have been there had he not rudely assaulted Mrs. Schultz in her endeavours to draw the bolts." Nothing was done to return Schultz to custody.

A large body, more than 800 residents, including a number of French mixed-bloods, signed a petition denying that the gaolbreak of Schultz had the approval of the general population. The editor of the *Nor'-Wester*, Walter Bown, refused to publish this document. He demanded protection from the authorities against a party of French mixed-bloods who were on their way to seize the newspaper's press. The immediate situation was resolved peaceably, although the dispute continued to simmer.

Bown eventually agreed to print a few copies of the petition, but when spokesmen for the French mixed-bloods took samples to the post office to have someone familiar with English proof-read them, Bown abused them and accused them of theft. The French mixed-bloods sued for defamation of character and at the May 1868 Quarterly Court won a verdict of twenty shillings in damages and costs. Bown refused to pay and was summarily imprisoned. His debt was paid by a supporter of the

Canadian party. The involvement of the French mixed-bloods in what had previously been infighting among the Anglophones added a new feature to the ongoing controversies.

French mixed-bloods were also involved in the case of the Queen v. Alex McLean, heard in the Quarterly Court in August and September of 1868, but in a different context. The defendant, a recent immigrant from Canada, was charged with manslaughter in the death of one Francis Desmarrais, a French mixed-blood trader. The alleged crime had been committed in Portage la Prairie, technically beyond the jurisdiction of the Council of Assiniboia and the Quarterly Court. The problem in the McLean case was less the breakdown of authority than the failure of the system of justice to expand in response to new settlement initiatives.

The McLean case was a contentious one with racist overtones. McLean had shot Desmarrais, who had harassed his family and threatened him with a shotgun. Unfortunately, the victim had been shot in the back while running away from the scene of the assault. It was necessary to petition the Council of Assiniboia to allow the Quarterly Court to hear the case. The Quarterly Court's jurisdiction was dubious to begin with, and more importantly, its traditional practices were nowhere near being in accordance with the standards of British justice.

The defence attorney was the American Enos Stutsman, hired by the McLean family because he was the only practising lawyer within 500 miles. The presence of a trained professional lawyer, previously unheard of in Red River, provided further evidence of the way the times were changing. Stutsman was born in Indiana with only stumps for legs. Despite his handicap he had come to the wild Dakota Territory in 1858 and resided in Pembina. Judge Black never knew what hit him. Stutsman successfully objected to a series of traditional court procedures, starting with his refusal to allow his client to speak for himself, carrying on with his insistence that all jurymen had to speak English, and could not query the witnesses, and continuing in his refusal to allow the judge to act as prosecuting attorney.

Stutsman rode roughshod over the fact that the British adversarial system had never existed in Red River. Judge Black failed to counter the assumptions of the defence about the nature of criminal practice with the obvious responses. There was no reason to assume that English law applied in Red River; Scottish criminal practice (which Black was employing) was just as legitimate as English or American; any colonial legal jurisdiction (especially in an area not officially a British colony) was entitled to its own rules of procedure so long as they were applied consistently. Conceding all these points to the aggressive defence attorney, Black was left in tatters.

Bereft of a proper prosecution – one juryman complained in the course of the proceedings that "no case has been made out" – Alex McLean was acquitted in ten minutes. The verdict meant that McLean did not need to use the escape plan worked out by his friends and relatives, which included having his sister sitting by the door to keep it open in the event a quick getaway was needed. In any event, the French mixed-blood community had once again been outmaneouvred by aggressive Canadian action.

The Famine of 1868

As if drought, grasshoppers, and prairie fires were not enough, on 3 July 1868, the settlement experienced another disaster in the form of a bout of unusual (although not entirely unique) weather. The weather had been extremely hot for days, with a good deal of heat lightning. About 2 a.m. in the morning, a monster thunderstorm began, waking the residents with the crash of the thunder. The sky was absolutely black, broken only by the lightning which lit the heavens with "perpetual brilliant flashes." Then the deluge began. Joseph Hargrave, who described the incident, does not record hail, although hail often accompanies storms of this nature. What Hargrave did note was the sudden appearance of a heavy wind, which lasted for about an hour.

The wind caused heavy damage to property and one life was lost. The building most damaged was the incomplete Church of the Holy Trinity, the unadorned timbers of which were summarily deposited on the ground. Peter Mathieson, a carpenter working on the structure, was sleeping nearby and was killed. The spire of St. Andrew's Church was blown onto the roof of the building. The *Nor'-Wester* office was nearly destroyed; it was saved only because the winds hit the building diagonally rather than head on. Many roofs were blown off, countless trees uprooted, and much fencing was carried away. The *Nor'-Wester* described the storm (which it labelled both a "hurricane" and a "tornado") as "the most serious ever witnessed in this country."

The rain of 3 July was both too late and too heavy. Much of it ran off without really soaking the ground. The settlement tried to clear up from the disaster, but by August of 1868, it was clear that an even greater disaster had come. This crisis was a combination of short-term and long-term ecological factors. Not only were there no crops, but the years of drought had completely devastated the wild vegetation on the prairie.

The buffalo disappeared, as did most game, and even fish stocks were hit hard.

While the total absence of game animals was probably to be associated with the drought, the disappearance of the buffalo may well have been part of a long-term trend which observers had been warning about for years. A temporary warming in water temperature was probably more responsible for the failure of the fisheries than over-fishing. The steamer *International*, had not been able to run regularly since 1865 because of the low volume of water in the Red River. The *Nor'-Wester* claimed that "within the whole Colony not one bushel of any kind of grain will be harvested," and there would be precious few potatoes either.

One of the most experienced farmers in Red River, Oliver Gowler, who had been brought to the settlement to run one of the many experimental farms, commented in the *Nor'-Wester* in 1860, that it was "next to impossible" for a serious famine to develop in Red River. His argument was based on the assumption that fish, game, and wild fruit were all available to supplement any crop failure. What Gowler did not realize was that a serious drought would take its toll on the bounty of nature as well as on Red River agriculture, which he admitted was not very sophisticated.

The *Nor'-Wester* invited comments on the impending crisis from the leading clergymen in the settlement, and published their replies in its issue of 11 August. Bishop A-A. Taché confirmed that there would be no crops, and opined that "the combined plagues of this year" were "the worst yet experienced as far as food is concerned." Anglican Archdeacon John McLean concurred, adding that there would be "a fearful amount of suffering from want among the poorer settlers during the coming winter, unless some steps are taken to make provision for them." Presbyterian John Black added that the buffalo hunt had also failed. Methodist George Young called for a public meeting "to appoint a committee from among the experienced and prominent and influential members of this community, whose duty it will be to present the case before a charitable public in the distance as fully as may be deemed advisable, and also to receive and distribute any contributions that may be sent." Although none of the clergymen made reference to the fact, all were well aware of the prospect, reported in the *Nor'-Wester* throughout its summer issues, that the settlement and the entire northwest would shortly be transferred to Canada.

The Council of Assiniboia voted all the funds it had available for relief in early August of 1868. Sixteen hundred pounds sterling was to be

Trials and Tribulations

spent immediately: 600 pounds on seed wheat, 500 pounds on flour, and 500 pounds on twine, hooks, and ammunition to encourage the settlers to try fishing. The *Nor'-Wester* newspaper appealed for aid to eastern Canada, and local religious leaders wrote to newspapers in Canada and the United States asking for help. A retired Pensioner named Michael Power wrote a letter to the *Times* in London outlining the disaster. The governor of the HBC in England, the Earl of Kimberley, added his voice in the newspaper as well. A letter from F. E. Kew, "Agent in England for the Red River traders," also appeared in the *Times*.

The *Nor'-Wester* was soon able to report on a meeting held in Ingersoll Hall in St. Paul, "to take measures to aid the sufferers of the Red River country," although it admitted it "was not very fully attended." The governor of Minnesota offered resolutions calling for assistance. Those present raised $1,137.75. The St. Paul Chamber of Commerce was soon soliciting aid "from the commercial and other organizations, from the churches, all benevolent associations, and from individual citizens of this State and elsewhere, for the people of the Red River Settlement."

The American committee (consisting of H. H. Sibley, R. Blakeley, R. N. McLaren, N. W. Kitson, and James J. Hill) thought that up to 5,000 people would have to be provided for over the winter. Ten thousand barrels of flour would be required. These supplies would cost $.75 per 100 pounds to transport to Red River before winter, and more thereafter. The appeal soon spread beyond Minnesota. In Milwaukee, Wisconsin, for example, $1,000 in contributions was raised at the Chamber of Commerce, and a local railroad executive offered to carry all supplies contributed to St. Paul without cost.

The probability of the transfer of Red River to Canada added some little public consciousness in the east of the existence of Red River, although the principal of the University at Kingston, Ontario, who had actively collected money for the settlement, reported, "I could have collected the money quite as easily, and the givers would have given it quite as intelligently, had the sufferers been in Central Abbyssinia." Nonetheless, Canadian newspapers did their best to publicize the need, and their efforts were thoroughly reported in the *Nor'-Wester*. The *Essex Record*, for example, noted that those who preferred "to limit their charity to those of their own faith" would find a resident clergyman in Red River "happy to receive and properly disburse any contributions."

The paper added that Nova Scotia fishermen had been assisted in 1867, "and we are sure the Assiniboians are not a whit less deserving than they." The *Canadian Free Press* of London began its appeal by describing the inhabitants of Red River as "Our fellow-colonists, that are soon to be." It added, "We are seeking to embrace this brave but distant people in our political system; to make them part and parcel of ourselves. Should we not then be the first to spring forward to their assistance?" The Kingston *British Whig* managed to support the appeal and blame the victims at the same time. It wrote: "The history of this Red River Settlement shows the great inconvenience of going far ahead of civilization with an isolated settlement. When population overflows, filling up a region of country by degrees, there is always help near, but when a small band of settlers go away far from all others – if they have no market for it – and it they suffer from scarcity there is no help near." The Toronto *Globe* soon reported that $195 had been collected in London, "with but a small part of the city canvassed."

The *Nor'-Wester* reported at length on the meeting at Mechanics' Hall, Hamilton, held by proclamation of the mayor upon the request of many of the leading merchants of the city. In his opening remarks, the mayor regretted that the attendance had not been larger, and several speakers echoed these sentiments. But an ecumenical collection of clergymen spoke eloquently on behalf of the Red River settlers. Wesleyan minister John Potts thought that sympathy was required both because of "our common humanity" and because of the "prospective political position" of the sufferers at Red River. "They desire to cast their lot in with us and become part of the Dominion of Canada; they have asked, and they wish to be one with us." He moved a resolution to that effect. In seconding that motion, Dr. Maclean observed that "the Red River country was not only a great necessity to Canada, but to the teeming millions of Europe. There were vast tracts of prairie, on the Assinniboine [sic] and Saskatchewan Rivers capable of maintaining millions of settlers, and it would not do to allow the pioneers of these settlements to be driven out now for want of support in their affliction."

The London newspaper had argued that the Dominion government should assist as well, and the Canadian government also contributed money to the relief effort. Moreover, as the *Nor'-Wester* reported in early October, the Canadian government had decided "to expend a considerable sum in the construction of Fort Garry and the opening up of the road to Red River." The man appointed as superintendent of the road was to be John Snow, who announced that he would need many carts to haul in his supplies from Georgetown, at the head of the American railroad.

As the Reverend George Young had suggested in his newspaper letter of 11 August, the "Red River Co-operative Relief Committee" was organized in the settlement to administer the incoming relief fund. It was

Trials and Tribulations

to consist of all the settlement's clergy, plus a lay delegate from each parish, and a number of local leaders. Subcommittees were also to be formed in each parish, composed of the local clergyman and four others. Their job was to identify those in need of relief and to guard "against any who would be included to impose upon this charity so kindly extended from abroad."

The general committee quickly organized an executive to do most of the business. The minutes of the executive still survive in the Provincial Archives of Manitoba. It was chaired by William McTavish, the governor of the HBC, and included most of the clergymen of Red River, both Protestant and Catholic, as well as the local newspaper editor and several public-spirited merchants. Most of these gentlemen had been named individually by easterners as local custodians of the funds remitted to Red River. In theory, a lay delegate from each parish was also a member of the committee. The first meeting of the executive was held at the court house near Upper Fort Garry on Monday, 19 October, 1868, and the committee agreed to meet every Wednesday afternoon at 3 p.m. at the same location. It did so until at least late January of 1869, when the minutes cease.

The chief function of the executive committee was to receive and distribute relief in the form of foodstuffs. At its second meeting, the committee deferred a request from the Ladies Bazaar that a portion of the relief fund be given to clothe the poor in the settlement, and never did respond to the request. Most contributions came as money, often gold, shipped west to St. Paul, Minnesota, which could be used to purchase food in the United States. The committee chartered over 100 Red River carts at 14 shillings per hundred pounds. Later, 100 sleds were hired to transport supplies to the colony. A detailed procedure was worked out for the parish subcommittees, organized by denomination, to report on cases of destitution. A printed form was drawn up to be sent to each parish delegate, "reporting the number in each case, and stating the age, also any male members in any family able to work who can leave home."

The famine was relatively nondiscriminatory in its effect, striking at Francophone and Anglophone alike. At one point, more than 2,500 people, about 20 percent of the population of Red River, were receiving aid, and most of the colony was on short rations. The committee noted that food assistance was limited to two pounds of flour per victim per week, and acknowledged that much of the money contributed was spent on transport.

The amount of money put at the disposal of the committee was considerably more than the inhabitants had expected. According to

Joseph Hargrave, by the winter of 1868/9, more than 3,000 pounds sterling from Britain, $3,600 from Canada, and over 900 pounds sterling from the United States had been collected. The final tally would be over 9,000 pounds sterling. The *Nor'-Wester*, in November 1868 estimated that the relief fund had already collected $26,000: $10,000 in England, $8,000 in the U.S., $5,000 from the Dominion government; and $3,000 from Canadian subscriptions. As Hargrave noted in his history of *Red River*, "the isolation of the colony had almost forbidden its inhabitants to believe in the possibility of a living interest being taken in its affairs by the busy people dwelling in the great outside world." The public response to the 1868 famine certainly demonstrated that Red River had come to the notice of the world.

At the same time the relief effort produced considerable controversy. Many criticized the HBC for not doing enough to help the victims. The Government of Canada attempted to integrate famine relief into its preparations for assuming control of the West when it announced that it would build a road from Thunder Bay to the settlement in order to provide employment for the destitute residents of Red River. Canada did not bother to consult with the local authorities before it sent the head of the roadbuilding crew, John Snow, into the settlement. Moreover, as Joseph Hargrave complained later, the amount of relief produced by the roadbuilding was relatively small. Snow never employed more than forty people, and he sold the workers their provisions at very high prices. There was much resentment that the Canadian government money pledged to famine relief was never paid, a fact noted in the pages of the minutes of the relief committee.

While some in Red River were suspicious of Canada's assistance, many rumours circulated that the crisis had been greatly exaggerated. The first sign of this critique was reported by the *Nor'-Wester*, which reprinted a story from the St. Paul *Pioneer* on the subject of the famine. The American newspaper noted the market prices of foodstuffs from the *Nor'-Wester*, claiming that they were only thirty to forty percent higher than normal. These prices "were far under famine prices and do not indicate a condition of terrible distress." The *Pioneer* continued, "we are inclined to think that the famine alarm exceeded in its proportions the depredations of the grasshoppers; or, at least, that the speculators were led to import largely, and that the price of provisions had not increased to the extent that might be expected." The *Pioneer* did admit that prices were controlled.

The *Nor'-Wester* had emphasized on 14 November 1868, that "Our readers must not judge the amount of supply by the amount of dollars

Trials and Tribulations

subscribed in the East. Because of the lateness of the season, the newspaper continued, much of the cost would be expended upon transporting emergency relief to the settlement." "U.S." wrote from Portage that it was mistaken policy to insist that sufferers had to be "perfectly destitute" before they could be assisted. He argued settlers should be aided to live through the winter without having to sacrifice their stock. He also answered the criticism that no one was actually starving, pointing out that it would be nearly a year before another harvest could be reaped. "The noble charities of our neighbors, should not be *misused* or *misdirected*, but there should be no cold, cramping, mean spirit exercised in its distribution." The *Nor'-Wester* used the letter to insist that every case of real distress should be relieved "without any reference to race, religion, or previous circumstance." The newspaper added that nearly a year's supply of food was needed before the settlement could return to normal.

The *Nor'-Wester* acknowledged the misrepresentation critique in its issue of 21 November. When he had first published reports from St. Paul that the famine had been exaggerated, wrote editor Walter Bown, he had been threatened with violence. Bown offered no substantiation of these reports. He noted that General Sibley had written Bishop Machray to say that the reason American subscriptions were less than expected was the rumour that the crisis had been overstated. The Milwaukee Chamber of Commerce had reported to the St. Paul Chamber of Commerce that an item originating in St. Paul had appeared in the local press to the effect that sufficient assistance had already been given to the Red River. The *Nor'-Wester*, and the local organizers of the relief efforts did their best to counter the rumours, and the controversy apparently died down, at least in its original form. The relief committee in the settlement certainly continued to receive contributions and dispense aid through the winter of 1868/9.

But the relief effort was never entirely free from controversy. "Philanthropist" took a slightly different tack in a letter to the editor of the *Nor'-Wester* dated 20 November 1868. This correspondent insisted that the suffering in Red River was real, but he feared that many who were not really needy would receive charity. He complained that the saloons in the settlement appeared to be flourishing. Moreover, many "able-bodied" men, refused to work "except for unreasonably high wages, evidently calculating on getting from the relief supply."

In the Quebec newspaper *Nouveau Monde* of 1 February 1869, a letter to the editor appeared from a "French mixed-blood" who signed himself "L.R." The letter answered one from Charles Mair, a recent arrival to Red

River, that had appeared in several Ontario newspapers. Mair had suggested that the only reason famine assistance had been necessary was because of "half-breed" indolence. "L.R." insisted that famine aid had been given to people of "all colours." He went on, "There are some half-breeds who do not ask for charity, as there are some English, some Germans, and some Scots, who receive it every week."

"L. R." continued, "It was not, of course, enough for these gentlemen to come to mock the distress of our country by making unfortunate people driven by hunger, work dirt cheap. They had also to spread falsehoods among the outside world, to lead people to believe that the relief sent to R.R. was not needed." He concluded, "in other circumstances than those in which we are, I should not have taken note of the falsehoods of this letter. We are accustomed to see strangers arrive every year who come to look us up and down, and who then print in the newspapers or in big books their reflections more or less queer on us and our country; but after the bad times which have befallen on us, driven as we are to have recourse to public charity, I have thought that it was my duty to protest against falsehoods which could give the impression elsewhere that there was no need of relief in Red River."

"L.R.," of course was Louis Riel, and this was his first known appearance in print. His response, probably reflecting that of many of the settlement's mixed-bloods, both French and English, suggests a sensitivity both to racial stereotyping and to condescending outsiders. Within a year Riel would be leading the French mixed-bloods in rebellion against the Canadian government.

The executive committee's final task was to distribute seed in the spring of 1869. The controversies of the previous winter had obviously had their effect. The committee's rules for the distribution of seed were quite careful to ascertain that only the "needy" were included among the recipients, who had to sign a declaration "that I cannot without great disadvantage supply myself otherwise." The committee also worried about misappropriation of its seed, insisting that recipients attest that they would sow the seed themselves. Quantities were strictly limited according to the number in a family, with 5 bushels the maximum, "which shall be given only to those in circumstances of actual poverty." Others would have to purchase the seed at "fair value" or on condition of making returns after harvest. There would be no free rides in the settlement in 1869.

Despite the suffering, the *Nor'-Wester* saw in the famine some advantages. It argued that the fields needed resting, and that the grasshoppers had destroyed noxious weeds as well as the crops.

Trials and Tribulations

Moreover, said the newspaper, the farmers of Red River would in future sow more widely. As for the buffalo hunters, they "will see that the cultivation of the ground is far likelier to supply their wants than the uncertain chase." And finally, the people of Red River had learned that "their brethren abroad have a regard for their welfare." Perhaps, although the buffalo hunters had probably been more influenced in any change of lifestyle by the absence of animals than by the famine of 1868. The concern of outsiders in Red River was a two-edged sword, influenced as much by imperialism as charity.

The Changing Mixed-Bloods

In an editorial in the *Nor'-Wester* in late 1860, entitled "The Plains-Hunting Business," James Ross had described the buffalo hunt "as the business, or regular, ordinary pursuit of a large proportion of the Red River people." In his opinion, the hunt created, and strengthened restless habits. It encouraged extravagance, and, repeating the earlier arguments of Alexander Ross, that six or seven hundred souls on the hunt consumed enough meat "as would suffice for six or seven thousand in Great Britain, France, or Germany." In addition, he maintained that it put every hunter into permanent debt, and led to the neglect of education for the young, who were permitted to wander about the prairie all summer, "like savages." The editorial spelled out its theory of social progress. Hunting represented a "rude or primitive state of society," the first "stage of civilization." The progression was from hunting, to pastoral, to agricultural, and ultimately to industrial. The *Nor'-Wester* doubted that this progression would ever occur in Red River, but the first link was clearly present. The hunt suited the "tastes of nature's children." But it was "an outlandish, temporary make-shift, quite unworthy of people pretending to a respectable degree of civilisation."

One of the problems with the Ross indictment was that it did not appreciate the dynamic nature of mixed-blood society in the settlement. The mixed-bloods were a complex people, constantly changing. Recent research on the French mixed-bloods has suggested that the Ross analysis of the economics of the hunt was hardly a complete one. The modern emphasis has been less directly on the question of profligacy, and more on the overall economic strategy of the mixed-bloods. By the evidence of Alexander Ross, and virtually every other observer of the Red River economy, the major problem with agriculture in the settlement was the want of market once the limited demands of the HBC had been satisfied.

Ross may have been accurate in his assessment of the future. But if the French mixed-bloods – or 'Métis' as they were beginning to call themselves – had rejected his appraisal and moved into farming before there was a market for their crops, the result could have been sheer disaster. Colonel John Ffolliot Crofton told the Select Parliamentary Committee in 1857, that he had attempted to talk the French mixed-bloods out of the hunt. They answered, "that they did not cultivate their lands for two reasons; one was, that they could not export corn which they might raise beyond that required for their mere subsistence, and that even it was better for them to purchase the means of subsistence with the produce of the plains, the pemmican which they made, than to cultivate their lands, for if they grew corn they did not know what to do with it; they could not export it, and they were not allowed to distil it."

Farming in the early settlement was on a strictly subsistence basis. The hunt offered the possibility of cash payment. Given the circumstances of the time, the hunt was the sensible and inevitable economic choice. The hunt complemented the agricultural economy of the early period, rather than conflicted with it, not least in its supply of food in years of bad harvest.

The economics of the hunt – and the behaviour of the French mixed-bloods – had changed substantially in the 1840s. Despite James Ross's reiteration of his father's earlier arguments, to generalize from his earlier criticism would be quite unfortunate. According to historian Gerhard Ens, the real choice for the Red River mixed-bloods, particularly in the post-1840 period, was "increasingly between a kin-based capitalist fur trade, wage labour, and peasant agriculture." Not the least part of the new economic regime was the employment of the carts, previously used mainly in the hunt, to carry goods between the United States and the settlement. This extensive haulage system, which employed upwards of 2,500 carts per year, would only last until the arrival of the railroad, but it was quite important, especially between 1850 and 1880.

Its appearance was joined by a new blurring of the lines between those mixed-bloods who lived for the hunt, and those who actively farmed, as the history of the famine of 1868 had revealed. In the newly developing transportation system, both Francophone and Anglophone mixed-bloods found employment, and there is some evidence – in the memoirs of Johnny Grant, for example – that a new group of mixed-bloods was slowly emerging who were relatively comfortable on both sides of the linguistic/religious divide in the settlement.

Both groups of mixed-bloods were involved in a meeting held in July 1869, called to consider the transfer of the territory to Canada by the

Trials and Tribulations

HBC. Its chairman, William Dease, called into question "the right of the Company to dispose of any territorial claims without the consent of the natives of the country." This gathering quickly turned into an open discussion about land ownership, with several mixed-bloods asserting that the question was whether the land belonged to the company or to the "halfbreeds" and First Nations.

William MacTavish, governor of both Assiniboia and the HBC, insisted that the Company had only sold the charter rights to the land, but Dease quoted from the report of the Canadian delegates who had gone to England to negotiate the transfer to the effect that the territorial rights of the country had been disposed of. McTavish insisted that this was not true, that land rights still belonged to the Aboriginal people, except for those rights which had been transferred to Lord Selkirk in 1817. Chief Pa-bat-or-kok-or-sis (aka Henry Prince), the son of Chief Peguis, insisted through an interpreter that the land had only been leased. The governor refused to enter into this discussion.

According to Alexander Begg, in his later history of the Red River rebellion, the meeting then heard a call for the mixed-bloods to seize the public funds of the settlement, and set up an independent government to negotiate with Canada. Begg did not really take this proposal seriously in his book, insisting that the business had been set afoot by land speculators who were trying to obtain land from the Aboriginals. In any case, a few days later a meeting of Francophone mixed-bloods resolved to organize mounted patrols to protect the settlement's land from speculators.

Whatever subterranean changes were occurring in mixed-blood society in the 1860s, land rights remained a critical issue in the settlement. Such rights would, of course, be profoundly affected by the events of 1869 and 1870, to which we now turn.

-8-

The Road to Rebellion

The actions of the Canadian government in advance of the actual takeover of Red River and Rupert's Land were singularly obtuse and blundering. The Canadian parliament had ratified the terms of the transfer of Rupert's Land in June 1869, setting the initial date of transfer at 1 October 1869; it was later pushed back to 1 December for financial reasons. Canada also passed "An Act for the Temporary Government of Rupert's Land," which called for a short-term administration of the territory by a lieutenant-governor and appointed council. However much Canadians may have disliked being colonists dependent on the British – as their rebellions of 1837 and 1838 suggested – they were quite prepared to turn westerners into such creatures.

Although the leading officials of the HBC would be offered seats on the council, Canadian newspapers reported the appointment of a whole suite of carpetbaggers as the government-to-be, headed by William McDougall as lieutenant-governor. Most of these officials had no connection with Red River, and many editorials pointed out the danger of this situation. Moreover, the Canadian government failed to advise anyone in Red River of either the new law or of its plans for the territory. On his way to Rome, Bishop Taché stopped in Ottawa to warn the government of the dissatisfaction in Red River. His advice was swept aside by George Étienne Cartier, who told him in no uncertain terms that the government had everything under control. "He knew it all a great deal better than I did," spluttered the bishop before a parliamentary committee in 1874, "and did not want any information."

Canadian Blundering

As if to compound its mistakes, Canada sent a team of surveyors, under John Stoughton Dennis, to prepare for the expected influx of settlement. This team was in addition to the roadbuilding

Trials and Tribulations

crew still working on the road from Lake of the Woods. Apart from residual Aboriginal rights, most land in Red River was held as river lots with unregistered title, extending two miles from the river on either side, and then with a "hay privilege" for unknown distances beyond. Surveying at any point would have been controversial, but to begin in advance of the transfer, surrounded by rumours, was the absolute height of folly. Governor William MacTavish received an order from the HBC to permit the surveys. He thought the decision "unfortunate," and warned the Company that he expected the "Halfbreeds and Indians" would "assert their rights to the land" and "probably stop the work until their claim is satisfied."

To MacTavish's amazement, Dennis not only wanted to proceed with all speed, but to begin by surveying the land occupied by the residents of the settlement. This was bound to generate ill will. Governor McTavish wrote to the HBC in late August, "some feeling has already been shewn by the Canadian halfbreed population who appear to think that there can be no necessity for surveying their lands until they desire it themselves." As a result, Father Georges Dugast wrote to Bishop Taché in Rome at the end of August that the country was "on fire."

On 11 September, the American consul in Winnipeg, Oscar Malmros, reported to his government that all the Francophones, and most of the other mixed-bloods were opposed to Canadian annexation. He thought that only the political inexperience of the people, combined with a lack of organizational ability, and considerable built-up apathy, would prevent an insurrection. But, Malmros added, a large number of settlers were "inclined however to get up a riot to expel the new Governor on his arrival here about the 15th of October."

Folly did not end with the surveying. In Ottawa, William McDougall, ordered arms for a prospective police force. The shipment arrived in early October and was observed with interest by Francophone mixed-bloods, who were not aware that the guns would be put in storage at Fort Abercrombie in the United States. At this time, the young man who was assuming the leadership of the Métis, Louis Riel, had his first meeting with Dennis. Riel was the eldest son of one of the leading Francophone mixed-blood families in the settlement. As we have seen, his father had been a political leader in the 1840s and was still protesting against abuses as late as the early 1860s, while his mother was a Lagimodière, the first Francophone family to settle in the region.

Young Riel had been sent to college in Montreal by Bishop Taché, and while he had not completed his studies, he had learned much about life in the big city. He had returned to Red River not long before the arrival of the surveyors, and he was at loose ends. Riel told Dennis that because he had some education, his Métis colleagues had requested that he consult with the surveyor, who tried, without success, to be reassuring. A letter, probably written by Riel a few days after this meeting, was published in a Quebec newspaper. The letter declared loyalty to the Queen and the HBC, but added that the surveyors had "disregarded the law of nations" by surveying in the name of "an alien authority." The letter asserted the "indisputable rights" of the Métis and their desire for the privileges of all Anglophone colonies.

Early in October, Red River was visited by Nova Scotia's Joseph Howe, the member of the government selected to supervise the West, a reward for Howe's decision to cease opposing Confederation. This visit was another example of the extraordinary lack of co-ordination on the part of the Canadian authorities. Howe had spent some weeks discussing railroad policies with the Americans in St. Paul, and apparently decided to head on to the Forks on a whim. In Red River, Howe did some research in the local records, and talked informally to a number of local residents. He would later have to deny in the House of Commons that he had met and drunk champagne with Louis Riel – and that he had not encouraged treason.

Even if Howe had said nothing untoward, however, he was well known as an opponent of union who had staunchly opposed Confederation because it was brought about without consulting the people. It would be surprising, indeed astonishing, if no Red River inhabitant thought of his presence as at least a symbolic encouragement to those opposed to joining Canada without consultation. His very presence encouraged rebellion, although that was not entirely Howe's fault. At the same time, what the man who would supervise Red River from Ottawa was doing informally in the settlement on the eve of its transfer has never been satisfactorily explained.

In an equally bizarre aftermath to his visit, Howe met William McDougall on the trail from St. Paul in the middle of a blinding storm, "facing sleet and wind enough to cut their throats." Howe later described the McDougall cavalcade as that of "a great satrap paying a visit to his Province, with an amount of following, a grandeur of equipage and a display of pomp that was enough to tempt the cupidity of all the half-breeds in the coun-try." It was "his first blunder," Howe insisted, "and a great blunder it was." The McDougall entourage consisted of Governor McDougall and Secretary, his daughter, Miss McDougall, and their servants, Captain Cameron, his wife and servants, Dr. A. G. Jacques, Mr.

Trials and Tribulations

Richards, Major Wallace, Mr. Charles Mair and wife. McDougall had his other three children along as well. This was understandable, as their mother had recently died. But if it was necessary to bring the children, McDougall probably should have declined the appointment.

In a letter to the Prime Minister, dated 16 October 1869, Howe had indicated that he had hoped to meet up with McDougall to "give him the benefit of my observations." In the event, the two men talked for about 15 minutes and went off toward their respective destinations. Although his private correspondence was apprehensive, by his own admission, Howe did not say anything to McDougall to suggest that there might be trouble with the takeover in Red River. According to McDougall, Howe said that the people of the settlement were well disposed, though restive. He certainly did not mention any armed insurrection.

In fairness to Howe, the resistance had not yet properly coalesced in the settlement, although two days after his arrival in Red River, one of the surveying parties had been obstructed by a group of Métis led by Louis Riel, who stood on the chains and refused to let them continue. It seems unlikely, after ten days in residence, and numerous conversations with local figures, that Howe came away without any clue that there might be trouble. On the other hand, Howe may have egotistically presumed that he had cleared the air with his various private meetings and there would be no further resistance. Perhaps more to the point, he had not bothered to meet with Louis Riel or any of the Métis. In any event, McDougall would subsequently charge that Howe had sandbagged him.

A Resistance Takes Shape

After Howe's departure, meetings were held in various parishes around the settlement. In the Francophone parishes, the mixed-bloods organized to repel the intruders, while at St. Andrews, the Anglophone mixed-bloods discussed how they should welcome Governor McDougall. Most of those present supported a fawning draft address prepared by Donald Gunn. However, Captain William Kennedy argued against this draft on the grounds that he was suspicious of McDougall, and thought that Red River should join Canada "on equal terms" with the other provinces. Mr. Hay supported Kennedy, and insisted on suffrage for "everyone capable of holding a plough." But the meeting eventually agreed to the Gunn draft.

Further debate over the welcoming address to McDougall occurred at a meeting of the governor and Council of Assiniboia. Here, the draft address was prepared by the Bishop of Rupert's Land, Robert Machray. It said that the incoming governor would "find old settlers of this country loyal subjects of Her Majesty, obedient to the laws, and ready to support Your Excellency in the just administration of them." Given the great changes occurring, it was hoped that "Your Excellency can understand mixed feelings in the community." The address further expressed "fullest confidence that all just rights of the old settlers will be respected." The Anglophone mixed-bloods and the settlement's ruling élite were obviously prepared to cross their fingers and hope for the best from the new regime.

The Francophone mixed-bloods intended a less accommodating strategy. They began by taking possession of the highways in St. Norbert. A roadblock was set up at a place called "Stinking River." It was manned by two armed sentries. One letter to the Montreal *Herald*, in late October, reported a discussion between the author and an unnamed mixed-blood, probably Riel himself. When asked what action they would take, the spokesman replied that the governor would be turned back, and there would be no compromise. "We want to govern ourselves. We will accept no concessions."

On Sunday, 24 October, Louis Riel addressed the congregation at the Catholic Cathedral. He told his compatriots that it would be easier to allow McDougall to enter the settlement, but to do so would compromise their ability to ensure their political rights. He suggested that should one mixed-blood fall, a handkerchief be dipped in his blood and it become their national flag. He said opposition to impending changes "must begin somewhere" and it should begin by opposing the entrance of the future governor.

A day later, an eight-hour meeting of the governor and Council of Assiniboia convened. Present were Messrs. Black, Machray, Cowan, Bird, Dease, Sutherland, McBeath, Fraser, and Bannatyne. Markedly absent were the Francophone councillors. John Black took the chair. He noted that despite the council address drafted the previous week, not everyone welcomed the arrival of Governor McDougall. He advised them that a large party had armed themselves to prevent the new lieutenant-governor's entrance into the settlement. The council unanimously condemned this action, but thought the parties might be forgetful or ignorant of the "highly criminal character" of their actions, and of the severe consequences. Council hoped by "calm reasoning and advice" the mixed-bloods could be induced to abandon "their dangerous schemes."

John Bruce and Louis Riel attended this meeting, and Riel addressed the council. He came with a list of 12 points, and his discussion was long, and according to the minutes of council, "somewhat irregular." Riel insisted the mixed-bloods were "perfectly satisifed with the present government and wanted no other." His people objected to a government being sent without previous negotiation. Riel continued that his people were "uneducated and only half civilized and felt that if a large immigration were to take place they would probably be crowded out of a country which they claimed as their own; that they knew they were in a sense poor and insignificant, but, that it was just because they were aware of this, that they had felt so much at being treated as if they were even more insignificant than they in reality were."

Once in, he maintained, McDougall could not be removed. Riel said he did not anticipate opposition from the English-speaking inhabitants, although he failed to note that he and John Bruce had been unable to persuade a meeting of mixed-bloods at St. Andrew's to join in the opposition to McDougall's entry. Riel insisted that his people were ready to resist the Canadian Party, but agreed to convey to his people the council's feelings, and report by the following Thursday.

After Riel and Bruce left the meeting, the council discussed the situation for some time. It explored several options. It decided against calling for an armed force to escort McDougall into the settlement, because such a force would come only from the Anglophone-speakers, and might raise a clash with the mixed-bloods in which the First Nations would join. Archbishop Machray later testified that he advocated raising a force and suppressing the rebellion, but was outvoted. The council did decide to send two of its members, William Dease and Roger Goulet, to head a party of loyal mixed-bloods to visit their compatriots at Rivière Sale and try to persuade them to disperse.

According to Joseph Hargrave, "It was agreed by all representative men at the Board that the great bulk of the Settlement was quite indifferent about Canadian rule, and the prevailing feeling was that, as the business had not yet practically come before them, they would decline to encounter danger at the hands of their fellow settlers in defence of a body of officials, in the appointment of which they had no voice, and in support of a government hitherto known to them only by report." The Canadian and British failure to consult and inform had come home to roost. Council had no control over the third option it discussed, which was that McDougall cool his heels at Pembina until affairs had calmed down. Only the lieutenant-governor himself could decide on this step.

On 27 October, John Dennis wrote a memo to McDougall reporting that the Anglophone mixed-bloods were generally well-disposed to the incoming government. They were unhappy with the Métis actions, he said, but added, "should an appeal to arms be necessary, we could hardly justify ourselves in engaging in a conflict which would be, in our opinion, certain to resolve itself into one of nationalities and religions, and of which we could hardly see the termination." The Anglophones were willing to accept Canadian rule, but, Dennis noted, they emphasized that they had not been consulted in any way. Thus they would not fight against the Métis, and possibly the First Nations, on behalf of the Dominion.

William McDougall finally reached Pembina on October 30. There he learned from John Dennis, and other correspondence, including a letter from Governor McTavish, about the unsettled state of Red River. McTavish thought that the assessments of Dennis were a reasonably accurate barometer of popular feelings among the Anglophone mixed-bloods in the settlement. He rehearsed the possible options, obviously preferring that McDougall remain on the American side of the border, which he insisted was the only "prudent or practicable" course of action. The incoming governor also received a report from one of his officials, J.A.N. Provencher, who had attempted to get to Red River, but was stopped at St. Norbert and returned to Pembina under escort.

In his discussions with the mixed-bloods at the barricade at St. Norbert, Provencher reported, he discovered that they knew nothing about the larger history of the transfer of the settlement. They complained they had not been consulted over the change of government, adding that they tolerated the HBC rule because it was not onerous. The insurrectionary movement had organized a new government, Provencher was told, had drafted a new constitution, and "were in negotiation with the English and Protestant half-breeds to arrange all matters relating to language, nationality, or religion." If this information was accurate, the leadership of the Francophone mixed-bloods were much better organized and prepared at the end of October than the unfolding of events would subsequently suggest.

At about the same time that Provencher left American territory, Captain Donald Cameron tried his luck, setting out in a buggy from Pembina with his wife. The British-born Cameron, the son-in-law of Charles Tupper, was a member of the government-in-waiting, in line to command some version of a mounted police force in the newly acquired territory. He got to Scratching River, and attempted to drive through the barricade, but his horses were seized, and he was brought to a halt. This incident would enter Red River folklore. A.C. Garrioch reported many years later that the Métis still "provoked much laughter by their clever

Trials and Tribulations

acting of the episode at Scratching River." On the other hand, Charles Boulton claimed that the rebels liked Cameron's pluck, and invited he and his wife to Father Ritchot's house for refreshments before returning them to the border.

The Escalation of Events

The arrival of Lieutenant-Governor MacDougall and his party at Pembina soon led to new initiatives by Louis Riel's forces. A party of mixed-bloods, led by Ambroise Lépine, rode to Pembina to warn McDougall not to attempt to cross the international boundary. At the same time, a much larger party of at least 100 horsemen took possession of Upper Fort Garry, offering to pay for the provisions they used in the name of the 'Council of the Republic of the Half-breeds.' Governor MacTavish wrote to McDougall, on 9 November, that on being asked what they meant by such a movement against the fort, the occupiers said it was their object to protect it. "Protect it from what?" they were asked. Their answer was – "from danger." "Against what danger," they were asked. To this question they replied that "they could not now specify the danger; but that they would do so hereafter." MacTavish, who was in bed dying of consumption, thought initially that the occupation was against Riel, but was soon disabused.

Whether the fort was occupied with MacTavish's approval has long been a question. William O'Donoghue insisted, in 1875, that MacTavish had aided and abetted the entire resistance, and that Riel was often under his instructions. Riel himself insisted that those in the Fort were angry at the occupation, and "would have stopped it if they could." MacTavish subsequently denied that Pensioners Mulligan and Power had warned of the occupation the day before it occurred, although they offered to expel the Francophones afterwards. According to MacTavish, there were 26 men remaining from the ranks of the Chelsea Pensioners and Royal Canadian Rifles. "They are absolutely inefficient in a military point of view. Most of them are old worn-out men, and those among them who are otherwise have already publicly and repeatedly refused to acknowledge the Company's right to command them to take up arms during civil disturbances." He vehemently denied that either he or Cowan had any suspicion of a seizure of Fort Garry in advance, but added, "even had we possessed such, we were powerless to prevent it."

A few days later, Louis Riel as secretary to the 'President and Representatives of the French-speaking population of Rupert's Land in Council publicly invited the Anglophone mixed-bloods to send 12 representatives to a meeting, to be held on 16 November, "to consider the present political state of this Country and to adopt such measures as may be deemed best for the future welfare of the same." There was trouble over the printing of this notice. A group of Francophone mixed-bloods took the notice to Dr. Bown at the *Nor'-Wester*, but after consultation with his "friends," he refused to print the copies. They then took Bown into custody, guarding him with two men in one of the rooms of his printing house, took possession of his press and type, and got two experienced hands, supervised by James Ross, to do the work. Although dated 6 November, the notice did not actually appear until the 9th. A day later, "Justitia" (the "nom de plume" of Alexander Begg) wrote his first letter to the Toronto *Globe*. This was the first serious effort to put the Red River case before an eastern audience. It was a powerful indictment of Canadian mismanagement. This fact helps explain the *Globe's* willingness to print it. The *Globe* supported western expansion, but was no friend of the Macdonald government.

The letter began, "That which has been foretold for some time past in this settlement has taken place." There has emerged "an open and decided resistance by the French half-breeds in preventing Mr. McDougall and his Council from entering the North-West Territory." Justitia notes that Canadian indignation would be great, and there would be charges of insults to Canadian honour. "But let the public of Canada pause before it accepts the one side of the story until it also hears the other." "Justitia" insisted that the Canadian government made a serious mistake in their assumption of rule over the North-West without prior consultation with the inhabitants of Red River. Because the locals had not been informed about the transfer, "Dame Rumour has full sway here," and "conjecture is the worst thing to be abroad in a country like this." Why were the locals not consulted and the views of the settlers taken into account? This question is, of course, unanswerable.

The Canadian government could hardly admit that nobody in Ottawa thought to pay any attention to a community of Indians and half-Indians. Serious mistakes were made by the government at Ottawa, argued the writer, of which the most important was in ignoring "a community of free British subjects" and their right to a "voice in the Government of their own country." "Justitia" questioned the wisdom of raising one side of the settlement against another, or of attempting to coerce it by force. He suggested sending delegates to take the views of the inhabitants over the winter, while McDougall returns home, and "take a new start in the spring in a proper direction." If the inhabitants were given their "just rights," he insisted, "no more faithful adherents to the

Trials and Tribulations

cause of Canada will be found in the Dominion than those same settlers of ours."

In what was called the The Convention of 24, Francophones and Anglophones met initially for two days, beginning on 16 November. They assembled at noon at the court house, with 150 armed men to escort the delegates into the council room. The armed men fired off a "feu de joie" to welcome the Anglophones, while there was a 24 gun salute fired from the fort. Of the 12 Anglophone-speaking representatives selected, only three were halfbreeds, one a full-blooded Indian, six long-time Scottish and Anglophone settlers, and the other two, a Canadian and an American, were known to be sympathetic to American annexation. One of the main reasons for the under-representation of the Anglophone mixed-bloods was that the proclamation calling for this convention had allowed the village of Winnipeg to have more delegates than it ought to have had, at the expense of the mixed-blood communities to the north and west.

None of the Francophone delegates were members of the Council of Assiniboia or the son of one, thus suggesting some shift in the nature of Francophones power in the settlement. This was not a public gathering and no reporters or visitors were allowed. The Francophones presented a relatively united front. Riel apparently did almost all of their talking. The Anglophones were not so united. Although outnumbered, it was a mixed-blood, James Ross, who became the spokesman for the Anglophones. Neither side seems to have much time for the First Nations. Riel spoke as if there were only two groups in the settlement, the Francophones and the Anglophones, and Ross didn't disagree. The only written record of the proceedings of this convention comes from notes taken by Louis Riel.

While the two groups jostled over preliminaries, James Hargrave brought a communication from Governor MacTavish – actually a copy a proclamation about the takeover of Fort Garry. In it, the governor observed that large bodies of armed men had avowed their intention of resisting the transfer of the government, and instead of adopting lawful and constitutional means had resorted to unlawful acts that threatened "the evils of anarchy and the horrors of war." He charged all to disperse peaceably before trouble got serious. James Ross insisted that this proclamation made clear that Fort Garry should be evacuated by the Francophones. Louis Riel refused, and denied the actions of his people were rebellion. "If we rebel against the Company which sold us and against Canada which wishes to buy us," he insisted, "we do not rebel against the English government, which has not yet given its approval to the actual transfer of the country."

These distinctions were more than mere hair-splitting, of course, because they raised the whole question of who, and what, represented the legitimate government of Red River. Before the gathering adjourned for the day, Riel called for united action by the mixed-bloods, a theme taken up on reassembly the following day. Further discussion revealed the extent of the gulf between what the Métis intended, and what the Anglophone mixed-bloods wanted to do with regard to the admission of Governor McDougall. The Francophones maintained that once McDougall was admitted all leverage was lost, and any action against him would truly be a rebellion. The Anglophones were prepared to take what they could get from Canada as an alternative to violence. One disturbing note in the proceedings was the complaint of Henry Prince, the Saulteaux chief, that he had not been allowed to express his opinions to the council the day before. Some reported that Prince was not allowed to speak to the council in his own language. These proceedings were interrupted so that the Quarterly Court could meet.

On 19 November, the principal case of the Quarterly Court involved John Snow, and an assault against him by his workers. The workers complained that Snow refused to pay their correct wages because of a previous work stoppage against him. The men, led by one of the defendants, Thomas Scott, had seized Snow and threatened to drown him, upon which the wages had been paid. Snow then had the ringleaders arrested. Alexander Begg claimed that a good case in favour of the workers was mismanaged by their legal counsel, and they were fined. Thomas Scott, was heard to say as he left the court, "it was a pity they had not ducked Snow when they were at it as they had not go their money's worth."

The convention of the delegates resumed on 22 November. James Ross raised the question of the gains that could come from admission to Confederation, insisting that the union "of this vast country to Canada is necessary to the dearest interests of British North America" and describing such union "as it were, the keystone of the arch of that grand undertaking" of Confederation. Louis Riel agreed, but added that the country had to be put on a footing that allowed existing settlers to continue to live prosperously, while outsiders "may find institutions all ready to make them happy by bestowing on them those liberties which all America likes to see its children enjoy without distinction."

Trials and Tribulations

Not all the delegates were impressed with the windy rhetoric of Ross and Riel. Old Donald Gunn stood up to complain of the amount of time wasted in reaching an understanding. He wanted the Métis to lay down their arms and urged that Governor McDougall be admitted so that complaints could be laid before him. Louis Riel replied yet again that it would be a mistake to lay down arms, and he reiterated, "McDougall shall not enter." The discussion continued until the 23 of November. The Anglophones wanted McDougall admitted, the Francophones were unwilling. Both sides agreed on the need for stronger government. Therefore, the Anglophones said, the Canadian government was a necessity. The Francophones responded by arguing that the people of the settlement should consider the formation of a provisional government to protect themselves, and to treat with Canada to "force it to grant us a form of responsible government." James Ross warned of a Canadian military expedition against Red River. Louis Riel insisted that winter gave Red River six months to arrive at an agreement. Riel finally recorded, "Adjournment, no understanding, little hope of one."

Following this adjournment the Francophone mixed-bloods met together for most of the night. Riel spoke for seven hours trying to bring the National Committee around to forming a provisional government. "No one was ready," Riel recorded, "What fears and hesitations there were to overcome. It is incredible what misgivings I had to overcome in them," The principal concern, of course, was the appearance that precipitous action meant rebellion against the Queen. Riel insisted that they would remain faithful to the Queen, but the government of Assiniboia was too weak to protect them. If the Queen knew what the Métis wanted, she would listen to them, said Riel.

In some ways it made good sense to form a provisional government. The Council of Assiniboia was still ostensibly in control, but obviously totally useless. As far as Riel and everyone else knew, Canada would assume title to the region on 1 December and the Council of Assiniboia would then be officially defunct. At this meeting, Riel advocated the seizure of the public records and funds, which he said belonged to the people. But he added that he was willing to wait until after 1 December to proclaim the formation of the provisional government, which suggests that he was unsure himself about the legal implications of his proposal.

After this overnight meeting, Riel did indeed act on his point about seizing the public funds of the colony. He went to Upper Fort Garry and woke up J.H. McTavish, the HBC accountant, ordering him to hand over to the "Republic" all documents in his possession, including the land register of the settlement, and the accounts of the Company. When McTavish refused, Riel chose the volumes he wanted and had them carried upstairs. Riel then demanded of Roger Goulait, the HBC collector of customs, all papers of the customs department. Goulait promptly surrendered them.

On 24 November the convention of delegates met once more. The Anglophones wanted to know what the Francophones were intending. Louis Riel wanted to know if the Anglophones would unite with the Francophones to deal with the present crisis. The Anglophones were equivocal. Riel told them, "You will know indeed what we want on our side. We want what all the French parishes want. And they want to form a provisional government for our protection and to treat with Canada. We invite you to join with us sincerely. That government will be composed equally of French and English. It will be only Provisional." The english delegates insisted on consulting their parishes, since their instructions did not authorize such actions. The convention then adjourned until 1 December.

In the wake of the adjournment, the citizens of the settlement met, publicly and privately, to discuss the fast-breaking developments in Red River. William McDougall, was still cooling its heels south of the 49th parallel, and the lieutenant-governor was blustering, but not taking decisive action. As for the Francophone mixed-bloods, they had finally resolved to establish a provisional government. The Anglophone leadership finally accepted that simply welcoming McDougall and his entourage to the settlement was not a viable strategy. One meeting of Anglophone leaders, held on 26 November at the house of Alexander Begg, did manage to come up with a reasonable alternative. The scheme proposed was to allow the HBC to continue to govern through the old Council of Assiniboia, while the people of the settlement would elect an executive council to negotiate with the Canadian government.

This proposal demonstrated that the Anglophone leadership was not prepared to give in to Canada, and also resolved one of the great concerns of the Anglophones, which was that they would be perceived by Canada and Britain (especially the latter) as being rebels. Had those discussing this proposal but known it, on this very day the Canadian government had requested a delay of the transfer of the settlement until "peaceable possession" of the territory could be guaranteed. As far as the Canadian government was concerned, this meant that the HBC was still the governing body in Red River. Had there been a means of communicating this decision to the settlement, the history of the region may well have taken a different course. As it was, the impasse between

Trials and Tribulations

the two mixed-blood communities had hardened Riel's resolve. In rejecting the Anglophone proposal Riel declared that the HBC government was "dead already & therefore not in force nor able to protect the people." By this point Louis Riel was well on his way to the establishment of a provisional government.

The Precipitate Actions of William McDougall

Everyone in the settlement understood that the critical day was 1 December 1869, the date earlier set for the formal transfer of the territory. Much depended on the action taken by William McDougall. The Convention of 24 was scheduled to reassemble on that date to finally decide on the Red River response to his entry into Red River. According to Alexander Begg, "The two sides in the settlement are armed and ready to fight against each other on provocation but the universal feeling is against fighting with each other. All are in favor of sticking together for the people's rights – representation." The Anglophone leadership met on the evening on 30 November, agreeing to support a reformed and representative Council of Assiniboia to negotiate appropriate terms with the Canadians. Nobody in the settlement disputed the need for better terms. Unfortunately, Begg and the Anglophones had not taken into account three volatile personalities – William McDougall, Louis Riel, and the leader of the "Canadian Party" in the settlement, John Christian Schultz.

William McDougall issued an official proclamation asserting Canadian control of Red River, and calling for lawful obedience to his administration. The proclamation had been sent in draft from Pembina, and was hastily copied by Canadian supporters in the settlement. Although no one knew it, this proclamation had no legal force because of the decision to delay the transfer. McDougall then issued a second proclamation supplanting Governor MacTavish and the HBC administration. While it is true that McDougall did not know of the delay, it is equally true that he had been instructed to wait for official authorization before proceeding. He had not done so. McDougall's impetuosity ended any hope of compromise in Red River.

A.G.B. Bannatyne took a copy of the McDougall proclamation to Fort Garry, where the Francophones were waiting for the Convention of 24 to resume for its final meeting. Louis Riel looked at the documents, and said laughingly that it indeed looked like a Queen's

Proclamation. He handed it back to Bannatyne, saying "Take that big sheet," but deliberately pronouncing the double "e" very short, so that it came out more like "shit." If it was indeed the Queen's Proclamation, said Riel, let us be prudent. He then went on to meet the Anglophone delegates. Riel told the delegates, "If Mr. McDougall is really our government today, our chances are better than ever. He has no more than to prove to us his desire to treat us well. If he guarantees our rights, I am one of those who will go to meet him in order to escort him as far as the seat of his government." A period of what Riel described as "disorderly discussion" followed, and the Francophones then asked for two hours to formulate what they wanted. Riel retired to prepare a list. In these two hours, he had obviously consulted with Enos Stutsman, because the document that resulted opens with four clauses initially sent by Stutsman a month earlier to the St. Paul *Daily Press* as a bill of rights for the Dakota Territory.

The Convention reconvened in the evening and sat late. It accepted a "List of Rights" submitted by the Francophones that called for the right of the people to elect their own legislature, and denied to the Dominion Parliament the right to make local acts binding on the territory without its consent. All local officials were to be popularly elected. The document called for a free homestead and pre-emption land law, and for bilingualism in both the courts and the legislature. It wanted a full and fair representation of Red River in the Canadian Parliament, and the continuation of "all privileges, customs and usages existing at the time of the transfer." These clauses were debated seriatim and were held generally to be "fair."

The Anglophone delegates were eager to send delegates to negotiate with Mr. McDougall on the basis of this list of rights, but Riel insisted that the Métis were not interested in any promises from McDougall. Let him secure these rights by an act of the Canadian parliament, said Riel. Then he would be admitted into the settlement. The Anglophones refused to meet with McDougall under these conditions. Riel then responded, "Go, return peacefully to your farms. Rest in the arms of your wives. Give that example to your children. But watch us act. We are going to work and obtain the guarantee of our rights and yours. You will come to share them in the end."

With this statement, the gathering broke up for the night. When it reassembled, the delegates found that Governor McDougall had also granted Colonel John Dennis a commission to raise an armed force to "attack, arrest, disarm or disperse" any men committing "unlawful" acts. Dennis in turn had appointed Charles Boulton to raise some volunteers

Trials and Tribulations

to implement his commission. Rumours of these actions prevented the Francophones from giving way on their insistence of guarantees. James Ross opposed any military action by Colonel Dennis, saying "I cannot see what in the world we are going to fight for. A civil war is far too dear a price to pay for anything wanted."

Confrontation with the Canadians

At this juncture a new sort of confrontation began to emerge, encouraged partly by McDougall's actions. Most of the Canadians in the settlement had been relatively quiet during November, while the mixed-bloods attempted to sort out their positions. On 21 November, Alexander Begg noted in his journal that Dr. John Christian Schultz had recently ceased his previous Sunday custom of hoisting the British flag with the word "Canada" sewn on it in white letters outside his drug store. But thanks to the commission to Colonel Dennis, many of the young Canadian hot-bloods were gathering in Winnipeg at the home of Dr. Schultz.

Rumours of other Canadians drilling in Kildonan soon reached Fort Garry. Riel had earlier warned Schultz not to cause trouble. In the early morning hours of 7 December, Riel led a large company of armed Métis, complete with cannon, to the Schultz house and demanded surrender. The good doctor's house was an unfortified wood-frame structure, and it now contained women and children as well as armed Canadian "volunteers." Dr. Schultz initially refused to surrender, but was outvoted by his supporters, who were disarmed and marched to Upper Fort Garry. As for Colonel Dennis, he disappeared from the settlement.

Most of the imprisoned Canadians were bachelors. They were housed in crowded and uncomfortable conditions in the upper flat of a two-storey building usually occupied by HBC accountants and clerks. The flat had a handful of small rooms which opened onto a central corridor that became a guard room. The small rooms themselves were "stoveless, bedless, and chairless," and "packed with prisoners." Later, some of the prisoners were removed to the small gaol outside the walls, described by one captive as "very filthy and crawling with vermin." Food supplied by the Francophones consisted mainly of pemmican, bannock and black tea, but it was supplemented by the kindness of the residents of Winnipeg, who provided baskets of bread, biscuits, and other items, including smuggled liquor.

J. M. Bumsted

The Proclamation of the Provisional Government

The surrender of the Canadians, and the disappearance of Colonel Dennis and his assistant Captain Boulton – the latter took refuge in Portage la Prairie – ended any possibility of armed resistance to a provisional government, which was announced under the presidency of John Bruce on 8 December, and formally proclaimed at Upper Fort Garry on 10 December. A flag-raising ceremony was held at the fort at 3 p.m. The new flag contained a fleur-de-lis and a shamrock (the latter supposedly in honour of William O'Donoghue, a recently-arrived Irishman who supported the Francophones). Following the ceremony, a boys brass band from St. Boniface played, and everyone marched up Main Road to "Dutch George's" hotel, where cakes and beverages were distributed to the crowd. James Ross reported in his diary, "Large parties going from saloon to saloon getting treats." American consul Oscar Malmros wrote to Washington that "the revolutionists" protected persons and property quite well.

Riel had all along insisted that his government was provisional only, and would give way when satisfactory terms of the transfer were negotiated. While there was disagreement in Red River over the means, the majority in the community agreed with the end. No takeover without consent. Time was of the essence, of course, as each passing day brought the possibility of armed intervention by the Canadian government one step closer.

In the short run, Riel's provisional government had to deal with a number of problems. One was public finance, resolved by seizing the cash in the coffers of the HBC. Another was expanding the support base of the government. During December, Riel suggested the creation of a new Council of 24, 12 members from each group, with a president elected from the council which would also serve as a court. The Canadian prisoners continued to be a thorny problem, with the government spending most of December trying to find a formula for release. Most of the prisoners refused to either swear loyalty to the new regime, or to promise not to oppose it; those few who were willing to make such commitments were pardoned and released. In January of 1870, a number – led by Charles Mair and Thomas Scott – escaped.

Despite many rumours, concrete evidence that the First Nations would cause trouble proved hard to find. Other rumours of American intervention in Red River, also encouraged by the American press, were never substantiated, although when a newspaper was finally allowed to

Trials and Tribulations

appear in Red River, in early January, it would advocate American annexation. The question of leadership of the provisional government was finally resolved on 25 December, by the resignation of John Bruce as president, and the assumption of that office by Louis Riel. Bruce had obviously been a figurehead, designed to garner support for the provisional government amongst the Anglophones, but the deed being done, the real leader took over without opposition. Regardless of who was its titular head, the most serious problem facing the new government was figuring out how to open negotiations with the Canadian government.

In early December, the Canadians had sent a series of emissaries to Red River. Colonel Charles de Salaberry, and the Reverend Jean-Baptiste Thibault left first, followed by Donald A. Smith, in company with Richard Hardisty, and Dr. Charles Tupper. The Canadians arrived in the settlement late in December. Unfortunately, none of them were empowered to negotiate, but merely to reassure the inhabitants of Red River that the Canadian government's intentions were honourable. Donald Smith had left his commission on the other side of the border, and so it was not immediately clear what authority he brought with him.

Dr. Tupper's arrival was another curiosity, like the earlier visit by Joseph Howe, for he appeared to be in Red River in a purely private capacity, to bring his daughter (married to one of Mr. McDougall's entourage) back to Canada. He spoke unofficially with Riel through the offices of Riel's sister Sarah, but had nothing concrete to offer, and left the settlement before the New Year. Men who were in the process of defying the Canadian government understandably wanted more than mere reassurances of Canadian good will, particularly when there was some question of whether that good will would be extended to the leaders of the opposition to the Dominion.

A greater degree of agreement among the resident factions would obviously be beneficial in any negotiations with the Canadians, and both the Francophones and the Anglophones sought a *modus vivendi*. By January of 1870, Louis Riel had come to suspect that none of the Canadians in the settlement had any power to negotiate, and he began to talk about unifying the settlement to produce a list of demands which could be carried back to Ottawa by the present emissaries. The Anglophone mixed-blood parishes began moving in the direction of unification with the Francophones, although most still preferred that the official government be the HBC, and not the provisional government of Riel.

J. M. Bumsted

In mid-January, De Salaberry and Father Thibault were pre-emptorily ordered back to Canada by the provisional government, when it was confirmed that they had no power to negotiate. Riel did not want them hanging around the settlement stirring up trouble. Donald A. Smith seemed a more likely candidate for discussions, or at least to serve as a go-between with the Canadian government. Rumours circulated that he had important documents from the Canadian and Imperial governments. The provisional government eventually summoned people from all over the settlement to a public gathering at Fort Garry to hear Smith's papers read. Smith hoped that he could use the occasion to persuade the people of Red River to give up their resistance to Canada.

The Meeting with Smith

Because of the size of the gathering – over 1,000 inhabitants were present at noon on 19 January – the meeting with Donald A. Smith had to be held in the open air of the courtyard of Upper Fort Garry. The weather was clear, and piercingly cold. As many as possible of those attending huddled inside the Company houses surrounding the courtyard, and others warmed themselves internally with large doses of alcohol. All present were bundled in fur caps and coats, belted at the waist with brightly coloured woollen scarves. The best shorthand reporter in the settlement was on hand to provide a record of the proceedings.

To Donald A. Smith's disappointment, the mixed-bloods had, at least temporarily, resolved their differences and displayed a united front at the meeting. As symbols of the new agreement, Anglophone mixed-blood Thomas Bunn was chosen as chairman, Louis Riel was elected to the key role of interpreter, and Judge John Black selected as secretary. After many preliminaries, Smith was given the floor, and he read his letter of appointment – which made clear that he had no negotiating powers – and a private letter from the governor-general, which emphasized that justice would be done to all inhabitants. A proclamation, issued by the governor-general on 7 December, and mentioned in Smith's letter of appointment, could not immediately be found. Had it been read, it would have stated that there would be amnesty for all those opposing Canada if they immediately put down their arms and dispersed. Smith failed to carry the crowd, despite his emotional expressions of loyalty to the Crown, and enthusiasm for Canada.

On the second day of this meeting, the audience decided it would be premature to release the remaining prisoners. They then listened to

Trials and Tribulations

Smith read several more letters reassuring the inhabitants of Red River of the honourable intentions of Canada. More to the point, Smith agreed to carry the wishes of Red River back to the government in Ottawa. After an adjournment, Louis Riel, seconded by A.G.B. Bannatyne, moved that "20 representatives shall be elected by the English population of Red River to meet 20 other representatives of the French population, on Tuesday the 25th inst., at noon, in the Court House, with the object of considering Mr. Smith's commission, and to decide what would be best for the welfare of the country." A broadly-based committee was chosen to apportion the Anglophone representatives. At the end of the meeting, Louis Riel emphasized that the two peoples of Red River shared "just rights," that "will be set forth by our representatives, and what is more, gentlemen, we will get them."

The Convention of Forty

The committee to select the English-speaking delegates met on 21 January, at the home of Bishop Robert Machray, and distributed the seats in a way that approximated the pattern of population in the settlement. In the ensuing elections, several delegates were given clear instructions by their constituents in favour of the restoration of the HBC as the legal government. Numerically, the Anglophone mixed-bloods were still under-represented, but not to the extent of the November meeting. A First Nations clergyman represented St. Peter's. A number of the Francophone districts also saw electoral contests, in which the supporters of Riel usually triumphed, but it is worth remarking that Riel did not have the unanimous support of his people, and in at least one constituency, the opposition was led by the group of mixed-bloods (Grant, McKay) that bridged the linguistic gap in the settlement

In the midst of the elections, Dr. Schultz escaped from Upper Fort Garry, and Louis Riel became virtually fixated with the good doctor's recapture, sending out men to turn the settlement upside down; he found refuge in Kildonan. The convention first convened at Upper Fort Garry on 26 January 1870. Judge John Black was in the chair, William Coldwell (the shorthand reporter) was the English-language secretary, and Louis Schmidt (a childhood chum of Riel) was French-language secretary. James Ross served as interpreter from French to English, and Riel from English to French.

The first resolution of the meeting, carried unanimously, was a declaration of loyalty to the Crown, "provided their rights, properties, usages and customs be respected." A committee was then appointed to prepare a draft Bill of Rights for the next day's session. This committee, chaired by James Ross, took longer than anticipated because of considerable disagreement. Ross introduced the draft on 29 January, with apologies for its "very crude shape." Nevertheless, the convention began debate, and adopted the first four clauses before breaking up late in the evening. None of these were particularly controversial within the settlement. The first article called for the continuation of existing import duties, the second forbade direction taxation from Ottawa so long as the country remained a territory of Canada, and the third insisted that while a territory, all public expenses were a Canadian responsibility. The fourth clause called for government by a lieutenant-governor, appointed in Canada, and an elected council, with heads of departments nominated by the Canadian governor-general. These clauses assumed that Red River would initially become a territory of Canada, and while Ottawa governed, it must pay the bills.

When the convention resumed sitting, it continued to find considerable agreement, accepting bilingualism in both the legislature and the courts. The first serious debate came over converting the haying privilege into fee simple ownership. The convention finally passed, by a vote of 21 to 18, an amended version of the clause, which called for the local legislature to have full control over all lands within a radius from Upper Fort Garry equal to the distance to the American border from the fort, or about 60 miles. The original clause had been designed to prevent land speculation, and the Francophones obviously preferred that the local legislature deal with it.

Only with the Bill of Rights completed did Louis Riel introduce the concept of admission of the settlement into Confederation as a province rather than as a territory. Riel insisted that provincial status would give the people of the country greater security for their rights and privileges, by keeping the hands of the Canadian government out of local affairs, particularly public lands and natural resources. But he was unable to carry the convention with him. The Anglophone delegates were almost unanimously opposed, and three Francophones broke ranks to vote against provincial status. Riel was quite unhappy about this defeat, and a subsequent one over the question of the status of the HBC. Both of these defeats he blamed on "traitors." This ending to the meeting of was quite unfortunate; the convention had achieved much. But Riel appeared to be unable to deal responsibly with his wishes being thwarted, and his behaviour became increasingly volatile and unpredictable.

In early February, Father Noel Ritchot, Judge John Black, and Alfred Scott were appointed to go to Ottawa to negotiate provincial status for

Trials and Tribulations

Red River within Confederation. Meanwhile, on 12 February 1870, an armed force of Canadian settlers, led by Charles A. Boulton, one of Canada's surveyors – and including Charles Mair and Thomas Scott – left Portage la Prairie to join a party led by John Schultz at Kildonan. The plan was to liberate the prisoners still being held, and when Riel independently released them, the armed parties began to disperse. On 17 February 1870, a small force of Riel's horsemen arrested and imprisoned a number of these men, including Thomas Scott, on their return march back to Portage.

Up to this point Riel's tactics had been little short of brilliant. He had managed to keep Francophone and Anglophone mixed-bloods united under the aegis of the provisional government. Despite some talk about negotiations with the Americans, mainly for effect, Riel clearly wanted Red River to be admitted to Confederation. In Ottawa, the Canadian cabinet agreed on 11 February to negotiate with the delegates from Red River. But it was also agreed that if negotiations broke down, a military force would be necessary. Steps were taken with the British government to organize such a force, to consist of British regulars and Canadian volunteers.

The Execution of Thomas Scott

Matters appeared to be in hand, and there was every chance that a peaceful resolution would follow. Then, inexplicably, Louis Riel allowed Thomas Scott, an unruly Anglophone prisoner to be tried by a Métis tribunal and sentenced to death. In accepting the sentence, Riel stated "We must make Canada respect us." On 4 March 1870, Scott was taken outside the gates of Fort Garry. His eyes were bandaged and he was shot by a firing squad. Riel apparently did not think much about the death of Scott, although it was the first fatality that had occurred in the course of Red River's resistance. But this treatment of Scott would have enormous repercussions. When word of Scott's death reached Ontario, which had been searching desperately for an excuse to condemn the insurgents, a secret society named "Canada First" undertook to orchestrate public reaction. The members of Canada First were inspired by the memory of D'Arcy McGee, who had been assassinated on the steps of the House of Commons on 7 April 1868.

They believed in the need to inculcate a national spirit. They also believed in Canadian westward expansion, and in the innate superiority of white Anglo-Saxon Protestants. Led by George Denison, the Canada Firsters – who included Charles Mair and John Schultz – organized their public campaign on the basis of their discovery that Thomas Scott had been a member of the Orange Order, a dominant force in Protestant Ontario. Nobody in Red River had been aware of Scott's Orange connections, and he had certainly not been executed because of them. But soon all Ontario was up in arms about the dastardly deed done to a young innocent Orangeman for his loyalty to Canada.

The Manitoba Act and the Wolseley Expedition

By the time that Red River's three-man delegation arrived in Ontario, the entire province was inflamed against Riel and the provisional government. Canada refused to meet officially with the delegates, and negotiations were conducted privately. Ritchot was able to gain concessions from the Canadian government that implemented most of the "List of Rights," including the demand for provincial status that had been added by Riel. However, Ritchot was not able to gain agreement for clause 19 which demanded that the federal government assume all debts contracted by the provisional government, and grant an amnesty to members of that government. The Canadians insisted that an amnesty was a question for the Imperial government, but Ritchot argued that negotiations were useless without immediate agreement. The Canadians said they would settle the matter, and Ritchot replied, "pourvu que l'affaire soit regleé, c'est tout ce qu'il nous faut." Ritchot would spend the remainder of his stay in Ottawa attempting, without success, to get some written assurance of this understanding. He was constantly put off with oral assurances, and legal explanations of why nothing could be put in writing.

At what the Canadian government always regarded as the point of a gun, the Manitoba Act was quickly passed. It granted provincial status to Manitoba (a name favoured by Riel), a province of only 1,000 square miles, with 1,400,000 acres set aside for the Francophone mixed-bloods and bilingual services guaranteed. The Scott execution provided the Canadian government with an excuse to deny Riel and his lieutenants an amnesty, although the Red River delegation always insisted that such an amnesty had been promised as part of the unofficial settlement. But there was nothing in writing. On 3 May, the Red River delegates had an important interview with Governor-General Sir John Young, and British envoy Sir Clinton Murdoch. These two worthies were charged, on behalf of the British government, with ensuring that the wishes of the people of

Trials and Tribulations

Red River were accommodated by the Canadian government. The British had agreed to commit troops to Red River only on condition that the local inhabitants were satisfied with the transfer.

According to Father Ritchot's testimony before a parliamentary commission in 1874, the governor-general had emphasized that if a satisfactory agreement could not be reached with the Canadians, "I am ready to hear you and Sir Clinton Murdoch has to do you justice." The delegates said they had consented to the Manitoba Act, but were not satisfied with the amnesty issue because they had no written guarantees. Ritchot further testified that the governor-general pointed to Murdoch and said, "He knows it is the intention of Her Majesty to declare a general amnesty in order to establish peace in the country. Besides you have seen my proclamation, are you familiar with it?" Ritchot responded that the proclamation only promised an amnesty and what he wanted was the "promulation of the actual amnesty promises." Murdoch answered, "You have nothing to fear, Her Majesty wishes but one thing, and that is to pass the sponge over all that has happened in the North-West and establish peace." Ritchot said he would still like something in writing, and Murdoch responded, "When you are treating with men such as those in whose presence you are today there is no necessity for written guarantees." He said in French, "tant mettre les points sur les i," adding, "you must leave us a certain latitude and you will gain by it." Ritchot responded, "since there is nothing to fear I trust to your words." In their testimony in 1874, neither Sir John Young nor Sir Clifford Murdoch, could remember making such statements, and Sir Clifford Murdoch could not even remember having met with the Red River delegates.

While it is tempting to say that Father Ritchot should have held out for a written commitment, he felt very much under the gun, fearing either an Anglo-Canadian invasion of Red River, or the withdrawal of the deal he had negotiated, or both. As a result of Ritchot's acceptance of British promises, later reneged upon, Louis Riel would be forced into long-term exile instead of becoming premier of the province he had created.* Whether the government would keep faith over its land guarantees to the Francophone mixed-bloods was another matter. The prospects were not good, for despite the passage of the Manitoba Act, the Canadian Government insisted on sending a military expedition to Red River, led by Colonel Garnet Wolseley.

---

*The Francophone mixed-blood leaders, including Riel, were finally granted amnesty in 1875. Riel's was conditional on his being banished form the country for five years as was Ambroise Lépine's. Lépine was also stripped of his civil rights. he decided to serve his sentence for the murder of Riel instead.

J. M. Bumsted

At Fort Garry, Louis Riel was waiting to hand over the government to Canada, but Wolseley insisted on having his force enter the settlement, in late August 1870, as a conquering army, and treating the members of the provisional government as rebels and murderers. Riel, and several his associates, fled the wrath of the expedition. "Personally," recorded Colonel Wolseley, "I was glad that Riel did not come out and surrender, as he at one time said he would, for I could not then have hanged him as I might have done had I taken him prisoner when in arms against his sovereign." Troops dragged some rifles from the fort and fired a royal salute of 21 guns as the Union Jack was run up the flagpole. Only a small gathering spectators gave three cheers for the Queen.

What followed was anticlimactic. Somewhat to his surprise, Wolseley found the main function of his troops was protecting the rebels from violent vengeance carried out by some of the locals and some of the arriving Canadian volunteers. One of the volunteers brought with him a warrant for the formation of Loyal Orange Lodge 1307, which was organized on 18 September 1870, and by February 1871, claimed a membership of 110 "good men and true," opposed to Catholic "bigotry" in "this priest-ridden country." In September 1870, Adams Archibald was formally installed as lieutenant-governor of Manitoba. Whether it was a fully autonomous province, or one occupied by the Canadian military was open to debate, as was the question of whether the Francophone mixed-bloods were to be fairly treated by the Canadian government.

For better or worse, the Red River Settlement was now officially a province within Canada. Ironically enough, the appropriate date for marking the official founding of Manitoba remains problematic. The Manitoba Act became law on 12 May 1870, but the territory of the new province had not yet been transferred from the Hudson's Bay Company to the British government to the Canadian government. The actual transfer occurred on 23 June, and the Manitoba Act was proclaimed in Ottawa on 15 July 1870. However, there was no officer of either the British or the Canadian government in the new province to exercise any authority under the proclamation. By default, the effective government in Manitoba on 15 July was the provisional government headed by Louis Riel.

Acceptance of this date as official would necessarily imply a recognition of the provisional government, which would have been unthinkable at the time. Wolseley's expedition did not actually arrive in the province until 20 August, and possession of Upper Fort Garry was not taken until 24 August. At that point Wolseley could well have

Trials and Tribulations

assumed authority, but instead he asked Donald A. Smith to govern in the name of the old Council of Assiniboia (thus presuming that Manitoba had not yet come into existence) until the new lieutenant-governor was sworn into office on 2 September 1870. Selection of any of these potential dates makes its own political statement. History, especially when recording the origins of a place like Manitoba, is almost never a simple and straightforward matter.

Select Bibliography

What follows does not pretend to be a full bibliography of material on Red River, but it does represent the material the author found of most value in preparing this work.

Primary Manuscript:

Douglas Library, Queen's University, Kingston, Ont.:
    Charles Mair Papers
    Alexander Morris Papers

Hudson Bay Company Archives, Winnipeg:
    Hargrave Papers
    William McTavish Correspondence
    Red River Miscellaneous Papers 1813-90
    Red River Rebellion, Miscellaneous Papers 1869-1879

Minnesota Historical Society:
    Alexander Ramsey Papers
    James Wickes Taylor Papers
    Robert Dickson Papers, (microfilm Provincial Archives of Manitoba, hereafter PAM.)

National Archives of Canada, Ottawa:
    Alexander Begg, Red River Journal
    Andrew Bulger Papers
    Campbell Papers
    William Cowan Diaries, 1852-71
    Simon J. Dawson Papers
    George Taylor Denison 3rd Papers
    Department of Justice Papers
    Hargrave Family Papers
    John A. Macdonald Papers
    William McDougall Papers
    Alexander Morris Papers
    Stephen Papers
    Charles Tupper Papers
    Garnet Wolseley Family Letters

National Archives, Washington:
    Consular Dispatches, Winnipeg
    Department of State, Red River Affairs

Public Archives of Manitoba, Winnipeg:

Trials and Tribulations

    Sergeant George Adshead Diary, 1871
    Adams G. Archibald Papers, 1870-73
    Charles Napier Bell Diary, 1870-1
    Charles Boulton Family Papers
    Court of Quarterly Sessions Records
    Council of Assiniboia Papers
    Famine Relief Committee Papers
    Kenneth McKenzie Diary
    P.G. Laurie, "Unpublished Narrative of events of 1869-70"
    Manitoba Provisional Government Papers
    George McVicar Papers
    Alexander Morris Lieutenant-governor's Papers
    James Ross Papers
    John Schultz Papers
    James Wickes Taylor Papers
    George B. Winship, "Account of Events at Red River 1869-1870"

Public Archives of Saskatchewan, Saskatoon:
    Four papers on Red River Rebellion by George Holmes Young
    Reminiscences of William Laurie
    Taché Papers

University of British Columbia Library, Vancouver, B.C.:
    John Stoughton Dennis letter transcription 27 October 1869
    William McDougall Papers

Winnipeg Public Library:
    Crofton, J. F., "Winnipeg in 1846: Copy of the
    Diary of the late Colonel J. F. Crofton."

Primary: Printed:

Anderson, David, *The Net in the Bay* (London, 1854)

Anderson, David, *Notes on the Flood at the Red River* (London, 1852).

Ballantyne, R. M., *Hudson's Bay* (Edinburgh, 1848)

Begg, Alexander, *The Creation of Manitoba* (Toronto, 1871).

Begg, Alexander and Walter Nursey, *Ten Years in Winnipeg* (Winnipeg, 1879).

Belcourt, George, "Autobiography of Father Belcourt," *Minn Hist Soc Coll*,

Boulton, Charles, *Reminiscences of the NW Rebellions* (Toronto, 1886)

Butler, W. F., *The Great Lone Land* (London, 1872).

Canada Legislative Assembly, *Report for the Exploration of the Country between Lake Superior and the Red River Settlement* (London, 1859).

Charette, Guillaume, ed., Ellenwood, Ray, trans. *Vanishing Spaces: Memoirs of Louis Goulet* (Winnipeg, 1976).

Corbett, G. W., *Notes on Rupert's America: its history and resources* (Dulwich,1868)

Cowley, A. T., "Lower Fort Garry in 1868," *The Beaver*, Sept. 1934, 39-41.

Dawson, G. T., *Report on the Exploration of the Country between Lake Superior and the RR Settlement* (Toronto, 1859).

Denison, *Reminiscences of the Red River Rebellion of 1869* (Toronto, 1873).

F., W., ed., "Selections from the Unpublished Recollections of Mrs. W. C. Pinkham, an Early Manitoban," *Manitoba Pageant*, winter 1974, 21-23, spring 1974, 19-22, autumn 1976, 11-17.

Franchère, Gabriel, *Adventure at Astoria*, 1810-1814 (Norman, Okla., 1967).

Garrioch, A.C., *First Furrows* (Winnipeg, 1923).

Garry, Francis, ed., , "Diary of Nicholas Garry," Trans. RSC, 2nd ser,. vii, sec 2 (1900), 73-204.

Glazebrook, G.P. de T., ed. *The Hargrave Correspondence*, 1821-43 (Toronto, 1947).

Great Britain, Colonial Office, *Papers relative to the Red River Settlement* (London, 1857)

____*Papers relative to the Hudson's Bay Company Charter* (London, 1859)

Great Britain, Parliament, House of Commons, *Report from Select Committee on HBC* (London, 1857)

Gunn, Donald, *History of Manitoba* (Ottawa, 1880)

Halkett, John *Statement respecting the Earl of Selkirk's settlement of Kildonan* (London, 1817).

Hind, Henry Youle, *Narrative of the Canadian RR Expedition of 1857*, 2 vol. (Toronto, 1860)

Hind, Henry Youle, "Red River Settlement and the Half-Breed Buffalo Hunters," *The Canadian Merchants' Magazine*, 3 (1858).

Hudson's Bay Company, *Charters, Statutes, Orders in Council & Relating to the HBC* (London, 1931).

Huyshe, G. L., *The Red River Expedition* (London, 1871).

Jacobs, Peter, *Journal of the Rev. Peter Jacobs* (Toronto, 1853)

Kane, Paul, *Wanderings of an Artist* (London, 1859)

Keating, William H., *Narrative of an Expedition to the Source of St. Peter's River* (Philadelphia,1825)

Paul Knapland, ed., "Gladstone on the Red River Rebellion, 1870," MVHR, 21 (1934), 76-7

Trials and Tribulations

MacBeth, R. G., *The Selkirk Settlers in Real Life* (Toronto, 1897)

M'Donnell, Alexander, *Narrative of Transactions in the Red River Country. . . till 1816* (London, 1819)

MacLeod, Margaret Arnett, *Letters of Letitia Hargrave* (Toronto, 1947).

McLean, John, *Notes of 25 Years' Service in the Hudson's Bay Territory*, 2 vol. (London, 1849).

Merk, Frederick, ed., *Fur Trade and Empire* (by George Simpson) (Cambridge, Mass., 1931)

Morton, W. L., ed., *Alexander Begg's Red River Journal* (Toronto, 1956)

Morton, W. L., intro, *Colvile Letter-Book* (Toronto, 1956)

Nute, Grace, ed., *Documents Relating to the Northwest Missions*, 1815-27 (St. Paul, 1942)

Oliver, E.H., ed., *The Canadian North West: Its Early Development and Legislative Records* (Ottawa, 1915)

Rich, E.E., ed., *Colin Robertson's Correspondence Book* (Toronto, 1939)

Ryerson, John, *Hudson's Bay* (Toronto, 1855)

Shrive, Norman, ed., "Charles Mair: A Document on the Red River Rebellion," CHR, 40 (1959), 218-26.

Simpson, Alexander, *The Life and Travels of Thomas Simpson, the Arctic Discoverer* (London, 1845)

Simpson, Thomas, *Narrative of the Discoveries of the North Coast of America* (Toronto, 1843)

Spry, Irene, ed., "The Memoiries of George William Sanderson," *Canadian Ethnic Studies*. 17 (1985), 115-34.

Stanley, George, ed., *Collected Writings of Louis Riel* (Edmonton, 1985).

Taché, A.A., *Sketch of the North-West of America* (translated by Captain D.R. Cameron) (Montreal, 1870).

Taché, A.A., *Vingt années de missions dans le nord-ouest de l'Amérique* (new ed., Montreal, 1888).

Taylor, W.H., "William H. Taylor's Journal, Assiniboia, 1851," *Journal of Canadian Church Historicalt Society.*, xii (1970), 24-36.

Tremaudan, A.H., "Louis Riel's Account of the Capture of Fort Garry, 1870," CHR, 5:2 (1924), 146-159.

Tucker, S., *The Rainbow in the North* (London, 1851)

U.S. Congress Senate, "Pembina Settlement," Exec. Doc 42, 31st Congress, 1st Session.

West, John, *The Substance of a Journal during a Residence at a Red River Colony* (London, 1824)

Secondary: Books:

Bayley, Denis, *A Londoner in Rupert's Land* (Winnipeg, 1969).

Begg. Alexander, *Seventeen Years in the Canadian North-West* (Toronto, 1884)

Bell, Charles N., *The Selkirk Settlement and the Settlers* (Winnipeg, 1887)

Benoit, Dom, *Vie de Mgr. Taché*, 2 vol. (Montreal, 1904)

Boon, T.C.B., *The Anglican Church from the Bay to the Rockies* (Toronto, 1962)

Brown, Jennifer, *Strangers in Blood* (Vancouver, 1980)

Bumsted, J. M., *Dictionary of Manitoba Biography* (Winnipeg, 1999).

Bumsted, J.M., *Floods of the Centuries: A History of Flood Disasters in the Red River Valley 1776-1997* (Winnipeg, 1997).

Bumsted, J.M., *Fur Trade Wars: The Founding of Western Canada* (Winnipeg, 1999).

Bumsted, J. M., *Louis Riel v. Canada: The Making of a Rebel* (Winnipeg, 2001).

Bumsted, J. M., *The Red River Rebellion of 1869-70* (Winnipeg, 1994).

Bumsted, J. M., *Thomas Scott's Body and Other Essays on Early Manitoba History* (Winnipeg, 2000).

Burley, Edith I., *Servants of the Honourable Company: Work, Discipline, and Conflict in the Hudson's Bay Company, 1770-1870* (Toronto, 1997).

Burrows, C. Acton, *The Canadian Pacific Railway Telegraph* (Winnipeg, 1880).

Bryce, George, *Manitoba: Its Infancy, Growth and Present Condition* (London, 1882)

Bryce, George, *The Romantic Settlement of Lord Selkirk's Colonists* (Winnipeg, 1909).

Champagne, Joseph Etienne, *Les Missions Catholiques dans L'Ouest Canadien 1818-75* (Ottawa, 1949).

Collins, Robert, *A Voice from Afar: The History of Telecommunications in Canada* (Toronto, 1977).

Cooper, Barry, *Alexander Kennedy Isbister: A Respectable Critic of the Honourable Company* (Ottawa, 1988)

Coutts, Robert and Richard Stuart, eds., *The Forks and the Battle of Seven Oaks in Manitoba History* (Winnipeg, 1994).

Cowie, Isaac, *The Company of Adventurers* (Toronto, 1913)

Cyr, J-E, *MonseigneurJoseph-Norbert Provencher; quelques considérations sur sa view et son temps* (St. Boniface, 1919).

David, L.O., *Msgr. Alexandre Antonin Taché, Archeveche de Saint-Boniface* (Montreal, 1883).

Douglas, William, *Free Masonry in Manitoba, 1864-1925* (Winnipeg, 1925).

Trials and Tribulations

Dugas, Georges, *Etablissement des Souers de Charité a la Riviere Rouge* (n.p., 1900?)

Dugas, Georges, *Monseigneur Provencher et Les Missions de la Riviere Rouge* (Montreal, 1889)

Ens, Gerhard, *Homeland to Hinterland: The Changing Worlds of the Red River Metis in the Nineteenth Century* (Toronto, 1996).

Ferguson, Barry, ed., *The Anglican Church and the World of Western Canada, 1820-1970* (Regina, 1991).

Findlay, G.G. and W.W. Holdsworth, *The History of the Wesleyan Methodist Missionary Society*, 5 vol. (Toronto, 1921).

Foster, John, ed., *The Developing West: Essays on Canadian History in Honor of LH Thomas* (Edmonton, 1983).

Francis, R. Douglas, *Images of the West: Changing Perceptions of the Prairies 1690-1960* (Saskatoon, 1989).

Fremont, D., *Provencher et sons temps* (Winnipeg, 1935)

Fremont, D., *Les Secretaries de Riel* (Prince Albert, 1953)

Friesen, G., *The Canadian Prairies: A History* (Toronto, 1984)

Galbraith, John S., *The Hudson's Bay Company as an Imperial Factor 1821-69* (Toronto, 1957)

Galbraith, John S., *The Little Emperor: Governor Simpson of the HBC* (Toronto, 1976)

Gibson, Dale and Lee, *Substantial Justice: Law and Lawyers in Manitoba, 1670-1970* (Winnipeg, 1970).

Giraud, Marcel, *The Metis in the Canadian West*, 2 vol. ((Edmonton, 1986)

Gluek, Alvin C., *Minnesota and the Manifest Destiny of the Canadian North-West* (Toronto, 1965)

Goldring, Philip, "Papers on the Labour System of the Hudson's Bay Company, 1821-1900: volume i and ii," *Manuscript Report Number 362, 412* (Ottawa, 1977).

Gosman, Robert, "The Riel and Lagimodiere Families in Metis Society, 1840-60," *Manuscript Report Series 171* (Ottawa, 1977).

Healy, William, *Women of Red River* (Winnipeg, 1923)

Heeney, William Bertal, *John West and His Red River Mission* (Toronto, 1920).

Heeney, W.B., ed., *Leaders of the Canadian Church*, 3rd ser., (Toronto, 1943)

Hill, Robert B., *Manitoba: History of its Early Settlement, Development and Resources* (Toronto, 1890

Howard, Joseph Kinsey, *Strange Empire* (New York, 1952)

Innis, Harold, *The Fur Trade in Canada: An Introduction to Canadian Economic History* (rev. ed., Toronto, 1956).

Kavanagh, Martin, *The Assiniboine Basin* (Winnipeg, 1946)

Knaplund, Paul, *Gladstone and Britain's Imperial Policy* (London, 1927, 1966).

Lent, Geneva D., *West of the Mountains: James Sinclair and the HBC* (Seattle, 1963)

Lord Selkirk Association of Rupert's Land, *The Selkirk Settlers of Red River and their Descendants 1812-1992* (no place, no publisher, 1992).

Lytwyn, Victor P., *The Fur Trade of the Little North: Indians, Pedlars and Englishmen East of Lake Winnipeg, 1760-1821* (Winnipeg, 1986).

MacBeth, George, *The Selkirk Settlers in Real Life* (Toronto, 1897)

Machray, Robert, *Life or Robert Machray* (Toronto, 1909)

MacDonald, Wilma, *Guide to the Holdings of the Archives of the Ecclesiastical Province and Dioceses of Rupert's Land* (Winnipeg, 1986).

MacKay, Douglas, *The Honourable Company* (London, 1937).

McDougall, John, *In The Days of the Red River Rebellion* (Toronto, 1903).

MacEwan, Grant, *Cornerstone Colony: Selkirk's Contribution to the Canadian West* (Saskatoon, 1977).

MacLean, John, *Henry Steinhauer* (n.d.)

MacLean, John, *James Evans, Inventor of the Syllabic System of the Cree Language* (Montreal, 1890)

MacLeod, M.A. and W.L. Morton, *Cuthbert Grant of Grantown* (Toronto, 1963).

Martin, Archer, *The HBC Land Tenures* (London, 1898)

Martin, Chester, *Lord Selkirk's Work in Canada* (Toronto, 1916)

Morice, A. G. *Histoire de l'Eglise Catholique dans l'Ouest Canadien, 4 vol.* (Winnipeg, 1921-3)

Morton, A.S., *A History of the Canadian West to 1870-1* (London, 1939)

Morton, A.S., Sir George Simpson: Overseas Governor of the Hudson's Bay Company: A Pen Picture of a Man of Action (Toronto and Vancouver, 1944)

Murray, Stanley Norman, *The Valley Comes of Age: A History of Agriculture in the Valley of the Red River of the North, 1812-1920* (Fargo, 1967).

Newman, Peter C., *A Company of Adventurers; Caesars in the Wilderness* (Markham, Ont., 1985).

Noel, Janet, *Canada Dry: Temperance Crusades before Confederation* (Toronto, 1995).

Pannekoek, Frits, *A Snug Little Flock: The Social Origins of the Riel Resistance of 1869-70* (Winnipeg, 1991).

Peel, Bruce, *Early Printing in the Red River Settlement 1859-1870* (Winnipeg, 1974).

Trials and Tribulations

Peterson, J. and J. Brown, eds., *The New Peoples: Being and Becoming Metis in North America* (Winnipeg, 1985)

Pritchett, John Perry, *The Red River Valley 1811-49* (NY, 1942)

Ray, Arthur, *Indians in the Fur Trade* (Toronto, 1974)

Reardon, James Michael, *George Anthony Belcourt, Pioneer Catholic Missionary of the Northwest, 1803-1874* (St. Paul, 1955)

Reid, W. Stanford, ed., *The Scottish Tradition in Canada* (Toronto, 1976).

Rich, E.E., *The Fur trade and the North-West to 1857* (Toronto, 1960)

Rich, E.E., *The Hudsons Bay Company 1670-1870, 3 vol.* (Toronto, 1960)

Roe, R.G., *The North American Buffalo* (Toronto, 1951)

Rundle, Edwin, *A Soldier's Life* (Toronto, 1909).

Schofield, F. H., *The Story of Manitoba* (Winnipeg, 1913)

Shrive, Norman, *Charles Mair: Literary Nationalist* (Toronto, 1965)

Sprague, D.N. and R.P. Frye, eds., *The Genealogy of the First Metis Nation* (Winnipeg, 1983).

Spry, Irene M., *The Palliser Expedition* (Toronto, 1963).

Stanley, G. F.G., *Louis Riel; The Birth of Western Canada* (London, 1936).

Stanley, G.F.G., *Louis Riel* (Toronto, 1985).

Stanley, G.F.G., *Toil and Trouble: Military Expeditions to Red River* (Toronto, 1989).

Stubbs, Roy St. G., *Four Recorders of Rupert's Land* (Winnipeg, 1967)

Szasz, Ferenc Morton, *Scots in the North American West, 1790-1917* (Norman, Okla., 2000).

Thomas, LH., ed., *Essays on Western History* (Edmonton, 1976).

Tremaudan, August-Henri, *Histoire de la Nation Metisse* (St. Boniface, 1936)

Van Kirk, Sylvia, *Many Tender Ties* (Winnipeg, 1980).

Williams, Glyndwr, The Hudson's Bay Company and the Fur Trade, 1670-1870, *The Beaver*, autumn 1983.

Wright, Richard Thomas, *Overlanders* (Saskatoon, 1985).

Secondary: Articles:

Anon, "The Company in London," *The Beaver*, Sept. 1935.

Artibise, Alan, "The Crucial Decade: Red River at the Outbreak of the American Civil War," *Transactions Historical and Scientific Society of Manitoba* [hereafter HSSM], 3rd ser., 23 (1966-7), 57-66   Ball, Tim, "Company Town" [Stromness in the Orkney Islands], The Beaver, 68:3 (May 1988), 43-52.

J. M. Bumsted

Barclay, Robert George, "Grey Nuns' Voyage to Red River 1844," *The Beaver*, outfit 297 (winter 1966), 15-23.

Barkwell, Laurence, "Early Law and Social Control among the Metis," in Samuel Corrigan and Laurence J. Barkwell, eds., *The Struggle for Recognition: Canadian Justice and the Metis Nation* 1991), 7-38.

Barron, F. L., "Victimizing His Lordship: Lord Selkirk and the Upper Canadian Courts," *Manitoba History* (spring 1984), 14-22.

Beresford, H. E., "Early surveys in Manitoba," *Transactions HSSM*, ser 3:9 (1954), 6-15.

Bieder, Robert E., "Scientific Attitudes toward Indian Mixed-Bloods in Early 19th century America," *Journal of Ethnic Studies*, 8 (1980), 17-30.

Bill, Fred, "Early Steamboating on the Red River," North Dakota Historical Quarterly, 9:2 (1942), 77.

Bindon, Kathryn M., "Hudson's Bay Company Law: Adam Thom and the Institution of Order in Rupert's Land 1839-54," in David Flaherty, ed., *Essays in the History of Canadian Law* (1981).

Blair, Danny and W.F. Rannie, "'Wading to Pembina': 1849 Spring and Summer weather in the Valley of the Red River of the North and Some Climatic Implications," *Great Plains Research 4* (February 1994), 3-26.

Boon, TCB, The Archdeacon and the Governor: William Cockran and George Simpson at the Red river colony, 1825-65," *Beaver*, outfit 298 (spring 1968), 41-49.

Boon, TCB, "St. Peter's Dynevor: The Original Indian Settlement of Western Canada," *Transactions HSSM*, 3 9 (1954), 16-32.

Bowsfield, Hartwell, "The United States and Red River Settlement," *Transactions HSSM* , 3rd ser., no 23 (1966-7), 33-55.

Bredin, Thomas, "The Red River Academy," *The Beaver*, winter 1974.

Bredin, Thomas, "The Reverend David Jones: Missionary at Red River 1823-38," *The Beaver*, outfit 312:2 (autumn 1981), 47-52.

Brown, Jennifer, "Changing Views of Fur Trade Marriage and Domesicity: James Hargrave, His Colleagues, and "the Sex", Western Canadian *Journal of Anthropology*, 6:3 (1976), 92-105.

Brown, Jennifer, "A Colony of Very Useful Hands," *The Beaver*, spring 1977, 39-45.

Brown, Jennifer, "Ultimate Respectability: Fur Trade Children in the Civilized World," *The Beaver*, winter 19777, 4-10 and spring 1978, 48-55.

Brown, Jennifer, "Linguistic Solitudes in the Fur Trade; Some Changing Social Categories and their Implications," in Carol Judd and Arthur Ray, eds., *Old Trails and New Directions* (1980)

Brown, Jennifer, "A Demographic Transition in the Fur trade Country: Family Sizes and Fertility of Company Officers and Country Wives 1750-1850," *Western Canadian Journal. of Anthropology,,* vi:1 (1976), 61-71.

Brown, Jennifer, :People of Myth, People of History: A Look at Recent Writing on the Metis," *Acadiensis*, 17:1 (1987), 150-162.

Brown, Jennifer, "Children of the Early Fur trades," in Joy Parr., ed., *Childhood and Family* (1982)

Brown, Jennifer, ":Woman as Centre and Symbol in the Emergence of Metis Communities," *Canadian Journal of Native Studies*, 3:1 (1983), 39-46.

Bryce, Marion, "Early Red River Culture," *Transactions HSSM*, no. 57 (1901).

Bourgeault, R., "The Indian, the Métis and the Fur Trade," *Studies in Political. Economy*, 12, 45-80.

Buck, Ruth M., "Keeping in Touch: Pioneer Mail Services Ended the North-West's Long Isolation," *The Beaver*, 66:5 (Oct/Nov 1986), 4-10.

Burley, David V. and Gayel A. Horsfall, "Vernacular Housea and Farmsteads of the Canadian Metis," *Journal of Cultural Geography*, 10:1 (1989), 19-33.

Campbell, John V., "The Sinclair Party – An Emigration Overland along the old HBC route from Manitoba to the Spokane Country in 1854," *Washington Historical Quarterly.*, 8 (1916), 187-201.

Carriere, Gaston, "Les Missions Catholiques dans l'est du Canada et l'honorable Compagnie de la Baie d'Hudson, 1844-1900," *Revue d'l'Université Ottawa*, 36 (1966), 15-39, 232-57.

Campbell, Robert, "A Journey to Kentucky for Sheep," *North Dakota Historical.Quarterly*, I (1926-7), 35-45.

Carrière, Gaston, "L'Honorable Compagnie de la Baie d'Hudson et les missions des Oblats 1844-61," *Revue d'lUniversité Ottawa*, 25 (1955), 33-364.

Carrière, Gaston, "Mgr Provencher à la recherece d'un coadjuteur," *Canadian Catholic Historical Association Study Sessions*, 37 (1970), 71-93.

Champagne, J. E., "Les Methodes Missionaries des Oblats dans l'Ouest Canadien (1845-75), *Etudes Oblats*, v (3), 506-23.

Chaput, Donald, "The 'Misses Nolin' of Red River," *The Beaver*, winter 1975.

Clarke, W. L., "The Place of the Metis within the Agricultural Economy of Red River during the 1840s and 1850s," *Canadian Journal of Native Studies*, III:1 (1983), 69-84.

Clouston, J. S., "Orkney and the HBC," *The Beaver*, 1936/7.

Coutts, Robert, "The Role of Agriculture in an English Speaking Halfbreed Economy: The case of ST. Andrew's Red River," *Native Studies Review*, nos 1-2 (1988), 67-94.

Coutts, Robert, "Anglican Missionaries as Agents of Acculturation: The Church Missionary Society at St. Andrew's, Red River, 1830-1870," in Ferguson, ed., *Anglican Church*, 50-60.

Cowan, Anna M. "Memories of Upper Fort Garry," *The Beaver*, Sept. 1935.

Craig, Irene, "Grease Paint on the Prairies," *Papers HSSM*, III, no. 3 (1947), 38-53.

Dafoe, J. W., "Early Winnipeg Newspapers," *Papers HSSM*, III, no. 3 (1947), 14-24.

de Moissac, Elisabeth, "Les Soeurs Grises et les evenements de 1869-70," *La Societé Canadienne d'Histoire de l'Eglise Catholique*, 37 (1970), 215-228.

den Otter, A.A., "An Environmental Perspective on the 1849 Sayer Trial," unpublished paper presented at 1849 Conference in Edinburgh, May 1999.

Dick, Lyle, "The Seven Oaks Incident and the Consturction of a Historical Tradition , 1816-1970," in *Journal of Canadian Historical Association*, new ser., 2 1991), 91-113.

Dick, Lyle, "Historical Writing on Seven Oaks: The assertion of Anglo-Canadian Cultural Dominance in the West," in Coutts and Stuart, eds., *The Forks*, 65-71.

Dickason, Olive, "From 'One Nation' in the Northeast to 'New Nation' in the Northwest: A Look at the emergence of the Métis," in Peterson/Brown,eds., *The New Peoples*, 15-36.

Dorge, Lionel, "Bishop Tache and the Confederation of Manitoba," *Papers HSSM*, 3rd ser., 26 (1944-5), 83-89.

Dorge, Lionel, "The Metis and Canadien Councillors of Assiniboia," *Beaver* 305 (1974), 1 (12-19, 2 (39-45) 3 (51-8).

Ens, Gerhard, "Dispossession or Adaptation? Migratio and Persistence of the Red River Metis," *Canadian Historical Association Hist Papers*, 1988.

Ens, Gerhard, "Metis Agriculture during the transition from peasant society to industrial capitalism: The Example of St. Francois Xavier, 1835-70," in R.C. Macleod, ed., *Swords into Ploughshares* (1992).

Flanagan, Thomas, "Louis Riel and the Dispersion of the American Metis," *Minnesota. History* (spring 1985), 179-190.

Flanagan, Thomas, "The Métis and Aboriginal Rights," in Menno Boldt et al., eds., *Aboriginal Rights in Canada* (Toronto, UTP, 1985), 230-45.

Flanagan, Thomas, "From Indian Title to Aboriginal Rights," in Louis Knafla, ed., *Law and Justice in a New Land: Essays in Western Canadian Legal History* (Toronto, 1986), 81-100.

Foster, John E., "Program for the Red River Mission: The Anglican Clergy 1820-1826," *Social History*, 4 (Nov. 1969), 49-75.

Trials and Tribulations

Foster, John, "Wintering, the Outsider Male and Ethnogenesis of the Western Plains Metis," *Prairie Forum* 19 (1994), 1-13.

Foster, John, "Missionaries, Mixed-Bloods and the Fur Trade: Four Letters of the Rev. William Cockran, Red River Settlement, 1830-33," *Western Canadian Journal of Anthropology.*, 3:1 (1972), 94-125.

Foster, John, "Rupert's Land and Red River Settlement, 1820-70," in Thomas, ed., *The Prairie West to 1905: A Source Book* (1975).

Foster, John, "The Metis: the People and the Term," *Prairie Forum*, 3:1 (1978)

Foster, John, "The Origins of the Mixed Bloods in the Canadian West," in Thomas, ed., *Essays in Western History* (1976).

Foster, John, "Some questions and perspectives on the problems of metis roots," in Peterson/Brown, eds. *The New Peoples.*

Foster, John, "The Plains Metis," in R. Bruce Morrison and C. Roderick Wilson, eds., *Native Peoples: The Canadian Experience* (1986).

Foster, John, "Paulet Paul: Metis or "House Indian" Folk Hero," *Manitoba History*, 9 (spring 1985), 2-7.

Francis, R. Douglas, "From Wasteland to Utopia: Changing Images of the Canadian West in the 19th Century," *Great Plains Quarterly*,7:3 (summer 1987), 178-194.

Gallagher, Brian, "A re-examination of Race, Class and Society in Red River," *Native Studies Review*, 4 1-2 (1988), 25-66.

Getty, Ian A.L., "The Failure of the Native Church Policy of the CMS in the Northwest," *Canadian Plains Studies*, 2 (1974).

Gibbons, Lillian, "Early Red River Homes," *Trans HSSM*, ser 3, no. 2 (1945/6), 26-42.

Gibson, Dale, "A Scandal at Red River," *The Beaver*, 70:5 (Oct/Nov 1990), 30-38.

Glover, Richard, "York Boats," *The Beaver*, March, 1949, 19-23.

Gluek, A. G., Jr., "The Riel Rebellion and Canadian-American Relations," *Canadian Historical Review*, 36 (1955),

Gluek, A.G., Jr., ""Imperial Protection for the Trading Interests of the HBC, 1857-1861," *Canadian Historical Review*, 37 (1956), 119-40.

Gluek, A.G., Jr., "The Sioux Uprising: A Problem in International Relations," *Minnesota History*, 34 (winter 1955), 317-24.

Goldring, Philip, "Governor Simpson's Officers: Elite Recruitment in a British Overseas Enterprise, 1834-1870," *Prairie Forum*, x (1985), 252-81.

Goldring, Philip, "Religion, Missions and Native Culture," *Journal of the Canadian Church Historical Society*, 26 (1984), 43-49.

Goldring, Philip, "Labour Records of the Hudson's Bay Company, 1821-1870," *Archivaria*, 11 (1980-81), 53-86.

Goldring, Philip, "Lewis and the Hudson's Bay Company in the Nineteenth Century," Scottish Studies, 24 (1980), 23-42.

Greenwood, L. M., "The Chartrand Murder Trial," *Criminal Justice History* 125:59.

Gressley, G.M., "The Red River Settlement: Chaos and Emerging Order," *North Dakota History* 27 (1960), 153-66.

Gunn, H. G., "Fight for Free Trade in Rupert's Land," *Proceedings of Mississippi Valley Historical Association*, 4 (1910-11)

Havard, V., "The French Half-Breeds of the North West," *Annual Report of the Board of Regents of the Smithsonian Institution* (1879), 309-27.

Hunt, Frank, "Britain's One Utopia," *Trans HSSM*, 61 (1902).

Hussey, "'Unpretending' but not Indecent': Living Quarters at Mid-19th Century HBC Posts," *The Beaver*, spring 1975.

Jaenen, C. J., "Foundations of Dual Education at Red River, 1811-34," *Papers HSSM*, 3 ser., 21 (1964-5), 22-28.

Kaye, Barry, "Flour Milling at Red River: Wind, Water and Steam," *Manitoba History*, 2 (1983), 12-20.

Kaye, Barry, "The Trade in Livestock between the Red River Settlement and the American Frontier, 1812-70," *Prairie Forum* 6:2 (1981), 163-181.

Kaye, Barry, "The Settlers Grand Difficulty: Haying in the Economy of the RRS, " *Prairie Forum*, 9 no. 1 (1984), 1-20.

Kermoal, Nathalie, "Les Roles et les soufrrances de femmes metisses lors de la Resistance de 1870 et de la Rebellion de 1885," *Prairie Forum* 19:2 (1993), 153-68.

Kienetz, Alvin, "The Rise and Decline of Hybrid (metis) Societies on the Frontier of Western Canada and southern Africa," *Can J of Nat Stud*, 3:1 (1983), 3-21.

Ladd, George van der Goes, "Father Cochran and His Children; Poisonous Pedagogy on the Banks of the Red," *Ferguson,* ed., 61-72.

le Chevalier, Jules, "Demembrement de vicariat de la Riviere Rouge durant l'administration de Mgr. Tache," *Etudes Oblats,* 4 (1945), 67-136.

Listenfelt, Hattie, "The HBC and the RR Trade," *Collections of State Historical Society of North Dakota*, 4 (1913),235-337.

Lussier, A. S., "Msgr. Provencher and the Native People of the Red River, 1818-1853," *Prairie Forum*, 10 (spring 1985), 1-15.

MacBeth, John, "The Social Customs and Amusements in the Early Days in the Red River Settlement and Rupert's Land," *Trans HSSM*, 1 ser., no. 44 (1893).

MacBeth, R. G., "Farm Life in the Selkirk Society," *Trans HSSM*, no. 50 (1897).

Trials and Tribulations

MacKay, Douglas, and W. K. Lamb, "More Light on Thomas Simpson," *The Beaver*, 269 (1938), 26-31.

MacLeod, Margaret Arnett, "Cuthbert Grant of Grantown," *Canadian Historical Review*, 21 (1940), 25-39.

MacLeod, Margarett Arnett, "The Lamp Shines in the Red River," *The Beaver*, outfit 267 (1936), 41-5.

Manore, Jack, "Mr. Dawson's Road, *The Beaver*, 71:1 (Feb./March 1991), 6-11.

Martin, Chester, "The Hudosn's Bay Company's Monopoly of the Fur Trade at the Red River Settlement, 1821-1850," *Proceedings Mississippi Valley Historical Association*, vii (1913-14), 254-65.

Martin, Ged, "British Attitudes to Prairie Settlement," *Alberta Historical Review*, 22:1 (winter 1974), 1-11.

Marwick, Ernest, "Chief Factor James Sutherland and his Orkney Correspondence," *The Beaver*, outfit 297 (winter 1966), 44-51.

Matheson, S. P., "Floods at Red River," *Papers HSSM*, ser. III, no. 3 (1947), 5-13.

Mayes, Hubert G., "Young Taché," *The Beaver*, 66:4 (Aug/Sept 1986), 30-34.

Mitchell, Elaine, ed., "A Red River Gossip," *The Beaver* outfit 291 (sping 1961), 4-11.

Mitchell, Elaine, "Edward Watkin and the Buying-Out of the HBC," *Canadian Historical Review*. 34:3 1953.

Morton, A.S., "The Place of the Red River Settlement in the Plans of the Hudson's Bay Company 1812-25," *Canadian Historical Association Reports*, 1929, 103-9.

Morton, W. L., "Agriculture in the Red River Colony," *Canadian Historical Review*, 30 (1949), 304-21.

Morton, W. L., "Red River on the Eve of Change, 1857-9," *Beaver*, outfit 293 (1962), 45-51.

Morton, W. L., "The Battle of the Grand Coteau July 13 and 14, 1851," in D. Swainson, ed., *Historical Essahys on the Prairie Provinces* (Toronto, 1970).

Morton, W. L., "The Historiography of the Great West," *Canadian Historical Association Report*, 1970, 48-59.

Morton, W. L., "The Red River Parish: Its Place in the Development of Manitoba," in R.C. Lodge, ed., *Manitoba Essays* (1937).

Morton, W. L., "Two Young Men, 1869: Charles Mair and Louis Riel,: *Trans HSSM*, ser 3:3 (1973-4), 33-43.

Nicks, John, "Orkneymen in the HBC, 1780-1821," in Judd and Ray, 102-26.

Pannekoek, Frits, "Some Comments on the Social Origins of the Riel Protest of 1869-70," in A.S. Lussier, ed., *Riel Mini-Conference Papers Louis Riel and the Metis* (1979), 65-76.

Pannekoek, Frits, "The Historiography of the Red River Settlement, 1830-68," *Prairie Forum*, 6:1 (1981), 75-85.

Pannekoek, Frits, "The Anglican Church and the Disintegration of Red River Society, 1818-1870," in Berger/Cook, eds., *The West and the Nation* (1976), 72-90.

Pannekoek, Frits, "The Rev. Griffiths Owen Corbett and the Red River Civil War of 1869-70," *Canadian Historical Review*, 57:2 (1976), 133-50.

Pannekoek, Frits, "A probe into the demographic structure of Nineteenth century Red River," in Thomas, ed., *Essays in Western History* (1976), 83-97.

Pannekoek, Frits, "The Rev. James Evans and the Social Antagonisms of Fur Trade Society 1840-1846," in Richard Allen ed., *Religion and Society in the Prairie West* (1974).

Pannekoek, Frits, "Protestant Agricultural Zions for the Western Indian," *Journal of the Canadian Church Historical Society*, 14 (1972), 55-67.

Pannekoek, Frits, "'Insidious' Sources and the Historical Interpretation of the Pre-1870 West," in Ferguson, ed., *Anglican Church*, 29-37.

Pannekoek, Frits, "The Flock Divided: Factions and Feuds at Red River," *The Beaver*, 70:6 (Dec.1990/Jan. 1991), 29-37.

Peake, Frank, "David Anderson, the First Lord Bishop of Rupert's Land," *Journal of Canadian Church Historical Society*, 24 (1982), 3-43.

Peake, Frank, "John Smithurst and the Ordination Controversy: Reflection on Red River Society in the 1840's," Ferguson, ed., 71-82.

Peake, Frank, "The Achievements and Frustrations of James Hunter," *Journal of the Canadian Church Historical Society*, 19 (1977).

Peers, Laura, "The Ojibwa, Red River, and The Forks, 1770-1870," in Coutts and Stuart, eds., 3-17.

Piers, Sir Charles, "Fire-Arms of the Hudson's Bay Company," *The Beaver*, March, 1934.

Pritchett, John Perry, "Some Red River Fur-trade Activities," *Minnesota Historical Bulletin*, 5:6 (may 1924), 401-23.

Ray, Arthur, "Smallpox: The Epidemic of 1837-8," *The Beaver*, autumn 1975.

Ray, Arthur, "Diffusion of Diseases in the Western interior of Canada, 1830-1850," *The Geographical Review*, 66: 2 (April 1976).

Rannie, W. F., "'Awful Splendour': Historical Accounts of Prairie Fire in Southern Manitoba Prior to 1870," *Prairie Forum*, 26/1 (spring 2002), 17-46.

Ready, W.B., "Early RR Schools," *Beaver* 278 (1947), 34-7.

Roe, F. G., "The Red River Hunt," *Transactions Royal Society of Canada*, sec 2 (1935), 171-218.

Roy, David, "Mgr Provencher et son clergé sèculiar," *Canadian Catholic Historical Society Study Sessions*, 37, 1-16.

St. Onge, Nicole, "Variations in Red River: The Traders and Freemen Metis of Saint-Laurent, Manitoba," *Can Eth. Stud.*, 24:2 (1992), 2-21.

Saw, Reginald, "Sir John H. Pelly, Bart," *British Columbia Historical Quarterly*, 13 (1949), 23-32.

Simonson, Gayle, "The Prayer Man: Ojibwa Henry Bird Steinhauer brought Religion to the Cree," *The Beaver*, 68:5 (oct.-nob. 1988), 28-33.

Sprague, Douglas and Ronald Frye, "Manitoba's Red River Settlement: Manuscript Sources for Economic and Demographica History," *Archivaria 9* (1inter 1979-80), 179-193.

Sprenger, G. Herman, "The Metis Nation: Buffalo Hunting vs. Agriculture in the Red River Settlement," *Western Canadian Journal of Anthropology*, 3:1 (1972), 158-78.

Spry, Irene, "The Metis and Mixed-Bloods of Rupert's Land before 1870" in Peterson/Brown.

Sprye, Irene, "The 'Private Adventurers' of Rupert's Land," in Foster, ed., *The Developing West*, 49-70.

Stanley, George, "The Metis and the Conflict of Cultures in Western Canada," *Canadian Historical Review*, 28 (1947), 428-33.

Stevenson, John, "The Unsolved Death of Thomas Simpson," *The Beaver*, outfit 266 (1935), 64-6.

Stubbs, Roy St. G., "Law and Authority in Red River," *The Beaver* outfit 299 (summer 1968), 17-21.

Swainson, Donald, "The North-West Transportation Company: Personnel and Attitudes," *Historical and Scientific Society of Manitoba, Transactions*, ser. III, no 26 (1969-70), 59-77.

Swainson, Donald, "Canada Annexes the West: Colonial Status Confirmed," in B.W. Hodgins et al, ed., *Federalism in Canada and Australia: The Early Years* (Waterloo, 1978), 137-157.

Thompson, A. N., "John West: A Study of the Conflict between Civilization and the Fur Trade," *Journal of Canadian Church Historical Society*, 12:3 (1970), 44-57.

Thompson, A. N., "The Wife of the Missionary," *Journal of Canadian Church Historical Society*, 15:2 (35-44).

Tway, Duane, "The Wintering partners and the HBC, 1863-1871," *Canadian Historical Review*, 33 (1952), 50-63.

Tway, Duane, "The Wintering Partners and the HBC, 1867-79," *Canadian Historical Review*, 41 (1960), 215-23.

Van Kirk, S., "Women and the Fur Trade," *The Beaver*, outfit 303 (1972), 4-21.

Van Kirk, S., "Women in Between: Indian Women in Fur trade Society," *CHA Historical Papers*,1977, 31-46.

Van Kirk, S., "What if Mama is an Indian?" The Cultural Ambivalence of the Alexander Ross Family," Foster, ed., *The Developing West* (1983).

Van Kirk, S.., "The Reputation of a Lady," *Manitoba History*, xi (1986), 4-11.

Van Kirk, S., "The Custom of the Country: An Examination of Fur Trade Marriage Practices," in L.H. Thomas, ed., *Essays in Western History* (Edmonton, 1976).

Walker, Peter, "The Origins, Organization and Role of the Bison Hunt in the Red River Valley," *Manitoba Archaeological Quaterly*, 6 (1982).

Weekes, Mary, "Three Prairie Folk-Songs," *The Beaver*, March 1934.

Williams, Glyndwr, "Governor George Simpson's Character Book," *The Beaver*, summer 1975.

Woolworth, Alan R., "A disgraceful proceeding: Intrigue in the Red River Country in 1864," *The Beaver*, outfit 300 (1969), 54-59,

Woolworth, N. L., "Gingras, St. Joseph and the Metis in the northern RR Valley, 1843-73," *North Dakota History.*, 42:4 (1973), 16-27.

Theses:

Bailey, Raymond R., "A Historical Study of the Public Education in West Kildonan to 1959," unpublished M.Ed. thesis, University of Manitoba, 1966.

Bartlett, Fred G., "William McTavish: The Last Governor of Assiniboia," unpublished M.A. thesis, U of M, 1964.

Boyce, G. E., "Canadian Interest in the Northwest, 1856-1860," unpublished M.A. thesis, U of M, 1960.

Brown, Jennifer, "Company Men and Native Families: Fur Trade Social and Domestic Relations in Canada's Old Northwest," Unpublished Ph.D thesis, University of Chicago, 1976.

Clarke, John, "Population and Economic Activity: A Georgraphical and Historical Analysis based on selected censuses of the RRV in the period 1832-56," Unpublished M.A.thesis, U of M, 1972.

Clarke, Margaret L., "Reconstituting the Fur Trade Community of the Assiniboine Basin, 1793 to 1812," unpublished. M.A.thesis, University of Winnipeg/University of Manitoba, 1997.

Czuboka, Michael, "St. Peter's: A Historical Study with Anthropological Observations on the Christian Aborigines of Red River 1811-76," unpublished M.A.thesis, U of M., 1960.

Dowker, G. H., "Life and Letters in Red River 1812-1863," unpublished M.A thesis., U of M., 1923.

Trials and Tribulations

Ens, Gerhard, "Kinship, Ethnicity, Class and the Red River Metis: the parishes of St. Francois Xavier and St. Andrews," unpublished Ph.D thesis., University of Alberta, 1989.

Fast, Vera, "The Protestant Missionary and Fur Trade Society: Initial Contact in the Hudson's Bay Territory, 1820-1850," unpublished. Ph.D. dissertation, U of M, 1984.

Gallagher, Brian, "The Whig Interpretation of the History of the Red River," unpublished M.A. thesis, UBC, 1986.

Foster, John, "The Anglican Clergy in Red River Settlement, 1820-26," unpublished. M.A. thesis, U of Alberta, 1966

Foster, John, "The Country-born in the Red River Settlement: 1820-50," unpublished Ph.D thesis., U of Alberta, 1972.

Fraser, William John, "A History of St. John's College, Winnipeg," unpublished. M.A thesis, U of M 1966.

Gainer, B. J., "The Catholic Missionaries as agents of social change among the Métis and Indians of Red River, 1818-1845," unpublished M.A. thesis, Carleton U, Ottawa, 1978.

Goossen, Jay, "The Relationship of the CMS and the HBC in Rupert's Land, 1821-1860, with a case study of Stanley Mission under the Direction of the Rev. Robert Hunt," unpublished. M.A. thesis, U of M., 1975.

Harvey, Golden, "The French Element in the RR Settlement' unpublished M. A. thesis, U of M., 1924.

Kaye, Barry, "Some Aspects of the Historical Geography of the RRS," unpublished M.A.thesis, U of M., 1967

Kaye, Barry, "The Historical Geography of Agriculture and Agricultural Settlement in the Canadian Northwest, 1774- ca. 1830," unpublished Ph.D. dissertation, U of London, 1976.

Klassen, Henry C., "The RRS and the St. Paul Route, 1858-70," unpublished M.A. thesis, U of M, 1963.

Moodie, D. W., "An Historical Geography of Agricultural Patterns and Resource Appraisals in Rupert's Land, 1670-1774," unpublished Ph. D dissertation, U of Alberta., 1972.

Pannekoek, Frits, "The Churches and the Social Structure in the Red River area 1818-70," unpublished . Ph.D thesis., Queens U., 1973.

Perfect, Mary, "One Hundred Years of History of the Rural schools of Manitoba: Their Formation, Reorganization and Dissolution, 1871-1971," Unpublished M.A. thesis, U of M, 1978.

Regnier, Paul, "A History of St. Boniface College," unpub. m.ed., u of m, 1964.

Rempel, Arthur, "The Influence of Religion on Education for Native People in Manitoba Prior to 1870", M.Ed. thesis, U of M., 1973.

Smith, W. D., "The Despatch of Troops to Red River, in 1846, in relation to the Oregon Question" unpub. U of M. M.A.

Sprenger, Herman G., "An Analysis of Selected Aspects of Metis Society 1810-70," M.A. U of M, 1972.

Wade, Jill, "Red River Architecture 1812-70," unpub. M.A., ubc, 1967.

Wilkinson, M. P., "The Episcopate of the Right Reverend David Anderson, 1849-64," unpub. M.A., U of M

Willie, Richard, "From Mission to Diocese: The Anglican Mission in the RRS, 1838-49," U of A M.A., 1979.

Trials and Tribulations

INDEX

-A-

A Few Reasons for a Crown Colony, 135
A Short Narrative of the Second Voyage of the Prince Albert, 128
Aberdeen, 61, 170
Aboriginal cession to Selkirk, 34
Aboriginal Rights, 99
Aboriginal Title, 69, 140-143, 187-8
Aborigines Friend and Colonial Intelligencer, 139-140
Aborigines Protection Society, 142
   Memorializes Colonial Office on Aboriginal title in Rupert's Land, 142
Abuse, sexual, 102-3
Act for the Temporary Government of Rupert's Land, 189
Agriculture, 15, 21-2, 36-40, 54, 72-3, 107, 132, 147, 178-187
   Potentiality of West for, 129-130, 132
   Famine of 1868 threatens favourable views of, 178-186
Allan, Dr. John, 26, 27
Allen, Miss, 78
American Fur Company, 97
Amnesty, 211-212
Anderson, Bishop David, 89, 113, 115, 117-8, 119-121, 127, 130, 135, 136, 161, 168
   Description of, 89
   And Presbyterians, 117-118, 122-123, 124
   And 1852 Flood, 119-121
   Behaviour in Corbett Affair, 161-4
Anderson, Miss, 89, 113, 115
Anglican Church, 41, 51, 59-60, 76-7, 88-89, 116
   Tensions in, in 1840s, 88-9
   David Anderson becomes first bishop, 89
   Conflict with Presbyterians, 115-119
   Gets First Nations clergymen, 135-6
   Involved in Corbett Affair, 159-164
   Reforms in, 169-172
Anglophones, 116

Annexation, to U.S., 118-119, 134
Annexation, to Canada, 139, 172-4
Archbishop of Canterbury, 170
Archibald, Adams
Anson Northup (steamboat), 137, 157
   Described, 137
Arabia (steamer), 131
Assiniboia, Council of, 51, 65, 71, 72, 75, 97, 109, 117, 123, 125, 128, 160, 167, 175, 177, 179-180, 192, 193-4, 198, 201, 202, 214
Assiniboia, District of, 48, 63, 97
Assiniboine River, 34, 43, 119, 131, 135, 142
Assiniboine Sheep and Wool Company, 65
Astor, John Jacob, 110
Astoria, 110
Athabasca District, 14, 21, 37, 38-9, 102, 103, 105, 149
Aubert, Pierre, 87

-B-

Baie Saint Paul, 61
Bailly, Alexis, 42
Ballantyne, Robert, 104-5, 110
Ballenden, John, 113-115
Ballenden, Sarah McLeod, 113-115
Bannatyne, A.G.B., 168, 193, 202,k 208
Bannerman, Alexander, 22
Bannerman, William, 22
Baring brothers, 165
Barnley, George, 77
Bas de la Riviére, 19, 24, 30, 63
Bathurst, Henry, Third Earl of, 31
Begg, Alexander, 188, 197, 199, 201, 204 (see also "Justitia")
Belcourt, Father George, 61, 67, 89, 92, 93, 94, 95, 100, 109, 125
Bern, Switzerland, 43
Big Stone Lake, 40
Bird, Curtis James, 193
Bird, James, 71, 72, 114
Black, John, 117-118, 179
Black, Recorder John, 161, 176, 177-8, 193, 207, 208, 209
Blakeley, Captain Russell, 134, 180
Blodgett, Lorne, 130, 132
Bond, H. Wesley, 118
Book of Common Prayer, 170-1

234

Books, in Settlement, 105, 143
Bown, Walter, 139, 158, 176, 184, 197
Boucher, François, 22
Bourgeau, Eugène, 130
Boulton, Charles, 196, 203, 205, 210
Bourke, John Palmer, 99
Brandon House, 14, 15, 20, 21, 25
Breland, Pacal, 141, 155
British Columbia, 133, 134, 142, 154-155
British House of Commons, 112, 129
  Votes for enquiry into legality of HBC, 112
British Wesleyan Missionary Society, 77
Brown, George, 126, 138, 172
Bruce, John, 193, 206
Bruneau, François-Jacques, 123
Budd, Henry, 88, 135
Budd, Henry, Jr., 135
Buffalo, 41-2, 125, 179
Buffalo, NY, 124
Buffalo hunt, 89-97, 125
  Described, 89-95
  Criticized, 95-97, 186-187
Buffalo Wood Company, 41-2, 90
Bulger, Andrew, 48, 49, 52, 57, 106
Bulger Papers, 46
Bunn, Dr. John, 71, 81-2, 114
Bunn, Thomas, 207
Burial Grounds, conflict over, 117-118, 122, 124

-C-
Cadieu, 74
Cadotte, Joseph, 30, 31
Caldwell, Major William Bletterman, 84, 105, 113-115
  Named Governor of Assiniboia, 105
Cambridge University, 112, 170
Cameron, Captain Donald Roderick, 191-2, 195
Cameron, Duncan, 13, 14, 15, 18, 19, 20
Canada, 16, 110, 134, 138, 147, 180
  Begins interest in Red River, 126-9
  Acts to acquire the West, 172-4
  Contributes to 1868 famine relief fund, 183-5
  Moves to take over Rupert's Land, 189-190
  Negotiates with Red River delegates, 210-212
Canada First, 210-211
Canadian Exploring Expedition, 131-2
  Reports of, published, 131-2
Canadian Free Press (newspaper), 180
Canadian House of Assembly, 129
Canadian Parliament, 189
Canadian Party in Red River, 194, 202
Canadians, 12, 28, 38, 42, 52
Capenesseweet, 85
Cart, Red River, 92, 149-150
  Described, 149-50
Carey, George, 73
Cariboo Gold Rush, 154
Carlton House, 150
Carlton Trail, 82, 154
Cartier, George-Etienne, 189
Cathedrals
  Anglican, 117, 121, 171
  Catholic, 62, 138, 193
  Burns down, 143-6
  Description of, 143-4
  St. Michael's Cathedral, Toronto, 144
Catholic Church, 35, 37, 60-2, 76-7, 86-8, 116, 123-4
  Builds cathedral, 62
  Cathedral burns down in 1860, 143-6
  Description of, 143-144
Cavalier, Charles, 133, 138
Censuses, 65
  1835 census, 72-73
Chapman, John
Chelsea Pensioners, 105-6, 108, 196
  Described, 106
Chicago, 124, 147
Chicago and North Western Railroad, 147-8
Chile, 128
Chipman, Mr., 174
Christianity, 127
Christie, Alexander, 63, 69, 76, 97, 98, 102, 105
Churches
  In 1831, 61
  In 1840s, 86-8
  In village of Winnipeg, 158

Trials and Tribulations

Destroyed in high wind of 1868, 178
Church Missionary Society, 60, 62, 88, 89, 117, 121, 129, 170
Church of the Holy Trinity, 178
Church of Scotland, 88, 115-119
Churches, 61
Clarke, John, 50
Clear Grits, 172
Climate, 129-131, 168-9, 178-180
Clouston, Robert, 84, 86, 99, 114
Cockran, William, 59, 61, 67, 70, 88, 109
   Biographical sketch, 60
Cockran, Ann, 60
Cochrane, Henry, 135, 171
Coldwell, William, 138, 162, 208
Collingwood, Canada, 131, 133
Colonial Office, 101-108, 130, 135, 141, 142, 160
Coltman, William, 22, 31-5, 36, 37
Coltman Commission, 31-5
Columbia River, 74, 83, 110
Colvile, Andrew, 41, 43, 47, 49, 50, 52, 54
Colvile, Eden, 112-113, 115, 117-118, 120, 121, 122
   Description of, 112-13
Confederation, 191
Convention of 24, 198-202
   Debate over establishment of provisional government, 200-202
Convention of Forty, 208-209
Cook, Charles, 88
Cook, Thomas, 135
Corbett, Abigail, 161-3
Corbett, Griffith Owen, 134-6
   Description of, 134, 159
   Trial of, 159-164
Council of 24, 205
Cowan, Ogle
Cowan, Dr. William, 122. 193, 196
Cowley, Abraham, 88
Cowlitz River, 83
Cree, 20, 34, 69, 82, 128, 141
Crofton, Colonel John Ffolliot, 187
Crown Colony status, for Red River, 135, 142, 160
Crusoe, Robinson, 110
Crosbie, 78
Crow Wing, 125, 134

Culture, amenities of in Red River Settlement, 153-4
   Libraries, 105, 143
   Bookshop, 153
   Music, 153
   Easter celebration, 153
   Christmas celebration, 153-4
   Hogmoney, 153-4
   Dancing, 154
Cunningham, Robert, 138, 153

-D-

Daily Press, (St. Paul newspaper), 203
Dakota Territory, 125, 147, 177, 203
Dallas, Alexander, 123, 161, 167
Darlington, Wisconsin, 56
Darwin, Charles, 130-
Davidson, John, 113-115
Dawson, Aeneas Macdonell, 126
Dawson, Simon James, 126, 131
Dawson, William Macdonell, 126
de May, Rudolf, 43-45
Dease, George, 67
Dease, Peter, 81
Dease, William, 188, 193, 194
de Meuron Regiment, 12, 16, 26, 27, 28-31, 36, 39, 42, 46, 52, 56
de Salaberry, Colonel Charles, 206, 207
de Watteville Regiment, 12, 16
Denison, George, 210
Dennis, John Stoughton, 189-90, 194-5, 203-4, 205
d'Equilly, Pierre Louis Morin, 73-4
DesCombe, David Louis, 50-51
Desmarrais, Francis, 177
Detroit, 124, 137, 147
Detroit Free Press, 137
Dick, Thomas, 133
Dickson, General James, 73
Dickson, Robert, 40
Dingwall, Scotland, 66
Disasters
   1817, 36-7
   Fire in 1818, 38
   Grasshoppers in 1818, 39-40, 42
   Food shortage of 1821, 48
   Winter of 1825-6, 54
   Flood of 1826, 55-57
   Flu Epidemic of 1846, 103
   Drought of 1846, 103-4

Beginning of shortage of game, 106
Cold year of 1849, 107
Flood of 1852, 119-122
Grasshoppers in 1857, 132-3
Catholic cathedral fire of 1860, 143-6
Flood of 1861, 145-7
drought and other problems of 1860s, 168-9
Famine of 1868, 178-186
Disease, 41, 70
   Consumption, 41
   Measles, 41
   Whooping cough, 41
   Epidemic disease, 69-70, 103
Donaldson, Captain Hugh S., 167
D'Orsennens, Captain Proteus, 27-31, 33, 43
Douglas, Thomas, FifthEarl of Selkirk, (see Selkirk)
Dousman, Michael, 40
Drever, William, 84
Drought, 168-9
Drummond, Sir Gordon, 16
Drummond's Island, 26
Dubach, John, 51
Ducharme, Antoine, 145
Dugast, Father Georges, 190
Dumoulin, Father Sévére Joseph, 37, 38
Durham, Lord, 74

-E-
Edmonton House, 82
Education, 42, 51
   Chief Peguis comments on, 52
   Anglican expansion of, 60
   Anglican Female School of 1827, 60
   Catholic female school of 1827, 60
   William Cockran opens school for mixed bloods, 61
   Red River Academy founded, 61
   Other Anglican schools, 62
   Catholic expansion of, 60, 63
   Grey Nuns open school, 87
Ellice, Edward, 129-130
Ellice Family, 112
Emmerling, George ("Dutch George"), 158
England, 64, 100, 102, 128, 147

Ens, Gerhard, 103, 187 Red River Valley, 90, 126, 146-7, 173
Epidemics, 69-70, 103
Essex Record (newspaper), 180
Eton Colllege, 112
Evans, James, 77, 83, 102-3
Every-day Life in the Wild of North America, 104
Experimental farms, 28, 30, 36, 38, 39, 40, 42, 73, 133
Extermination of the American Bison (1887), 95

-F-
Faribault District, Minnesota, 133
Faribault Party, 133-4
Ferry across Red River at St. Boniface, 157
   Described, 157
Fidler, Peter, 14, 16, 25, 33, 34, 105
Finlayson, Duncan, 75, 78
Finlayson, Isabel, 78
   Describes settlement, 78-81
Fire, 38, 143-6
   Prairie fires, 168-9
First Nations, 17, 127, 137, 166-8, 194, 208
   Sioux Uprising in Minnesota of 1862, 166-8
Flag, 205
Flett, Mr. 92
Flett, George, 154-5
Flooding, 64
   In 1826, 55-57
   In 1852, 119-122
   In 1861, 146-147
Fond du Lac (Superior, Wisconsin),
Forks, 11-12, 15, 18, 20, 25,29, 30, 32-34, 35, 55, 59, 61, 72, 73, 121, 134, 159
Fort Abercrombie, 125, 138
   Canadian government stores arms there, 190
Fort Ellice, 154
Fort des Prairies, 18
Fort Daer, 29, 34, 141
Fort Douglas, 13, 17, 18, 20, 21, 23, 24, 28, 29-31, 34, 38,46, 48, 51, 141
Fort Edmonton, 82, 155
Fort Garry, 54, 121, 132, 134, 137, 140, 148, 150, 155, 156, 162
Fort Garry Hotel, 159

237

Trials and Tribulations

Fort Gibraltar, 13, 15, 16, 17, 18, 19, 20, 21, 24, 35
Fort Maurepas, 19
Fort Pelly, 107
Fort Simpson, 67, 148
Fort Snelling, 66
Fort Vancouver, 82
Fort William, 13, 15, 26, 27, 28, 31, 32, 131, 133, 143
Forty-ninth parallel, 40
Foss, Captain Christopher, 106, 113-115
Foss-Pelly Affair, 113-115
France, 87
Fraser, John, 193
Fraser River, 133
Franklin, Sir John, 108, 128
Franklin, Lady, 108, 128
Franklin Expedition, 108, 128
Fraser, Alexander, 24
Free Kirk of Scotland, 117-118
Free Trade Question of 1840s, 97-111
   Free Trade Protest Deflected, 102-108
Freemen, 17
Frog Plain, 62, 118, 122, 124

-G-
"G.W.N.," 146-7
Gale, Samuel, 34, 37
Galena, Illinois, 124
Gardens, 107
Garrioch, A.C., 195
Garrioch, Peter, 62
Garry, Nicholas, 42-3, 46
Gazden, Joseph, 106, 139
General Palmer (ship), 105
George III, 141
Georgetown, 134, 148, 155
German Street, 38
Gladman, George, 131
Globe (Toronto), 107, 126, 128, 137, 138, 181, 197
Goiffin, Father, 145
Gold, 133
Gold Rush, 133, 154-155
Gosselin, Sister, 145
Gossip, 84
Goulet, Roger, 98, 194
Gowler, Oliver, 179
Graham's Point, 126
Grand Trunk Railway, 147, 165-6

Grant, Cuthbert, 22-4, 30-1, 38, 53, 72, 73, 75, 91, 114
Grant, Johnny, 187, 208
Graffenreid, Lieutenant Antoine, 31, 36-7
Grand Coteau herd of buffalo, 96
Grand Forks, 141
Grand Rapids, 59, 61, 85
Grasshoppers, 39-40, 42, 62, 132, 168-9, 178, 185
Great Britain (ship), 132
Green, John, 139
Grey Nuns, 87, 143, 153
Guelph Advertiser, 107-8
Gunn, Donald, 12, 55, 90, 135, 140, 192, 200
Gunn, George, 154

-H-
"Half-breeds, 127" 17 (see also mixed bloods, Métis)
Halkett, John, 48-49
Hallett, William (the elder), 91
Hallett, William (the younger), 69
Hamilton, Canada, 181
Harbidge, George, 42, 52
Harbidge, Mrs., 52
Hardisty, Richard, 206
Hargrave, Laetitia, 78
Hargrave, James, 60, 64
Hargrave, Joseph James, 137, 147-8, 149, 150, 153, 155, 162, 169, 175, 178, 183, 194, 198
Hassell, Thomas, 102
Hatch, Edwin, 167
Hay, Mr., 192
Headingly, 132, 134-5, 142, 160, 161
Hector, James, 130
Heron, Francis, 55-6, 58
Heurter, Frederick, 25, 32
Hibernian (steamship), 147
Hill, J. J., 180
Hind, Henry Youle, 96, 107, 125, 131-2, 143-4, 146
Hornaday, William, 95
House of Commons, Canadian, 173, 191
House of Commons Select Committee of 1857, 129-130, 133, 187

Houses, 78
  Described by Isobel Finlayson, 78-9
Howe, Joseph, 173, 175
  Visits Red River1869, 191-2
Hudson Bay, 12
Hudson's Bay Company, 11-35, 37, 41, 42, 50, 63, 67, 73, 116, 142
  Merges with NWC, 42
  Conflict with government of settlement, 51
  Introduces cash system at store in 1834, 70
  Purchases Selkirk interests in Settlement, 70-1
  And Oregon, 74
  Responds to threat from American Fur Company in 1843, 97-101
  Responds to Red River Petition of 1846, 101-102
  Negotiates replacement for Sixth Regiment, 105-6
  British House of Commons votes to enquire into, 112
  Red River officers of a Settlement faction, 115-116
  London Committee rules on churchyard, 118
  William Kennedy provides political alternative to, 128-9
  British Parliament holds hearings on, 129-130
  Syndicate owned by purchases Anson Northup, 138
  Opposes gold rush, 155
  Reorganized in 1863 in London, 165
  Proposed to continue as government of Red River, 201
Hudson Strait, 45
Hudsons Bay Territories and Vancouver's Island, The, 105
Hunter, James, 129, 161-3, 169-70

-I-
Image Plain (see also Middlechurch), 59, 61, 62
India, 78
Ingersoll Hall, St. Paul, 180
International (steamboat), 155, 179
Intercolonial Railway, 165-6

Irish, 12
Irvine, John R., 134
Isbister, Alexander Kennedy, 76, 101-2, 108, 128-129, 141

-J-
Jack River, 14, 15
Jacques (an Iroquois), 88
Jacques, Dr. A. G., 191
Jailbreaks, 160-64, 176
James Robert, 85-6, 107
James, Mrs. Robert, 85-6
Joly, Mr., 174
Jones, David, 51, 52, 54, 58, 60, 61
Jones, Mrs. David, 60
Journals, Detailed reports, and Observations of Palliser expedition, 131-2
Justice, Administration of, 52, 72, 85
  District courts established in 1835, 72
  Quarterly Court established, 72
  New court system of 1839, 75
  Sayer Trial, 108-109
  Aboriginal trials, 85, 143
  Court House, 159
  Described, 159
  Trial of G.O. Corbett, 162-5
  In the 1860s, 175-178
  In 1869,199
"Justitia," (see also Alexander Begg), 197\

-K-
Kaministiquia River, 27
Kennedy, Roderick, 128
Kennedy, Captain William, 108, 126, 128, 133, 135, 192
  Described, 128
Kentucky, 28, 66
Kew, Frederick, 176, 180
Kildonan (Sutherlandshire), 12, 13, 116
Kildonan (Red River), 54, 116. 117, 155, 204
King, William Cornwallis, 148
Kingston, Canada, 180
Kingston BritishWhig (newspaper), 181
King's College, Aberdeen, 61, 66, 74, 170, 171
King's College, London, 135

239

Trials and Tribulations

Kirkcudbright, 15
Kitson, Norman, 97, 100, 180
Klyne, Adam, 125
Knox Church, 158

-L-
Labrador, 128, 132
Lacrosse, Wisconsin, 148
Ladies Bazaar, 182
Lafayette, Minnesota, 134, 137
Lafleche, Father Louis-François, 123
La Grave, Eulalie, 144
La Mar, Seraphim, 30
Laroque, Antoine, 66-7, 69
La-Terre-qui Brule, 69
La Verendrye, 19
Lac la Pluie, 27-9, 31
Lachine, 64, 70, 81, 888
Lagimodière, Jean-Baptiste, 12, 15, 16
Laidlaw, William, 28, 30, 36, 38, 39, 40, 42
Lake of the Woods, 28, 131, 190
Lake Superior, 131, 173
Lake Winnipeg, 146, 149
Lavigne, 23
Law Code, 75, 85
LeBlanc, Pierre
Leith, James, 89
Lépine, Ambroise, 196
Libraries, 105, 143
Little Mountain, 121
Little Six, 169
Little Souris River, 96
Lillie, Alexander, 133
Liverpool, 78, 147
Livestock, 40, 42, 44, 49, 65, 107
    Merino Sheep, 44, 65
    1832/3 Expedition to U.S. for, 65-66
    Breeding programmes, 107
    Horses, 107
    Stallion named "Melbourne," 107
    In 1852 flood, 120
    In 1861 flood, 146
Livingstone, Donald, 25
Logan, Robert, 42, 71, 72, 105, 116
London, England, 180
London, Canada, 180
Lord Wellington (ship), 45
Love, Timoleon, 154
Lowe, David, 120

Lower Canada, 14, 15, 16, 31, 37, 64, 74, 112
Lower Church, 62, 88
Lower Fort Garry, 64, 74, 78, 113, 131, 133, 148
Lowman, Mary, 62
"L.R.", 184-5
Lyons, George, 106

-Mc-
McBeath, Robert, 193
McDermot, Andrew, 71, 99, 100, 114, 140, 142, 151
McDermot, Mary Sarah, 159-160
McDonald, Lieutenant, 29
Macdonald, Sir John A., 172
Macdonald, John Sandfield, 172
MacDonald, Robert, 135
Macdonell, Alexander Greenfield, 13, 15, 18, 21, 22, 24, 25
Macdonell, Sheriff Alexander, 19, 21, 23-5, 34, 36, 39, 41, 45, 48
Macdonell, Allan, 126
Macdonell, Miles, 13, 14, 16-17, 26, 28-31
McDougall, William, 126, 172-4, 189-190, 191, 193-5, 196, 199, 201, 202, 203
    Described, 172
    Appointed lieutenant-governor of the Northwest Territory, 175, 189
    Meets with Howe on prairie, 192
McDougall, Miss, 191
McGee, D'Arcy, 210
McGill, Peter, 74
McKay, James, 208
McKenney, Henry, 145, 157-8, 176
    Described, 157
McKenney and Company, 176
McKenzie, Daniel, 26-7, 33
McKenzie, Donald, 25, 54
McKenzie, Nancy, 63, 64
Mackenzie River, 149
McLalren, R. N., 180
McLaughlin, John, 99-100
McLean, Alex, 177
McLean, John, 126
McLean, John (of Hamilton), 181
McLean, Warden John, 171, 179
    Described, 171
McLellan, Archibald, 25, 30

240

MacLeod, John, 19
McLeod, Archibald Norman, 24-5
McMicking, Thomas, 155
McPherson, Donald, 37
McTavish, John George, 63, 64
McTavish, J. H., 200
MacTavish, William, 159-160, 182, 187, 190, 195, 198

-M-
Macallum, John, 61, 88
Machicabaou, 23
Mackipictoon, 82
Machray, Robert, 170-1, 184, 193, 194
  Described, 170
Main Road, 205
Mainville, François, 30
Mair, Charles, 92, 159, 184, 192, 205, 210, 211
Mair, Elizabeth, 192
Malmros, Oscar, 190, 205
Manitoba, 175, 211
Manitoba Act, 211-212
Manitoba, Provincial Archives, 182
Manitobah, Republic of, 164
Manitoulin Island, 172in Island, 172
Mapleton, 162
Mason, William, 77
Matthey, Captain Frederick, 16, 26, 38-9, 41
Mazenod, Charles-Joseph-Eugené de, Bishop of Marseilles, 87
Mechanics Hall, Hamilton, 181
Medicine Bottle (Sioux), 168
Mestre, Father, 144
Métis, 187, 190, 192-214
Michilimackinac, 28, 40
Middlechurch, 59, 61, 88, 122, 146
Mill Creek, 146
Minneapolis, 134
Milton, Viscount William Fitzwilliam, 89, 91-2
Milton and Cheadle, 92
Michigan, 116
Michigan Centrail Railroad, 147
Milwaukee, Wisconsin, 180
Milwaukee Chamber of Commerce, 184
Minnesota, 118, 180
Missions
  Catholic, 37-40
    Building of first chapel, 40
    New arrivals of 1840s, 76-7
  Anglican, 41
    Arrival of David Jones, 51
    Expansion in Settlement, 59-60
    New arrivals of 1840s, 76-7
    Reform, 169-72
  Methodist, 77, 93, 102-3, 172
Mississippi River, 35
Mixed-bloods, 17, 43
  Described by Selkirk, 17-18
  Described as threatening Red River, 18
  Attack James Sutherland, 20
  Over-run Brandon House, 20
  Conflict with settlers at Seven Oaks, 21-23
  Occupying Fort Douglas at its Capture, 30-31
  Not under control of NWC, 32
  Missionaries organized for, 37-38
  Simpson policy toward in 1824, 53
  Replace Swiss in Settlement after 1826, 59
  Settle Grand Rapids, 59
  "Turning off" native wives, 63
  Mixed-blood women snubbed by Frances Simpson, 64
  Thomas Simpson contempt for, 66-7
  Attitude of Europeans toward, 67-68
  New mixed-blood consciousness, 69
  Described by Isobel Finlayson, 78
  Anglophone mixed bloods depart for Oregon, 82
  And buffalo hunt, 89-97
  French mixed bloods and buffalo hunt, 91
  And free trade agitation, 97-111
  Suffer in drought of 1846, 104
  Francophones especially suffer from thin harvests in late 1840s, 106
  Confrontation, especially by Francophone mixed bloods, with authorities, 1848-9
  Social attitudes towards mixed bloods in Foss-Pelly Affair, 113-115

French mixed bloods a faction in settlement, 115-116
Scottish-Orcadian mixed bloods lack identity after 1851, 118
1852 flood confirms division between French and English, 121
Treatment in Ross's TheRed River Settlement, 127-8
Testimony about in 1857 parliamentary hearing, 130
Royal Canadian Rifles arrive in (1857), 133
Grasshoppers infest in 1857, 132-3
Canadians try new postal service, 133
Settlement becomes staging area for Gold Rush, 133
Anglophone mixed bloods search for identity, 134-136
Mixed blood claims to aboriginal land, 140-143
Anglophone mixed bloods led by G.O. Corbett, 160-2
Francophone mixed bloods support HBC in 1862, 160
Francophone mixed bloods sue Walter Bown, 176-7
The Queen v. McLean pits French v. English mixed bloods, 177-178
Louis Riel defends mixed bloods in Famine Controversy, 184-5
Mixed blood society in the 1860s, 186-8
Differential response to Canada from, 192
Resistance to Canadian takeover, 189—211
Moffat, George, 74
Montgomery, Robert, 105
Montreal, 15, 37, 45, 87, 147, 190
Montreal Herald, 74
Moose Factory, 77
Morin, Magloire, 145
Mosquitoes, 122
Mountain, Bishop George, 83, 88
Moustache, 21
Mulligan, James, 196
Murdoch, Sir Clinton, 211-212
Murray, Alexander, 22

-N-
Napoleonic Wars, 44

National Archives of Canada, 46
Newcastle, Duke of, 142, 167
Newfoundland, 48
New York, 15, 73
Niagara, 124
Niagara Frontier, 48
Nolin, Angélique, 60
Nolin, Jean-Baptiste, 30, 60
Nolin, Louis, 38
North American (newspaper), 126, 172
North Star (steamer), 134
Northup, Anson, 134
Norway House, 70, 77, 102-3, 108, 149, 150
North West Company. 12-35
    Disperses Red River Settlement, 14-15
    Threatens Settlement, 16-17
    Reoccupies the Forks, 24-5
    Negotiates with Selkirk at Red River, 31-35
North West Trading and Colonization Company, 128
Nor'-Wester, 68, 84, 92, 105, 106, 136, 138-9, 140-1, 142, 144, 147, 153, 154, 155, 160, 161, 162, 168, 174, 178, 179, 180, 181, 183-4, 185, 186, 197
    Described, 138-139
Northern Department, 150
Northern packet, 150
Nouveau Monde (newspaper), 184

-O-
Oblate Missionaries of Mary Immaculate, Congregation of, 87, 123
O'Connor, Mr., 173-4
O'Donoghue, William, 196, 205
Ojibwa language, 77
Ontario, 210
Orange Order, 134, 211, 213
Oregon, 74, 76, 82-3
Oregon Crisis, 74, 76, 103
Orkney Islands, 128
Ottawa, 175, 190, 197, 207
Ottawa Valley, 127

-P-
Pacific Fur Company, 53
Pacific Ocean, 172

Paketay-Hoond, 140 (see Peguis)
Palliser, Captain John, 130-132
  Described, 130
Palliser Expedition, 132
  Reports of published, 131-2
Pambrun, P. C., 19
Palliser's Triangle, 132
Papers Relative to the Exploration by Palliser expedition, 131-2
Parisien, 69
Parker, Dr., 174
Parliament, 75
Peguis, 14, 29-30, 52, 61, 140-141. 142, 188
Pelly, Augustus E., 113-115
  Mrs. Pelly, 114
Pelly, Sir John H., 101-2
Pelly, Robert Parker, 51, 52, 57
Pembina, 13, 19, 20, 29-30, 37, 40, 42, 47, 49, 53, 61, 90, 91, 97, 99, 118, 120, 125, 141, 148, 177, 195, 196
Pembina Mountain, 146
Pemmican, 94-5
Pemmican Proclamation, 13
Penetanguishene, 133
Pensioners, 105-6, 108, 113, 121, 196 (see also Chelsea Pensioners)
Petition to Crown of 1846, 108
  Described, 100-101
  Fate of, 101-102
Petitions, 99-102, 128-9
  Petition for expansion of Canada to Red River, 128-9
  Petitions of 1861, 160
  Petition for troops, 1863, 167
:"Philanthropist," 184
Pin-panche, 29
Pioneer (steamboat), 154, 166
Pioneer (St. Paul newspaper), 183
Plessis, Bishop J.O.
Ploughboy (steamer), 133
Police, 52, 71
Point Douglas, 146
Portage and Main, 157
Portage La Loche brigade, 149
Portage la Prairie, 21, 134, 155, 177, 205, 210
Postal Service in Red River, 125, 133
Potatoes, 107
Potts, John, 181
Power, Michael, 180, 196
Prairie du Chien, 40-41

Presbyterian Church, 41, 60, 88, 89, 115-119, 122-123, 124, 136, 170, 171, 172 (see also Church of Scotland)
Presbyterian Church of Canada, 117-8
Presbyterians, 136
Prince, Hendry (Chief Pa-bat-or-kok-or-sis), 188, 199
Prince Rupert (ship), 89
Printing press, 135, 138-9
Pritchard, John, 22, 23, 24, 25, 41, 53, 55, 56, 59, 62
Pritchard, Samuel, 171
Prisoners, 204, 207
Provencher, J.A.N., 195
Provencher, Father J.N., 37, 38, 39, 41, 49, 60, 62, 63, 71, 75, 86-8, 109, 120
  Death and Achievements, 123
Provincial Archives of Manitoba, 182
Provisional government, 200-202
  Debated, 200-202
  Proclaimed, 205-206

-Q-
Qu'Appelle, 18, 20, 24
Qu'Appelle River Valley, 131
Quarterly Court of Assinobia, 83-84, 85, 112-114, 159-164, 177-178
Quebec, 147
Queen v. Alex McLean, 177-178
Queen Victoria, 100, 200
Queenston, Canada, 124

-R-
Racette, Charles (Rossette), 155
Racette, George ("Shaman"), 155
Railroads, 124, 127, 131, 132, 147, 161-2
Rainy River, 131
Ramsey, Alexander, 118-119
Rebellions of 1837 and 1838, 74, 189
Red Lake River, 147
Red River, 11, 13, 14, 15, 32, 34, 43, 55-7, 119-122, 131
  Low water levels in 1860s, 179
Red River (book), 147, 175
Red River Academy, 61
Red River Co-operative Relief Committee, 181-4

243

Trials and Tribulations

Red River Company, 167
Red River Hall, 158
Red River Relief Fund, 182-184
Red River Settlement, The (book), 127
 Discussed, 127-8
Red River Settlement
 Origins, 11-12
 Early establishment, 12-13
 First dispersal in 1815, 14-15
 Restoration in 1815 by Colin Robertson, 15
 Dispersed in 1816, 23-25
 Reoccupied by de Meurons, 27-30
 Visited by Lord Selkirk, 31-35
 Re-established in 1817, 36-7
 Compared to Athabasca, 37
 Described 1818-21, 38-42
 Swiss settlers of 1821 in, 43-48
 Described by Simpson in 1822, 48
 And Flood of 1826, 55-57
 New European standard in, 64
 Administrative reforms, 72-76
 Rumour and gossip in, 84
 Meetings in over free trade issue, 98-99
 And Foss-Pelly Affair, 112-114
 Presbyterian demands in, 117-118
 Flood of 1852, 119-122
 Petititon for Canadian takeover circulated in, 1857, 128-129
 G.O. Corbett advocates Crown Colony status for, 135
 First steamboat arrives in 1859, 137-8
 Catholic cathedral burns, 143-146
 Transportation to and from in 1860s, 147-150
 Cultural amenities in, 153-4
 BC Gold Rush in, 154-5
 Founding of Winnipeg, 156-9
 Responds to Sioux War in U.S., 166-8
 Breakdown of justice, 175-177
 And famine of 1868, 178-186
 Canadians move to take over, 190-92
 Resistance to Canada begins, 192-196
 Debate over strategy, 200-204
 Provisional Government proclaimed, 205
 Enters Confederation as Manitoba, 213
Red River Valley, 90, 126, 146-7, 173
"Red River Voyageur," by Whittier, 143
Reid, Dr. Alexander, 154
Reinhard, Charles, 25
Report of Progress of Hind expedition, 131-132
Richards, A. N., 192
Riel, Louis Sr., 109, 114, 160
Riel, Louis, 144, 184-5, 190, 192, 193-4, 198, 199, 200, 201, 202-214
 Described, 190-1
Riel, Sara, 144, 206

Rindisbacher, Peter, 57
Rights, Bill of, 209-210
Rights, List of, 203, 211
Ritchot, Father Noel, 196, 209-210, 211
River Sale, 29
Roadbuilding, 133, 173, 181, 183, 189-190
Robertson, Colin, 14-15, 17, 18-19, 20, 21, 22, 24, 38, 65
Rockford, Illinois, 124
Rocky Mountains, 82, 131, 132, 134
Roe, Frank, 90, 95
Rome, 87, 189
Ross, Alexander, 12, 35, 48, 53, 64, 71, 75, 82, 85, 88, 89, 90, 91, 92, 94, 98, 103, 108, 113, 116, 117-118, 124, 168,
 Critical of buffalo hunt, 95-7
 Describes Sayer Trial, 109
 Publishes Adventures on the Columbia
 Publishes The Red River Settlement
Ross, Donald, 60, 71, 108, 118
Ross, Henrietta, 118
Ross, James, 97, 124, 135, 138, 139. 141, 153-4, 160, 197, 200, 202, 205, 208-9
 Travels to Toronto by steamer and train in 1853, 124
 Dismissed from his official appointments in 1862, 160
 Serves as G.O Corbett's lawyer, 162
 Critical of buffalo hunt, 186

Becomes spokesman for anglophone mixed bloods, 198-202
Ross, William, 124, 125
Rothney, Helen, 83-4
Rotterdam, 45
Royal Canadian Rifles, 132, 134, 196
Royal Geographical Society, 130
Royal Hotel, 140, 157
Royal Warwickshires, 103-4
Rumour, 84, 197
Rundle, Robert, 77
Rupert's Land, 74, 98, 112

-S-
St. Andrews, 64, 72, 103, 106-7, 117, 121, 155, 167-8, 169, 192, 194
St. Andrews Church, 178
St. Boniface, 38, 59, 60, 91, 121, 123, 143, 146, 205
St. Clair River, 147
St. Cloud, 126
St. Cloud Democrat, 146-7
St. Denis, Louis, 72
St. Francois Xavier, 53, 91, 103
St. James, 121
St. John's Collegiate School, 122, 124
St. John's College, 88, 135, 136
Re-established in 1866, 170-172
St. John's Park, 42
St. Joseph, 125, 146
St, Lawrence Hall, Toronto, 134
St. Louis, 35, 41, 65, 66
St. Norbert, 193, 195
St. Paul, Minnesota, 124, 133, 137, 138, 147, 150, 180, 182, 184, 191
St. Paul Chamber of Commerce, 137, 180, 184
St. Paul's Choral Society, 153
St.. Peter's, 60, 62, 88, 208
St. Peter's, Minnesota, 155
St. Peter's River, 35
Sarnia, 147
Saskatchewan, 96
Saskatchewan Gold Expedition, 155
Saskatchewan River, 77, 149
Saskatchewan River Valley, 131
Sault Ste. Marie, 38, 60, 131, 133
Saulteaux, 14, 21, 24, 29-30, 34, 52, 69, 85, 141, 143, 199
Sayer, Pierre-Guillaume, 108-109
Sayer Trial, 76, 77-8
Scandal, 84, 102-3,

Foss-Pelly Affair, 113-115
Corbett Trial, 159-164
Scandinavians, 12
Schmidt, Louis, 208
Schultz, Agnes Farquaharson, 176
Schultz, John Christian, 139, 175-6, 202, 204, 208, 210, 211
Science and Red River, 130-131
Scotland, 67
Scott, Alfred, 209
Scott, Thomas, 199, 205
Trial and execution of, 210-211
Scots, 12-13, 36, 37, 39, 40, 41, 42, 52. 67, 72, 88
Highlanders, 12-13, 44
Orkneymen, 12, 59, 104
Leave for U.S., 72-3
Experience in 1846 drought, 104
Fight for Presbyterian Church, 115-119, 122-4
Scratching River, 195
Secretary of State for the Colonies, 106
"Selkirk Settlers", 12, 34-5, 41, 49
Selkirk, Earl of, 11-35, 37, 49, 60, 63, 89, 100, 114, 116, 127, 140, 188
Founds Red River 11-13
Travels to North America in 1815, 15-16
Negotiates with North West Company, 15-16
Departs for West, 26
Captures Fort William, 26
Negotiates with Daniel McKenzie, 26-7
Orders capture of Fort Douglas, 28-31
Is ordered arrested by Lord Bathurst, 31
Travels to Red River, 32
At Red River, 32-35
Negotiates with First Nations, 34, 140
Death of, 41
Promises about Presbyterian clergyman, 116
Selkirk, Lady Jean 35
Selkirk Estate, 43-51, 58
Sells interest in Settlement, 70-1
Servants, 78, 83, 114, 161-3
Semple, Robert, 15-16, 17, 18, 19, 20, 21, 22, 43

245

Trials and Tribulations

Setter, George, 120
Seven Oaks, 21-23, 25, 26, 32, 40
Shaw, John, 32
Shaw, William, 18, 32
Sheyenne River, 134, 146
Sherbrooke, Sir John, 31, 33, 37
Shoal Lake, 153
Sibley, H. H., 180, 184
Sicotte, Louis-Victor, 172
Sidney Sussex College, Cambridge University, 170
Simpson, Alexander, 82
Simpson, Frances, 58, 61, 63, 64, 78
Simpson, George, 41, 45, 46, 48, 49, 50, 52, 53, 54, 56, 62, 64, 66, 70, 71, 72, 74-5,82,   83, 97, 99, 102, 104, 108, 109, 115, 117, 123, 126, 129, 133, 138, 155
  Resides year-round in Red River, 58, 63-4
  Marriage, 63
  Moves to Canada, 65
  Invites Adam Thom to be recorder, 74-5
  Becomes governor of Rupert's Land, 75
Simpson, Thomas, 66-7, 69, 81
  His suicide in 1840, 81-82
Sinclair, James, 69, 100, 109, 116, 125
  Leads overland party to Oregon, 82-3
  Writes Governor Christie about fur trade in 1845, 98-9
Sioux, 66, 69, 118, 125, 126, 143, 160, 168
  Uprising in Minnesota and Dakota in 1862. 166-8
Sioux War, 166-168
Sisters of Charity of the Hôpital Général in Montreal (see also Grey Nuns), 87, 144, 158
Sixth Royal Regiment of Foot, 103 (see also Royal Warwickshires), 105
Siveright, John, 18
Smith, Donald A., 206-8, 214
  Meeting between Smith and people of Red River in January 1870, 207-8
Smith, W. R., 105
Smithurst, John, 86
Snow, John, 181, 183, 199

Society for the Propagation of the Gospel, 170
Society of the Propagation of the Faith at Lyons, 87
Souris River, 131
Southesk, Earl of, 137, 138, 153, 168
Spence, Thomas, 163-4
Steamboats, 124, 131, 133, 134, 137, 147
  Anson Northup, 137-138
Stewart, Adam, 40, 49
Stinking River, 193
Stutsman, Enos, 177-8, 203
  Described, 177
Stony Mountain, 121
Sugar Point (see St. Peter's)
Surveys, 189-190
Sutherland, Alexander, 22
Sutherland, James, 20, 38, 72, 83
Sutherland, John, 193
Sutherland, Roderick, 105
Swan River, 18, 150
Swiss, 12, 36
  Swiss Settlers of 1821, 43-51
  Swiss depart to United States in 1826
  Swiss soldiers, 16, 26-7
Stewart, Adam, 40-1

-T-
Taché, Alexandre-Antonin, 87, 88, 123-124, 127, 137, 139, 145-6, 179, 189, 190
Tait, John, 162
Tallow Company, 66
Tanner, John ("The American"), 28-31
Taylor, George, 72
Taylor, James W., 134
Taylor, John, 161-3
Taylor, Samuel S., 167-9
Taylor, William, 122, 132
Telegraph, 165
Telegraph, Montreal, 168
Temperance, 87-8
Thibault, Reverend Jean-Baptiste, 206, 207
Thom, Adam, 74-5, 76, 86, 88, 97
  Sketch of, 74
  Appointed Recorder of Rupert's Land, 75
  And "Ordination Controversy,"

83, 88
  Sued by Helen Rothney, 83-4
  Judicial harshness, 84-5
  And Sayer Trial, 109
  And Foss-Pelly Affair
Thom, Ann, 78
Thomas, Maria, 161-3
Thomas, Simon, 161
Thunder Bay, 26
Todd, William, 45
Toronto, 125, 127, 128, 131, 134, 147
Toronto Board of Trade, 128
Traill, Walter, 149
Transportation, 78, 104-5, 124, 133-4, 147-152
  By railroad in 1861, 147-8
  By York Boat, 148-9
  By Red River Cart, 149-150
  By Northern Packet (dog teams pulling sledges), 150
Treaty, with First Nations by Selkirk in 1817, 141
Trinity College, Cambridge University, 112
Trinity College, Toronto, 131
Troops, 103, 126
  In Red River 1846-8, 103
  Royal Canadian Rifles (1857), 132
  Petition for in 1862, 160
  Petition for in 1863, 167
Truck System, 96
Truttier, André, 140-1
Tupper, Charles, 195
  Visits Red River, 206
Twenty-five Years Service in the Hudson's BayTerritories, 126
Turner, Catherine, 63
Turtle Mountain, 96

-U, V, W-
University of Manitoba, 88
United States, 40, 51, 65, 72-3, 74, 90, 93, 99-100, 111, 118, 124, 125, 126, 132, 138, 147, 160, 180, 182, 205-206
  Covets Red River, 119
"U.S", 184
Upper Canada, 14. 16, 56, 127
Upper Church, 88
  Burial ground of, 117
Upper Fort Garry, 64, 66, 72, 78, 81, 99, 105, 113, 134, 143, 146, 156,

182, 198, 204, 205, 209, 213-4
  Description of, 156-157
  Seized by Métis in 1869, 196
  Site of meeting with Donald A. Smith, 207-8
Vancouver Island, 112, 129
Victorian values, 88, 112-113
Vincent, Thomas, 135
von Huser, Walter, 45, 46, 47
Voudrie, Soussants, 30
Wallace, Major James, 192
War of 1812, 48, 65, 110
Washington, D.C.., 100
Watkin, Edward, 165
Wesleyan Methodist Missionary Society, 102
West, John, 41, 42, 51, 57, 116
Wheat, cultivation of, 106-107
  Prairie de Chien variety, 107
  Black Sea variety, 107
White, John, 19
White Horse Plain, 53, 61, 72, 82, 91, 92, 123, 155
  Buffalo hunt brigade of, 91-2
Whittier, John Greenleaf, 143
Wilkie, Jean-Baptiste, 9
Willamette River, 83
Wind damage, 178
  Destruction of Church of the Holy Trinity and other buildings, 178
Winegart, Catherine, 114
Winnipeg, 139, 156-8, 198
  Establishment of Winnipeg, 156
  Description of early Winnipeg, 156-8
Winnipeg River, 131
Winslow House hotel, 148
Wisconsin Herald, 110
Wolseley, Colonel Garnet, 212-213
Wolseley Expedition, 212-214
Woodlands, 153
Wyss, Rudolf, 47, 51

-X, Y, Z-
York boats, 78, 104-5, 132, 148-9
  Described, 148-9
York Factory, 38, 42, 45, 46, 47, 51, 61, 71, 73, 78, 103, 104, 132, 149, 150
Young, George, 158, 179, 181
Young, Sir John, 211-212